THE BRITISH ARMY

Copyright © R & F (Defence Publications) 2000

ISBN 0 8052 710 4

Price £4.95

Pen & Sword Books Ltd
47 Church Street
Barnsley S70 2AS

Telephone: 01226-734222   Fax: 01226-734438

The Information in this publication has been gathered from unclassified sources.

Front Cover: The British Army's new attack helicopter - WAH64 Longbow Apache.

Rear Cover: A Warrior armoured vehicle belonging to the Irish Guards enters Kosovo during June 1999.

Kosovo 1999

In addition to being the editor of this publication I am also the editor of Jane's World Armies. As such, I have visited over 50 armies worldwide and, having served with the British Army for over 20 years, it is impossible for me not to have made comparisons. Indeed, I am always being asked about how the British Army compares with the rest.

One of the answers is that I have seen a few good armies, lots of mediocre armies and some appalling armies. However, being naturally biased I will leave it to others to make a judgement regarding the British Army. Independent Television News reporter Julian Manyon watched British troops entering Kosovo at the beginning of June 1999. His comments appeared in "The Spectator" later in June.

*"NATO or rather the British Army, entered Kosovo, according to the letter of the agreement extracted from the Serbs, at dawn on Saturday. Racing down the road to meet them I came upon a surprisingly modest advance guard: four Land Rovers containing Gurkha soldiers who, with a mixture of Eastern politeness and menace, set about searching the vehicles of surprised and equally angry Serbs at a makeshift checkpoint. Behind them came General Jackson's spearhead force, lines of paratroopers supported by Scimitar and Warrior armoured vehicles, and behind them the heavy Challenger tanks. The best assessment of them came from my newly arrived cameraman, Ezra, an Israeli whose own military experience includes commanding the second boat in Arik Sharon's stunning night counter-attack across the Suez Canal in the Yom Kippur war. **"This is a real army"** said Ezra as we drove alongside the British lines of advance, observing the soldiers relaxed professionalism and the immaculate condition of their equipment **"It's the real thing"**.*

CONTENTS

CHAPTER 1 - OVERVIEW

General Information

Populations - European Union - Top Five Nations
(1998 estimates)

Germany	82.05 million
United Kingdom	58.7 million (1999 estimate)
France	59.1 million
Italy	57.9 million
Spain	39.2 million

Finance - European Union - Top Five Nations
(1998 figures)

	GDP		Per Capita Income
Germany	DM3,800 bn	(US$2,100 bn)	US$23,000
France	Ff8,500 bn	(US$1,400 bn)	US$23,100
United Kingdom	£812 bn	(US$1,300 bn)	US$21,600
Italy	L2,017 tr	(US$1,200 bn)	US$21,500
Spain	P82.7 tr	(US$553 bn)	US$16,900

UK Population

England	-	47,055,204
Wales	-	2,835,073
Scotland	-	4,998,567
Northern Ireland	-	1,573,282
Total	-	56,462,166

Figures are from the 1991 census. The population split in Northern Ireland is approximately 56% Protestant and 41% Roman Catholic with the remaining 3% not falling into either classification. The latest (1999) estimate is that the overall UK population is approximately 58.7 million.

UK Population Breakdown - Military Service Groups

Age Group:	13-17	18-22	23-32
Men	1,883,000	1,817,000	4,194,000
Women	1,796,000	1,732,000	4,025,000

UK Area (in square kilometres)

England	-	130,423
Wales	-	20,766
Scotland	-	77,167
Northern Ireland	-	14,121
Total	-	242,477

UK Government

The executive government is vested nominally in the Crown, but for practical purposes in a committee of Ministers that is known as the Cabinet. The head of the ministry and leader of the Cabinet is the Prime Minister. For the implementation of policy, the Cabinet is dependent upon the support of a majority of the Members of Parliament in the House of Commons. Within the Cabinet defence matters are the responsibility of the Secretary of State for Defence.

United Kingdom - Defence Overview

Total British Armed Forces (as at 1 April 1999)

Regular: 212,600; Locally Entered 4,000; Regular Reserves 247,500; Volunteer Reserves 57,400; Cadet Forces 128,000; MoD Civilians 115,600 (of which 100,800 are employed in the UK).

Regular Army 109,700; Royal Navy 43,700; Royal Air Force 55,200; (Note: Royal Naval figure includes some 5,800 Royal Marines.

Strategic Forces:
3 x Vanguard Class submarines each with 16 x Trident (D5) Submarine Launched Ballistic Missiles (SLBM). The 4th Vanguard Class submarine with 16 x Trident D5 SLBM - probably becoming operational "early in the next century". Future plans are for a stockpile of 200 operationally available warheads and 58 missile bodies.

Royal Navy: 43,700: 3 x SSBN; 12 x Tactical Submarines; 3 x Aircraft Carriers (1 in refit); 31 x Destroyers and Frigates; 8 x Amphibious Vessels; 19 x Mine Counter Measures Vessels; 8 x Offshore Patrol Craft; 24 x Coastal Patrol Craft; 1 x Ice Patrol Ship; 6 x Survey Vessels; 3 x Harrier Squadrons; 12 x Helicopter Squadrons; 3 x Royal Marines Commando Groups: Royal Fleet Auxiliary - 2 x Large Fleet Tankers; 3 x Small Fleet Tankers; 3 x Support Tankers; 5 x Fleet Replenishment Ships; 1 x Helicopter Support Ship; 5 x Landing Ships; 1 x Forward Repair Ship.

Merchant Navy: Merchant Naval Vessels Registered in the UK and Crown Dependencies: 104 x Tankers; 22 x Bulk Carriers; 12 x Specialised Carriers; 29 x Cellular Container Ships; 79 x Ro-Ro Passenger and Cargo Ships; 82 x Other General Cargo Ships; 11 x Passenger Ships; 69 x Tugs.

Note: This listing refers to vessels of 500 gross tons and over.

Air Force: 55,200; 6 x Strike/Attack Squadrons with 78 x Tornado GR1; 5 x Offensive Support Squadrons with 51 x Harrier GR7/T10 and 30 x Jaguar GR1A/B; 5 x Air Defence Squadrons with 69 x Tornado F3; 3 x Maritime Patrol Squadrons with 23 x Nimrod MR2; 3 x Reconnaissance Squadrons with 39 x Tornado GR1A, 2 x Intelligence and Electronic Warfare Squadrons with 2 x Nimrod R1 and 7 x Canberra; 2 x Airborne Early Warning Squadrons with 7 x AEW Sentry; 17 x Transport, Tanker and Helicopter Squadrons with 10 x VC10 C1K, 9 x Tristar, 47 x Hercules, 29 x Chinook, 33 x Puma, 15 x Wessex, 15 x VC10 Tankers ; 2 x Search and Rescue Squadrons with 16 x Sea King HAR3; 4 x RAF Regiment Surface to Air Missile Squadrons; 5 x RAF Regiment Ground Defence Squadrons.

Army: 109,700 (including some 3,500 Gurkhas); 1 x Corps Headquarters in Germany (ARRC); 1 x Armoured Divisional HQ in Germany; 1 x Mechanised Divisional HQ in UK ; 3 x Brigade Headquarters in Germany; 14 x Brigade Headquarters in UK plus 1 x Air Assault Brigade.

British Army Major Units

(at 1 Jan 1999)	Germany	UK	Elsewhere	TA
Armoured Regts	6	3	-	-
Armoured Recce Regts	1	1	-	6
Armoured Infantry Bns	6	2	-	-
Mechanised Bns	-	4	-	-
Airmobile Bns	-	2	-	-
Parachute Bns	-	3	-	2
Light Role Bns	-	18	2	31
Gurkha Bns	-	1	2	-
Total Infantry (1)	6	30	4	33
Army Air Corps Regiments	1	4	-	1
Artillery Field Regts	3	9	-	3
Air Defence Regts	1	2	-	3
Engineer Regiments	4	6	-	9
Signals Regiments	3	7	1	11
EW Regiment	-	-	-	-
Equipment Support Bns	3	2	-	5
Logistic Regiments	9	15	2	11
Fd Ambulances/Hospitals	3	9	-	18

Note (1) Excludes the 6 x Home Service Battalions of the Royal Irish Regiment and 1 x Battalion of the Gibraltar Regiment.

British Army Equipment Summary

Armour: 300 x Challenger 1 - estimate 105 x Challenger 2 in service during early 2000, in total 386 x Challenger 2 on order; 134 x Sabre; 88 x Striker; 315 x Scimitar; 1,650 x Fv 432; 736 x MCV 80 Warrior; 520 x Spartan; 590 x Saxon; 11 x Fuchs (NBC).

Artillery and Mortars: 540 x 81 mm mortar (including 110 x self propelled); 2093 x 51 mm Light Mortar; 179 x AS 90; 64 x 227 mm MLRS; 31 x 155 mm FH 70; 140 x 105 mm Light Gun.

Air Defence: 64 x Rapier Fire Units; 298 x Javelin and Starburst Launchers; 135 x Starstreak Launchers.

Army Aviation: 115 x Lynx; 154 Gazelle; 7 x BN-2; 7 x DHC2 and 21 Chipmunk (for training); 67 x WAH-64D Apache on order. Helicopters available from RAF- 29 x Chinook; 15 x Wessex; 33 x Puma.

Defence Roles and Responsibilities

The aim of the United Kingdom's Armed Forces is to deliver and sustain an operational capability wherever and whenever it is required. This overall aim is translated into the three major National Defence Roles.

The Missions of the Armed Forces

The MoD mission statement for the armed forces reads as follows "Defence policy requires the provision of forces with a high degree of military effectiveness, at sufficient readiness and with a clear sense of purpose, for conflict prevention, crisis management and combat operations. Their demonstrable capability, conventional and nuclear, is intended to act as an effective deterrent to a potential aggressor, both in peacetime and during a crisis. They must be able to undertake a range of Military Tasks to fulfil the missions set out below, matched to changing strategic circumstances." These missions are not listed in any order of priority:

A: Peacetime Security: To provide forces needed in peace time to ensure the protection and security of the United Kingdom. To assist as required with the evacuation of British nationals overseas, to afford Military Aid to the Civil Authorities in the United Kingdom, including Military Aid to the Civil Power, Military Aid to Other Government Departments and Military Aid to the Civil Community.

B: Security of the Overseas Territories: To provide forces to meet any challenges to the external security of a British Overseas Territory (including overseas possession and the Sovereign Base Areas) or to assist the civil authorities in meeting a challenge to internal security.

C: Defence Diplomacy: To provide forces to meet the varied activities undertaken by the Ministry of Defence to dispel hostility, build and maintain trust, and assist in the development of democratically accountable armed forces (thereby making a significant contribution to conflict prevention and resolution).

D: Support to Wider British Interests: To provide forces to conduct activities to promote British interests, influence and standing abroad.

E: Peace Support and Humanitarian Operations: To contribute forces to operations other than war in support of British interests and international order and humanitarian principles, the latter most likely under UN auspices.

F: Regional Conflict Outside the NATO Area: To contribute forces for a regional conflict (but on an attack on NATO or one of its members) which, if unchecked, could adversely affect European security, or which could pose a serious threat to British interests elsewhere, or to international security. Operations are usually under UN or Organisation for Security Co-operation in Europe auspices.

G: Regional Conflict Inside the NATO Area: To provide forces needed to respond to a regional crisis or conflict involving a NATO ally who calls for assistance under Article 5 of the Washington Treaty.

H: Strategic Attack on NATO: To provide, within the expected warning and readiness preparation times, the forces required to counter a strategic attack against NATO.

This mission statement is further sub-divided into a number of Military Tasks (MT) which accurately define the way in which the missions are actually accomplished.

Ministry of Defence (MoD)

In 1963 the three independent service ministries were merged to form the present Ministry of Defence (MoD). This massive organisation which directly affects the lives of about half a million servicemen, reservists and MoD employed civilians, is controlled by The Secretary of State for Defence who is assisted by two ministers. The first of these is the Minister of State for the Armed Forces and the second the Minister of State for Defence Procurement.

The Secretary of State for Defence chairs The Defence Council. This Defence Council is the body that makes the policy decisions that ensure the three services are run efficiently, and in accordance with the wishes of the government of the day.

Defence Council

The composition of The Defence Council is as follows:

The Secretary of State for Defence
Minister of State (Armed Forces)
Minister of State (Defence Procurement)
Parliamentary Under-Secretary of State for Defence
Chief of the Defence Staff
Vice-Chief of the Defence Staff
Chief of the Naval Staff and First Sea Lord
Chief of the Air Staff
Chief of the General Staff
Permanent Under-Secretary of State
Chief of Defence Procurement
Chief Scientific Adviser
Second Permanent Under Secretary of State

Chief of The Defence Staff

The Chief of the Defence Staff (CDS) is the officer responsible to the Secretary of State for Defence for the co-ordinated effort of all three fighting services. He has his own Central Staff Organisation and has a Vice Chief of the Defence Staff (VCDS) who ranks as number four in the services hierarchy, following the three single service commanders. The November 1996 announcement that General Sir Charles Guthrie was to replace Field Marshal Sir Peter Inge in the post of CDS probably means that the previous policy of rotating the post of CDS between the heads of the three armed services has ceased.

General Sir Charles Guthrie GCB LVO OBE ADC Gen
Chief of The Defence Staff (with effect from 1 May 1997)

General Sir Charles Guthrie was born on 17 November 1938. He went to The Royal Military Academy Sandhurst in 1957 and was commissioned into the Welsh Guards in 1959. He served with his Regiment as a young officer in the United Kingdom, Germany and Aden. In 1966 he became a

Troop Commander with 22nd Special Air Service Regiment and served in Aden, the Persian Gulf, Malaysia and East Africa. In 1968 as a Squadron Commander, still serving with 22nd Special Air Service Regiment he served in the Persian Gulf and the United Kingdom.

He returned to 1st Battalion Welsh Guards in Münster in 1970 to command a mechanised infantry company prior to attending the Staff College at Camberley in 1972. His first appointment after attending the Staff College was Military Assistant to the Chief of the General Staff (Field Marshal Lord Carver and General Sir Peter Hunt). After a year as Second in Command of 1st Battalion Welsh Guards in London and Cyprus in 1976 he assumed the appointment of Brigade Major, Household Division. In 1977 he commanded 1st Battalion Welsh Guards in Berlin and Northern Ireland.

General Guthrie became Colonel General Staff, Ministry of Defence in 1980 (Col GS MO2) responsible for military operations and planning worldwide, less Germany and Northern Ireland. In the same year he was Commander British Forces New Hebrides (Vanuatu). In 1981 he was appointed Commander of the 4th Armoured Brigade in Münster, following which he was Chief of Staff, Headquarters 1st (British) Corps in Bielefeld.

He was appointed General Officer Commanding the 2nd Infantry Division and North East District in 1985. He was appointed Colonel Commandant of the Intelligence Corps in 1986. He became Assistant Chief of the General Staff in November 1987 and assumed command of the 1st (British) Corps in October 1989. In January 1992 he became Commander Northern Army Group and Commander-in-Chief British Army of the Rhine. Northern Army Group was disbanded in June 1993. He was appointed ADC Gen on 13 July 1993 and GCB in The Queen's Birthday Honours List in 1994. On 15 March 1994 he was appointed Chief of the General Staff and on the 1st May 1997 he was appointed Chief of the Defence Staff. In late 1999 it was announced that General Gutherie would remain as Chief of the Defence Staff until May 2001.

Chain of Command

The Chief of the Defence Staff (CDS) commands and co-ordinates the activities of the three service through the following chain-of-command:

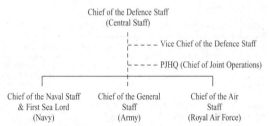

The three single service commanders exercise command of their services through their respective headquarters. However, the complex inter-service nature of the majority of modern military operations, where military, air and naval support must be co-ordinated, has led to the recent plans for a permanent tri-service Joint Headquarters.

● *General Sir Charles Guthrie*

Permanent Joint Headquarters (PJHQ)

The UK MoD established a Permanent Joint Headquarters at Northwood in Middlesex for joint military operations on 1 April 1996. This headquarters brings together on a permanent basis, intelligence, planning, operational and logistics staffs. It contains elements of a rapidly deployable in-theatre Joint Force Headquarters that will command rapid deployment front line forces.

MoD officials have described the role of PJHQ as "Working proactively to anticipate crises and monitoring developments in areas of interest to the UK. The establishment of PJHQ has set in place a proper, clear and unambiguous connection between policy and the strategic direction and conduct of operations. Because it will exist on a permanent basis rather than being established for a particular operation, the permanent Joint HQ will be involved from the very start of planning for a possible operation. It will then take responsibility for the subsequent execution of those plans if necessary."

PJHQ, commanded by the Chief of Joint Operations (CJO), (currently a 3 star officer) occupies existing accommodation above and below ground and brings together at Northwood some 330 civilian, specialist and tri-Service military staff from across the MoD. There are approximately 90 Royal Navy, 100 Army, 100 RAF and 40 civilian staff. PJHQ is responsible for planning all UK-led joint, potentially joint, combined and multinational operations and will work in close partnership with MoD Head Office in the planning of operations and policy formulation, thus ensuring PJHQ is well placed to implement policy. Having planned the operation, and contributed advice to Ministers, PJHQ will then conduct such operations.

When another nation is in the lead, PJHQ will exercise operational command of UK forces deployed on the operation.

Being a permanent joint Headquarters, PJHQ will provide continuity of experience from the planning phase to the execution of the operation, and on to post-operation evaluation and learning of lessons.

From 1 Aug 1996 PJHQ assumed responsibility for current operations in the Middle East and the Former Yugoslavia. Non-core functions, such as the day-to-day management of the Overseas Commands in Cyprus, Falkland Islands, and Gibraltar, are also being delegated by MoD Head Office to PJHQ. This will allow MoD Head Office to concentrate in particular on policy formulation and strategic direction. The annual running costs of the Headquarters is estimated to be between £20 - £23 million. The Headquarters structure follows the normal Divisional organisation, but staff will operate within multidisciplinary groups which draw from across the HQ.

Notes:
(1) CJO - Chief of Joint Operations; (2) Deputies to the single Service Commanders in Chief. They provide high level single Service advice to CJO and direct links with single Service commands; (3) COS - Chief of Staff; (4) ACOS - Assistant Chief of Staff; (5) CJRDFO - Chief of the Joint Rapid Deployment Force Operations.

PJHQ Headquarters Structure

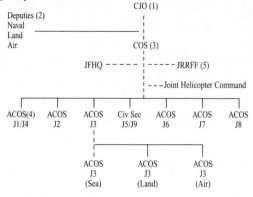

J1 Personnel and Admin
J2 Intelligence
J3 Operations
J4 Logistics
J5 Policy

J6 Communication and Information Systems
J7 Doctrine and Training
J8 Plans
J9 Finance

Joint Rapid Reaction Force (JRRF)

The successor of the JRDF established in August 1996, the new JRRF provides a force for rapid deployment operations using a core operational group of the Army's 16 Air Assault Brigade and the Royal Navy's 3rd Commando Brigade, supported by a wide range of air force and maritime assets. The force uses what the MoD has described as a "golfbag" approach with a wide range of units available for specific operations. For example, if the operational situation demands assets such as heavy armour, long range artillery and attack helicopters, these assets can easily be assigned to the force. This approach means that the JRRF can be tailored for specific operations ranging from support for a humanitarian crisis to operations including high intensity operations.

The "reach" of the JRRF will be enhanced by the Royal Navy's new amphibious vessels HMS Albion and HMS Bulwark, due to enter service after 2001. Both of these ships will be able to carry 650 troops plus a range of armoured vehicles including main battle tanks. A flight deck will allow ship-to-shore helicopter operations. The cost of each ship is believed to be in the region of £220 million.

Responsibility for providing units to the JRRF remains with the single service commands who ensure that units assigned are at an extremely high state of readiness. JRRF units remain committed to NATO and a JRRF-assigned battalion group provides the first wave assets for any rapid deployment.

The force commander is the CJRRF (Chief of the Joint Rapid Reaction Force) who is responsible to the Chief of Joint Operations (CJO) at PJHQ. CJRRF is supported by the Joint Force Headquarters (JFHQ) at PJHQ which would provide the deployable staff element of the JRRF when the force be deployed on operations. JFHQ has a staff of 55 of whom just over 30% are army personnel.

The United Kingdom Defence Budget

"You need three things to win a war, Money, money and more money".

Trivulzio (1441-1518)

In general terms defence is related to money. Estimates for the world's top six defence budgets for 1999 (in billions of US$ and the latest year for which accurate figures are available) are as follows:

United States	-	$277.6 billion
Japan	-	$41.1 billion
United Kingdom	-	$34.6 billion
Russia	-	$31.0 billion
France	-	$29.5 billion
Germany	-	$24.7 billion
China	-	$12.6 billion

In the 1999-00 Financial Year (FY) the UK Government planned to spend £22.28 billion on defence. Over the following two years planned expenditure is as follows:

FY 2000-01	-	£22.83 billion
FY 2001-02	-	£22.98 billion

Expenditure in FY 1999-00 represents about 2.4 per cent of GDP. In 1985 UK defence expenditure represented 5.2% of GDP.

The breakdown of the 1999-00 Defence Budget figure of £22.28 billion can be shown in percentage terms for all three services as follows:

Equipment Purchases	-	44.0%
Service Personnel	-	28.0%
Civilian Personnel	-	10.1%
Works Buildings & Land	-	7.8%
Miscellaneous Stores etc	-	10.1%

The equipment expenditure figure can be broken down further, to reveal that during the 1999-00 Financial Year a total of £9.803 billion will be spent, with money going to the services as follows:

Sea Systems	-	£2.299 billion
Land/Army Systems	-	£1.652 billion
Air Systems	-	£4.532 billion
General Support	-	£1.321 billion*
Total	-	£9.803 billion

10

Note: In general Sea, Land and Air Systems relate to Naval, Army and Air Force expenditure.
* General Support usually refers to finance for research and development.

Land Equipment Procurement

Some of the more interesting Army equipment expenditure figures (production and repair estimates) for the 1997-98 Financial Year (the latest year for which figures are available) are amongst the following:

Guns, Small Arms and NBC Defence Stores	-	£24 million
Ammunition, Mines and Explosives	-	£131 million
Fighting Vehicles	-	£131 million
Load Carrying Vehicles	-	£352 million
Engineering Equipment	-	£57 million
Guided Weapons	-	£178 million
Communications	-	£174 million
Surveillance Equipment	-	£47 million
Maintenance	-	£421 million

Defence Expenditure (Top Level Budget Holders - TLB)

During 1999-00 Defence expenditure figures for the top level budget holders are as follows:

GOC Northern Ireland	-	£525 million
CinC Land Command	-	£3,017 million
Adjutant General (personnel & Training)	-	£1,141 million
CinC Fleet	-	£1,058 million
RAF Strike Command	-	£1,560 million
Chief of Joint Operations	-	£317 million
Chief of Defence Logistics	-	£4,627 million
CinC Naval Home Command	-	£541 million
RAF Personnel & Training Command	-	£683 million
2nd PUS & VCDS	-	£1,892 million
Defence Procurement Agency & Nuclear	-	£667 million
Defence Systems Procurement	-	£5,917 million
Major Customers' Research Budgets	-	£453 million

This listing totals £22,800 million when £17 million in loans and grants repaid from the Meteorological Office and the Defence Evaluation and Research Agency are repaid.

The high unit costs of individual items of equipment illustrate the problems faced by defence planners when working out their annual budgets. At 1996 prices the following items cost:

Kinetic Energy Round for Challenger	£1,750 each
155 mm High Explosive Round	£500 each
Individual Weapon (IW)	£600 each
5.56mm round for IW	.90p
One Rapier Missile	£40,000
One Challenger Tank	£3 million (approx)
Tornado Air Defence Fighter	£23 million

PRC 351 VHF Radio	£7,000 each
Combat High Boot	£50 per pair
Harrier GR5	£14.2 million
Lynx Helicopter	£6.25 million
Starstreak Missile	£100,000 each
Trigat (MR) Missile	£35,000 each (estimate)
Attack Helicopter	£25 million (region)
Eurofighter	£40 million (estimate)

Defence Budgets - NATO Comparison (in US$)

The nations of the North Atlantic Treaty Organisation (NATO), of which the United Kingdom is a member state, spent some US$437.2 billion on defence during 1999

NATO Defence Expenditure 1999	- US$429.99 billion
NATO Defence Expenditure 1999 (less USA)	- US$152.39 billion
NATO (European Nations) Defence Expenditure 1999	- US$145.69 billion

The next table shows the defence budget for each NATO nation during 1999.

USA	US$ 277.6 billion
UK	US$ 34.6 billion
France	US$ 29.5 billion
Germany	US$ 24.7 billion
Italy	US$ 16.2 billion
Turkey	US$ 8.9 billion
Netherlands	US$ 7.0 billion
Canada	US$ 6.7 billion
Spain	US$ 6.0 billion
Greece	US$ 3.8 billion
Norway	US$ 3.2 billion
Poland	US$ 3.2 billion
Denmark	US$ 2.6 billion
Belgium	US$ 2.5 billion
Portugal	US$ 1.6 billion
Czech Republic	US$ 1.1 billion
Hungary	US$ 688 million
Luxembourg	US$ 102 million

Iceland has no military expenditure although it remains a member of NATO.

An interesting comparison is made by the total national defence budget divided by the total number of full time personnel in all three services. Figures for the top seven world defence spending nations are as follows:-

Ranking	Nation	1999 Defence Budget	Total Service Personnel	Cost Per Serviceman
1	USA	US$277.6 bn	1,371,000	US$ 202,479
2	Japan	US$41.1 bn	236,300	US$ 173,931
3	UK	US$34.6 bn	212,400	US$ 162,900
4	Russia	US$31.0 bn	1,004,000	US$ 30,876

5	France	US$29.5 bn	317,300	US$ 92,971
6	Germany	US$24.7 bn	332,800	US$ 74,218
7	China	US$12.6 bn	2,480,000	US$ 5,080

British Army Statistics

Strength of the Regular Army (1 April 1999)

Armour	11 Regiments (1)
Royal Artillery	15 Regiments (2)
Royal Engineers	10 Regiments
Infantry	40 Battalions (3)
Special Air Service	1 Regiment
Army Air Corps	5 Regiments
Signals	11 Regiments (4)
Equipment Support	6 Battalions
Logistics	24 Regiments (5)
Medical	12 Hospitals/Field Ambulances

Notes: (1) Includes 1 x Training Regiment. (2) Includes 1 x Training Regiment. (3) Excludes the 6 x Battalions that comprise the Home Service Element of the Royal Irish Regiment and 1 x Battalion of the Gibraltar Regiment. (5) Includes 3 x Combat Service Support Battalions that have a mix of REME, RAMC and RLC personnel. In general these Battalions/Regiments are commanded by Lt Colonels and have a strength of between 500 and 800 personnel.

Strength of the Territorial Army (1 April 1999)

Armour	6 Regiments (1)
Royal Artillery	5 Regiments (2)
Royal Engineers	9 Regiments
Infantry	33 Battalions
Special Air Service	2 Regiments
Signals	11 Regiments
Equipment Support	4 Battalions
Logistics	14 Regiments
Medical	19 Hospitals/Field Ambulances

Notes: (1) Includes 4 x Regional National Defence Reconnaissance Regiments and 1 x Armoured Reconnaissance Regiment. (2) Includes Honourable Artillery Company (HAC). For the latest changes to the Territorial Army see Chapter 13.

Deployment of the Regular Army (As at 1 April 1999)

Land Command	Officers	Soldiers
1st (UK) Armoured Division	1,200	16,000
2nd Division	300	1,300
3rd (UK) Division	1,000	13,400
4th Division	1,000	9,800
5th Division	400	2,600
Scotland	200	1,700
London District	400	3,900
Northern Ireland	800	8,800

UK Support Command (Germany)	200	600
Command and Training	1,700	13,800
Land Support	100	200
	7,300	**72,100**

Adjutant General (Personnel & Training Command)

Manning & Training	700	1,600
Army Personnel Centre	100	-
Army Trainees	800	11,800
Chief of Staff	600	600
Recruitment & Training Agency	1,400	600
Assistant CGS	300	300
RMC Shrivenham	100	-
	4,000	**14,900**

Quartermaster General

Equipment Support	200	300
Logistic Support	300	600
Logistic Policy & Services	100	-
	600	**900**

Overseas Garrisons

	Army		
Falkland Islands	800	(1,700)	approx
Gibraltar	72	(435)	
Other Far East	261	(333)	
Brunei	853	(865)	
Cyprus	2,331	(3657)	
Other Near East & Gulf	216	(616)	approx
Other Locations	2,767	(7098)	approx

Note: The figures in brackets relate to tri-service garrisons. Figures for other locations include personnel on short tours and detached from HQ Land. These figures do not include UK Army personnel in the Former Yugoslavia.

Manning Figures (Including personnel under training)

Regular Army (As at 1 April 1999)

	1999	1995	1990
Trained Officers	12,700	13,100	16,200
Trained Soldiers	83,600	91,500	121,000
Untrained Officers	900	900	1,200
Untrained Soldiers	12,500	6,300	14,400
	109,700	**111,800**	**152,800**

Note: Previous years figures are given for comparison purposes. At 1 April 1999 there was a shortfall of 6,089 trained soldiers. This figure does not include the Gurkhas where there was a surplus of 492 and the Home Service element of the Royal Irish Regiment. Overall the army is about 5.9% short of its target figure for trained soldiers.

Regular Army Reserves (As at 1 April 1999)

	1999
Army Reserves	34,800
Individuals liable to recall	145,600
Territorial Army	51,800

Recruitment - Regular Army (During Financial Year 1998/99)

	(1998/99)	(1980/81)
Officers	696	1,489
Soldiers	16,267	27,382
Total	16,963	28,871

Note: 1980/81 figures are given for comparison. 1998/99. Figures for soldiers include 1,729 apprentices.

Outflow - Regular Army (During Financial Year 1998/99)

	(1998/99)	(1990/91)	(1980/81)
Officers	1,353	1,860	1,497
Soldiers	15,662	20,964	20,422
Total	17,015	22,824	21,919

Figures for army personnel discharged on medical grounds are:
1998 - 756; 1997 - 1,064; 1996 - 1,186.

Army Cadet Force

	(1 Apr 1999)	(1 Apr 1980)
Total Cadets	65,700	74,600

Totai expenditure on the Cadet Forces during FY 1995-96 (the last year for which figures are available) was £22.55 million for the Army Cadet Force (ACF) and £3.74 million for the Combined Cadet Force (CCF) Army Detachment.

UK Army Establishment Figures 1 May 1996 (Trained Personnel)
(the latest year for which we have accurate figures)

	Soldiers	Officers
Household Cavalry/Royal Armoured Corps	5,121	884
Royal Artillery	7,652	1,132
Royal Engineers	7,810	1,147
Royal Signals	8,321	999
Infantry	24,913	2,915
Army Air Corps	1,317	350
Royal Logistic Corps	14,807	1,821
Royal Army Medical Corps	1,878	704
Royal Electrical and Mechanical Engineers	9,476	895
Adjutant General's Corps	5,990	1,116

Royal Army Veterinary Corps	159	24
Small Arms School Corps	100	27
Royal Army Dental Corps	243	160
Intelligence Corps	1,055	273
Army Physical Training Corps	300	39
Queen Alexandra's Royal Army Nursing Corps	556	395
RAChD	-	144
Long Service List	496	-
Army Musicians	1,136	35
Gurkhas	4,325	155
	95,655	**13,215**

Animals on Strength (As at 1 Nov 1999)

Horses	422
Dogs	1,300
Goats	2 (Regimental Mascots)
Black Buck	1 (Regimental Mascot)
Ram	1 (Regimental Mascot)
Shetland Pony	2 (Regimental Mascots)
Wolf Hound	1 (Regimental Mascot)
Drum Horse	1 (Regimental Mascot)
Ferret	1 (Regimental Mascot)*

Note: The ferret held by 1st Battalion the Prince of Wales' Own Regiment of Yorkshire is not a charge to public funds and the cost for feeding and accommodation is borne by the regiment.

100 Years Ago - Strength of the British Army at 1 Jan 1900

Household Cavalry	1,316
Cavalry of the Line	18,388
Horse Artillery	3,781
Field Artillery	14,308
Mountain Artillery	1,293
Garrison Artillery	17,312
Royal Engineers	7,424
Foot Guards	6,032
Infantry of the Line	135,175
Colonial Corps	5,070
Army Service Corps	3,523
Ordnance Staff	857
Armourers	318
Medical Services	2,482
	217,279

CHAPTER 2 - ARMY ORGANISATIONS

"In war the outcome corresponds to expectations less than in any other activity".
                                                                    Titus Livy 59 BC - 17AD

"Nothing is so good for the morale of the troops as occasionally to see a dead general".
                                                                    Field Marshal Slim 1891-1970

The routine management of the Army is the responsibility of The Army Board the composition of which is shown in the next diagram.

The Army Board
The Secretary of State for Defence
Minister of State (Armed Forces)
Minister of State (Defence Procurement)
Parliamentary Under-Secretary of State for the Armed Forces
Chief of the General Staff
Second Permanent Under Secretary of State
Adjutant General
Quartermaster General
Master General of the Ordnance
Commander in Chief (Land Command)
Commander UK Support Command (Germany)
Assistant Chief of the General Staff

Decisions made by the Army Board are acted upon by the military staff at the various headquarters world-wide. The Chief of the General Staff is the officer responsible for the Army's contribution to the national defence effort and he maintains control through the commander and the staff branches of each of these headquarters. Each military headquarters is organised along exactly the same lines with identical branches at each level in the chain of command.

General Sir Michael Walker KCB CMG CBE ADC Gen
Chief of the General Staff (CGS)
General Sir Michael Walker was born on 7 July 1944 in Salisbury, Southern Rhodesia. He was educated partly in Rhodesia and partly in Yorkshire. On leaving school he taught at a preparatory school for 18 months before attending the Royal Military Academy, Sandhurst. He was commissioned into the Royal Anglian Regiment in 1966 and served with the 1st Battalion as a platoon commander in Celle and Catterick. In 1969 he was posted to Cyprus as an ADC to the GOC Near East Land Forces. He returned to his battalion in 1971 and during the course of the next five years served in Northern Ireland, Cyprus and Tidworth variously as Operations Officer, Regimental Signals Officer and Adjutant. In 1975 he was posted to the Ministry of Defence as a Staff Officer.

He attended the Army Staff Course at Shrivenham and Camberley, returning to his battalion in Tidworth as a Company Commander. At the end of 1979 he was posted back to the Ministry of Defence to the Directorate of Military Operations. On promotion to Lieutenant Colonel he was appointed Military Assistant to the CGS from 1982 to 1985. He then commanded his battalion in Londonderry and Gibraltar. He commanded 20 Armoured Brigade in Detmold from December 1987 and after three years in command was appointed Chief of Staff 1 (British Corps) in Bielefeld (Germany). General Walker assumed the appointment of GOC North East District and Command 2 Infantry Division on 30 September 1991 and then GOC Eastern District on 1 April 1992. In December 1992 he returned to the Ministry of Defence as Assistant Chief of the General Staff.

17

In December 1994, as a Lieutenant General, he assumed command of the ARRC in Rheindahlen, Germany, and deployed with HQ ARRC to Bosnia Herzegovina from December 1995 to November 1996 to command the multinational land component of IFOR. On relinquishing command of the ARRC he became the Commander-in-Chief Land Command, based at Wilton in Wiltshire and became Chief of the General Staff on 14 April 2000.

Staff Branches
The Staff Branches that you would expect to find at every military headquarters from the Ministry of Defence (MoD) down to Brigade level are as follows:

Commander   -   Usually a general who commands the formation.

Chief of Staff   -   The officer who runs the headquarters on a day-to-day basis and who often acts as a second-in-command.

G1 Branch   -   Responsible for personnel matters including manning, discipline and personal services.

G2 Branch   -   Responsible for intelligence and security

G3 Branch   -   Responsible for operations including staff duties, exercise planning, training, operational requirements, combat development & tactical doctrine.

G4 Branch   -   Logistics and quartering.

G5 Branch   -   Civil and military co-operation

● *General Sir Michael Walker*

The Army is controlled from the MoD via two subsidiary headquarters and a number of smaller headquarters world-wide. The Joint Headquarters (JHQ) at Northwood in Middlesex has an important input into this chain-of-command and it is almost certain that any operation with which the army is involved will be under the overall command of PJHQ. The following diagram illustrates this chain-of-command.

Chain of Command

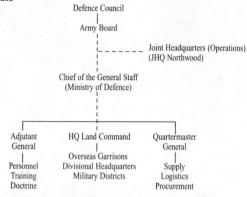

Note: Garrisons in Northern Ireland, Cyprus and the Falkland Islands are commanded from the MoD via JHQ.

HQ Land Command

Following the MoD's "Front Line First" study, plans were drawn up to reorganise HQ United Kingdom Land Forces (HQ UKLF) in a new formation designated HQ Land Command that became operational on 1 April 1995. HQ Land Command is located at Erskine Barracks, Wilton near Salisbury and controls about 75% of the troops in the British Isles and almost 100% of its fighting capability.

Land Command's role is to deliver and sustain the Army's operational capability, whenever required throughout the world, and the Command comprises all operational troops in Great Britain, Germany, Nepal and Brunei, together with the Army Training Teams in Canada, Belize and Kenya. Land Command has almost 70,000 trained Army personnel - the largest single Top Level Budget in Defence, with a budget of just over £3 billion. It contains all the Army's fighting equipment, including attack helicopters, Challenger 2 tanks, Warrior Infantry Fighting Vehicles, AS90 and the Multi-Launch Rocket System (MLRS).

Land Command is one of the three central commands in the British Army, the other two being the Adjutant General (with responsibility for administration, personnel and training) and the Quartermaster General (responsible for supply and logistics). The Command is responsible for providing all the Army's fighting troops throughout the world. These are organised into eight formations and are commanded by Major Generals.

Ready Divisions

There are two "Ready" Divisions: the 1st (UK) Armoured Division, based in Germany, and the 3rd (UK) Division in the United Kingdom. Both of these divisions are earmarked to form part of the Allied Command Europe Rapid Reaction Corps (ARRC), NATO's premier strategic formation; but they also have the flexibility to be employed on rapid reaction tasks or in support of other Defence Roles.

In addition to their operational roles, they also command the Army units in specified geographic areas: in the case of the 1st Division, this area is made up of the garrisons in Germany where the Division's units are based; and in the case of the 3rd Division the South West of England.

Regenerative Divisions

There are three Regenerative Divisions, based on old Districts in the United Kingdom. These are the 2nd Division with its Headquarters at York (Edinburgh from 1st April 2000), the 4th Division with its Headquarters at Aldershot, and the 5th Division (replacing the old Wales and Western District) with its Headquarters at Shrewsbury. These Regenerative divisions are responsible for all non deployable Army units within their boundaries, and could provide the core for three new divisions, should the Army be required to expand to meet a major international threat.

Districts

From Ist April 2000 two Districts will remain: London (although subordinated to 4th Division for budgetary purposes), and the United Kingdom Support Command (Germany). London is responsible for all Army units within the M25 boundary. The United Kingdom Support Command (Germany) with its Headquarters at Rheindahlen has similar responsibilities, but also provides essential support functions for the 1st Division and the Headquarters of the ARRC.

These divisional and district areas are further sub-divided into brigades and garrisons, which also have a varying mix of operational and infrastructure support responsibilities. As a result of the Defence Costs Studies, some brigade headquarters, which previously had purely operational functions, have been amalgamated with garrison headquarters to achieve savings and greater efficiency.

Embedded into this structure are all the other force elements which represent Land Command's operational capability. They include:

16 Air Assault Brigade, based in Colchester and under the command of the Joint Helicopter Command from 1st April 2000.

The United Kingdom element of the ACE Mobile Force (Land), with its Headquarters and logistic elements at Bulford and an infantry battalion at Dover.

Three signal Brigades (one of which is in Germany).

Two Combat Service Support Groups (one of which is in Germany).

Various additional units which are earmarked for the ACE Rapid Reaction Corps or for National Defence tasks.

The overseas detachments in Canada, Belize, Brunei and Nepal are commanded directly from Headquarters Land Command at Wilton. The Review of the Army Command Structure recommended that the Army should be organised into three central commands and that doctrine and training should be the responsibility of the Adjutant General rather than the Command-in-Chief. Therefore Headquarters Doctrine and Training at Upavon, Wiltshire, does not form part of Land Command (although it was part of United Kingdom Land Forces until 1993).

Although Land Command is not responsible for running operations in Northern Ireland, Cyprus and the Falkland Islands (a responsibility of PJHQ), it will provide the operational troops for these areas. Some 12,000 troops are involved in Northern Ireland at present, either deployed in the Province or training for deployment; and a further 5,000 are deployed to Cyprus and the Falklands.

National operations and operations in support of the United Nations/NATO, the most significant of which are 10,000 troops deployed in Bosnia and Kosovo.

Some 500 troops are involved at any one time in MoD-sponsored equipment trials, demonstrations and exhibitions. Public Duties in London taking up two/three battalions at any one time. All troops not otherwise operationally committed are also available to provide Military Aid to the Civil Authorities in the United Kingdom.

Headquarters Land Command has assumed a number of new responsibilities, some of which have been delegated from MoD as part of recent reviews. These include:

The Commitments Plot - Control of the Operational Tour Plot, the Arms Plot (the rotation of Armoured, Artillery and Infantry units between stations), the Formation Training Plot, and the provision of assistance to trials and studies.

Collective Training - Including responsibility for armoured battlegroup training at the British Army Training Unit at Suffield in Canada.

Land Command Divisional/District Summaries
1 (UK) Armoured Division & British Forces Germany (BFG)

The 1st Armoured Division was formed in 1940 adopting the charging rhino (the most heavily "armoured" animal) as its insignia in 1942 prior to El Alamein. Since the Second World War the Division has been retitled three times and became the 1st (United Kingdom) Armoured Division in 1993, having successfully fought in the Gulf War of 1991. The Division has its headquarters at Herford in Germany and commands three Armoured Brigades situated throughout North West Germany and is the major component of British Forces Germany.

British Forces Germany (BFG) is the composite name given to the British Army, Royal Air Force and supporting civil elements stationed in Germany. The terms British Army of the Rhine (BAOR) and Royal Air Force Germany (RAFG), until recently were the traditional names used to describe the two Service elements of the British Forces stationed in Germany.

For many years following WWII, and as a result of the confrontation between NATO and the former Warsaw Treaty Organisation, the UK Government had stationed four Army divisions and a considerable part of its Air Force at five airbases in the Federal Republic of Germany. On the whole, this level of commitment was maintained until 1992 and, although these forces appeared to be solely national, they were in fact closely integrated with the NATO Northern Army Group (NORTHAG) and the 2nd Allied Tactical Air Force (2 ATAF).

As a result of political changes in Europe and the UK Government's "Options for Change" programme, the British Army's presence in Germany has been reduced to three armoured brigades and a divisional headquarters. The RAF presence has been concentrated on one airbase

Composition of 1(UK) Armoured Division

1 (UK) Armoured Division has its headquarters at Herford in Germany (about 50kms from Hanover) and the three Armoured Brigades under command are located at Osnabruck, Bergen-Hohne and Paderborn.

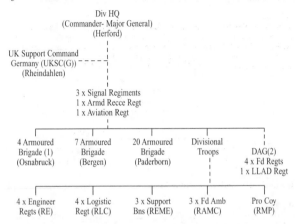

Note: (1) Current plans appear to be for all three armoured brigades to have an identical organisation. (2) DAG (Divisional Artillery Group) This DAG could be reinforced by Rapier Air Defence and MLRS units from the UK as necessary. (3) Personnel total in Germany is 18,000; 17,200 in 1 (UK) Armoured Division and 800 in UKSC(G).

During 1999 this Division could provide the Headquarters (HQs) for 12 Battlegroups.

Force Levels in 1 (UK) Armoured Division (1 April 1999)

Army Personnel	17,200
Challenger MBT	250
Tracked Vehicles	1,350
Army Helicopters	35
Artillery Guns	52
MLRS	0
AVLB	21

It is probable that in the event of hostilities considerable numbers of officers and soldiers from the Territorial Army (TA) would be used to reinforce this division. These reinforcements would consist of individuals, drafts of specialists, or by properly formed TA units varying in size from Mobile Bath Units of 20 men, to Major Units over 500 strong. For example the UK MoD recently announced that eight TA infantry battalions had a role that entailed possible support for the ARRC.

UKSC(G) - The United Kingdom Support Command (Germany) has responsibility for British Army Troops on the Continent of Europe that are not part of 1st (United Kingdom) Armoured Division. Its headquarters replaces that of the British Army of the Rhine, whose sign it has adopted. The new headquarters is located at Rheindahlen and has 800 personnel under command.

2nd Division

The 2nd Division has responsibility for the whole of England north of the Humber, and Scotland. The Division was first formed in 1809 to fight in the Peninsular War, although the crossed keys sign was not adopted until 1940 when the division was reconstituted in England following the withdrawal from Dunkirk. Its most famous engagement was during the Burma Campaign in 1944 when, at the battle for Kohima, the tide against the Japanese Army finally turned. The Divisional Headquarters is in York.

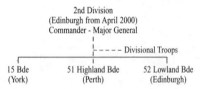

2nd Division
(Edinburgh from April 2000)
Commander - Major General

- - - - Divisional Troops

| 15 Bde | 51 Highland Bde | 52 Lowland Bde |
| (York) | (Perth) | (Edinburgh) |

Force Levels in 2nd Division (1 April 1999)

Army Personnel   1,600

3 (UK) Division

The 3rd (United Kingdom) Division is the only operational (Ready) Division in the UK. The Division has a mix of capabilities encompassing armoured, airborne and wheeled elements in its two mechanised brigades and one airborne brigade. The Division which was first formed during the Napoleonic Wars now also has responsibility for South-West England. The"Iron-Triangle" insignia was chosen for it in the early part of World War II by its commander the then, Major General B L Montgomery.

Following plans for the reorganisation of NATO Forces on the Central Front during 1992, the HQ of the 3rd (UK) Armoured Division moved from its old location at Soest in Germany to Bulford in Wiltshire, where it became 3(UK) Division part of the NATO ARRC (Allied Rapid Reaction Corps). In the event of hostilities it will move to the ARRC area of operations on the European mainland or worldwide as necessary.

HQ 3 (UK) Division

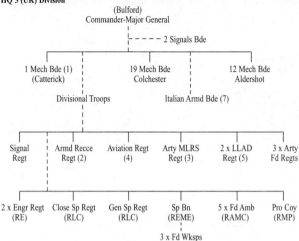

HQ 3 (UK) Division

(Bulford)
Commander-Major General

2 Signals Bde

- 1 Mech Bde (1) (Catterick)
- 19 Mech Bde Colchester
- 12 Mech Bde Aldershot

Divisional Troops — Italian Armd Bde (7)

- Signal Regt
- Armd Recce Regt (2)
- Aviation Regt (4)
- Arty MLRS Regt (3)
- 2 x LLAD Regt (5)
- 3 x Arty Fd Regts

- 2 x Engr Regt (RE)
- Close Sp Regt (RLC)
- Gen Sp Regt (RLC)
- Sp Bn (REME)
- 5 x Fd Amb (RAMC)
- Pro Coy (RMP)

3 x Fd Wksps

Note: (1) 1 Mechanised Brigade; ; (2) Armoured Reconnaissance Regiment; (3) Artillery Regiment with Multi Launch Rocket System; (4) Army Air Corps Regiment with Lynx & Gazelle; (5) Air Defence Regiments with Rapier and Javelin/Starstreak missiles; (6) The composition of this division allows the UK MoD to retain a balanced force for out of NATO area operations should that become necessary (7) Under Allied Rapid Reaction Corps framework agreements this division could be reinforced by an Italian Armoured Brigade (Ariete). 3 Commando Brigade, a Royal Naval formation is available to support 3(UK) Div if necessary. Details of the organisation of 3 Cdo Bde are given in the Miscellaneous Chapter. 3 Cdo Bde is not under the command of 3 Div.

Force Levels in 3 (UK) Division (1 April 1999)

Army Personnel	14,400
Challenger MBT	95
Tracked Vehicles	1,280
Army Helicopters	21
Artillery Guns	154
MLRS	24
AVLB	27

4th Division

The 4th Division has military responsibility for South East England, including Bedfordshire, Essex and Hertfordshire and its headquarters is in Aldershot. Until 1992 it was based in Germany as an armoured division. The division now has three brigades under command, 2 South East Brigade based in Shorncliffe, 145 Home Counties Brigade in Aldershot and 49 Eastern Brigade based in Chilwell The divisional symbol is the Tiger.

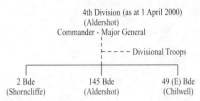

4th Division (as at 1 April 2000)
(Aldershot)
Commander - Major General

- - - - Divisional Troops

| 2 Bde | 145 Bde | 49 (E) Bde |
| (Shorncliffe) | (Aldershot) | (Chilwell) |

Force Levels in 4th Division (1 April 2000)

Army Personnel	10,800
Challenger MBT	26
Tracked Vehicles	1,280
Army Helicopters	21
Artillery Guns	154
MLRS	24
AVLB	27

5th Division

The 5th Division has responsibility for military units and establishments in Wales, the West Midlands and the North West of England and the Headquarters is in Shrewsbury. The Division emblem, inherited from Wales and Western District, depicts the Welsh Dragon, the cross of St Chad (7th Century Bishop of Mercia), and the Red Rose of Lancaster. The 5th Division fought at Waterloo and played a significant part in the endeavours of the BEF in both World Wars.

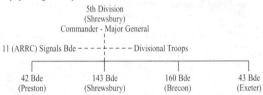

5th Division
(Shrewsbury)
Commander - Major General

11 (ARRC) Signals Bde - - - - - - - Divisional Troops

| 42 Bde | 143 Bde | 160 Bde | 43 Bde |
| (Preston) | (Shrewsbury) | (Brecon) | (Exeter) |

Force Levels in 5th Division (1 April 1999)

Army Personnel	3,000

Scottish District

From 1st April 2000 Scottish District will merge with 2nd Division. The new 2nd Division will have its Headquarters in Edinburgh

London District

Headquarters London District was formed in 1906. It has responsibility for units that are located within the Greater London Area as well as in Windsor. The activity for which the Headquarters and the District is most well known is State Ceremonial and Public Duties in the Capital. The district insignia shows the Sword of St Paul representing the City of London and the Mural Crown representing the County of London. The District has its Headquarters in Horse Guards. London District is now subordinated to HQ 4th Division for budgetary purposes.

London District
(Horse Guards)
Commander - Major General

Public Duties
Battalions

District
Troops

Army Brigades

The Armoured Brigade

The following diagram illustrates the possible composition of an Armoured Brigade in 1(UK) Armd Div on operations.

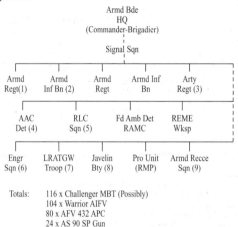

Armd Bde
HQ
(Commander-Brigadier)

Signal Sqn

| Armd Regt(1) | Armd Inf Bn (2) | Armd Regt | Armd Inf Bn | Arty Regt (3) |

| AAC Det (4) | RLC Sqn (5) | Fd Amb Det RAMC | REME Wksp |

| Engr Sqn (6) | LRATGW Troop (7) | Javelin Bty (8) | Pro Unit (RMP) | Armd Recce Sqn (9) |

Totals: 116 x Challenger MBT (Possibly)
104 x Warrior AIFV
80 x AFV 432 APC
24 x AS 90 SP Gun
Approx 4,500 men

Notes: (1) Armoured Regiment with approx 58 x Challenger MBT - from mid to late 2000 there will only be one armoured regiment with a brigade in 1 (UK) Armoured Division; (2) Armoured Inf Battalion with approx 52 x Warrior (with rifle coys) and approx 40 x FV432; (3) Artillery Regiment with 32 x AS90 SP Guns; (4) Army Air Corps Detachment (possibly 9 x Lynx & 4 x Gazelle); (5) Transport Squadron RLC with approximately 60 -70 trucks; (6) Engineer Squadron with 68 vehicles but depending upon the task could involve a complete engineer battalion; (7) Long Range Anti-Tank Guided Weapon Troop (Swingfire) but due to be replaced by Trigat(LR) in the longer term; (8) RA Bty with 36 x Javelin AD missiles and 40 vehicles; (9) Armoured Recce Squadron.

This Brigade could provide the HQs for 4 Battlegroups

Mechanised Brigade Organisation

The following is an example of the 3 (UK) Division Mechanised Brigade organisation.
Note: (1) Long Range Anti-Tank Guided Weapons-Currently Striker/Swingfire.

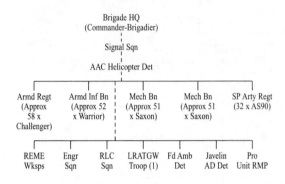

Equipment	Qty
Challenger MBT	50
Chieftain ARRV	5
Warrior Command	9
Warrior Section	47
Warrior Repair	8
Warrior Recovery	4
Combat Vehicle Reconnaissance (Tracked)	8
CVR(T) Sultan-Command	8
CVR(T) Spartan-Multi-role transport vehicle	14
CVR(T) Samson-REME variant (winch)	4
SAXON Command Vehicles	38
SAXON Section Vehicles	82
SAXON Maintenance	10
Fighting Vehicle (FV) 432 Command	2
FV432 Section Vehicles	28
FV432 Ambulance	10
FV434 REME Repair Vehicle	5
FV436 Communications Vehicle	10
FV439 Radio Relay	2
FV439 Secondary Access Message Centre	2

16 Air Assault Brigade

Nearly 10,000 personnel will form the new 16 Air Assault Brigade. It will be able to punch deep and fast into enemy territory, and radically change Britain's ability to react rapidly to conflicts. Using everything from the latest Apache helicopter to air-mobile artillery equipment and high velocity air defence missiles, the new Brigade marks a giant leap forward in Britain's defence capability.

The new Brigade will embody a unique warrior spirit, able to operate far in advance of the front line, deep into enemy territory in isolation from other friendly forces. Combining cutting edge technology with ground breaking doctrine and highly professional well trained troops, the creation of 16 Air Assault Brigade gives the British Army a powerful and potent air manoeuvre force which will be capable of meeting the challenges of the next century.

The Brigade capitalises on the combat capabilities of the former 24 Airmobile Brigade and 5 Airborne Brigade, including two parachute battalions with an increase in combat service support. The introduction of the Apache Attack Helicopter, due in March 2000, will provide a new generation of weapons systems bringing major improvements in military capability. The newly launched Brigade will pull together its various elements over the next three years and is expected to be fully capable in the air manoeuvre role in June 2004, when the last Aviation Regiment is combat-ready.

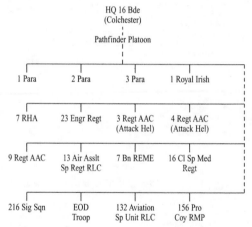

Note: Although much of the brigade in already in locations around the Colchester area, some units will be arriving at various stages during 2000. 23 Engineer Regiment is forming and as yet we have no date for when it will join the brigade.

Support helicopters are provided by the RAF and the Brigade would normally expect to operate with 18 x Chinook and 18 x Puma. An airmobile infantry battalion can be moved by 20 x Chinook equivalents. Each airmobile infantry battalion is equipped with 42 x Milan firing posts - a total of 84 within the Brigade.

The Battlegroup

A division usually consists of 3 brigades. These brigades are further sub-divided into smaller formations known as battlegroups. The Battlegroup is the basic building brick of the fighting formations.

A battlegroup is commanded by a Lieutenant Colonel and the infantry battalion or armoured regiment that he commands, provides the command and staff element of the formation. The battlegroup is then structured according to task, with the correct mix of infantry, armour and supporting arms.

The battlegroup organisation is very flexible and the units assigned can be quickly regrouped to cope with a change in the threat. A typical battlegroup fighting a defensive battle on the FEBA (Forward Edge of the Battle Area), and based upon an organisation of one armoured squadron and two mechanised companies, could contain about 600 men, 16 tanks and about 80 armoured personnel carriers.

The number of battlegroups in a division and a brigade could vary according to the task the formation has been given. As a general rule you could expect a division to have as many as 12 battlegroups and a brigade to have up to 4. The following diagram shows a possible organisation for an armoured battlegroup in either 1(UK) Armd Div or 3(UK) Div.

(1)   Armoured Squadron
(2)   Mechanised Company
(3)   LLAD-Low Level Air Defence - Javelin
(4)   LRATGW - Long Range Anti Tank Guided Weapon- Swingfire.
(5)   Engineer Detachment

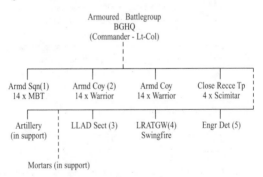

Company Groups/Task Group/Combat Team

Each battlegroup will operate with smaller organisations called combat teams, task groups or company groups. These groups which are commanded by a Major, will be allocated tanks, armoured personnel carriers and supporting elements depending upon the aim of the formation. Supporting elements such as air defence, anti-tank missiles, fire support and engineer expertise ensure that the combat team is a balanced all arms grouping, tailored specifically for the task. In general a battlegroup similar to the one in the previous diagram could be expected to form 3 company groups.

Expect a Group organisation to resemble the following diagram:
Notes: (1) Forward Observation Officer (FOO - usually a Captain) with his party from the Royal Artillery. This FOO will be in direct communication with a battery of eight guns and the Artillery Fire Direction Centre. The MFC is usually a sergeant from an infantry battalion mortar platoon who may have up to six mortar tubes on call. In most Combat Teams both the FOO and MFC will travel in close proximity to the Combat Team Commander; (2) Possibly 2 x Striker with Swingfire; (3) Possibly 2 x Spartan with Javelin; (4) Possibly 2 x Scimitar.

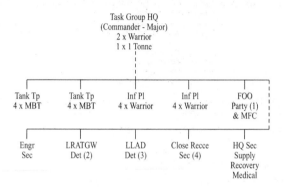

Allied Command Europe Mobile Force Land AMF(L) Contingent

This contingent is the UK's contribution to the Allied Command Europe Mobile Force (AMF) which is tasked with the reinforcement of the flanks of NATO. On mobilisation, operations would probably take place in either Norway or Turkey and the UK MoD has recently stated that the UK's contribution to the AMF will be retained. The AMF is a Brigade+ NATO formation with about 6,000 men and 1,500 vehicles.

In 1995, the UK contingent on an AMF(L) exercise in Norway included 1 x Infantry Bn, 1 x Armoured Sqn, 1 Locating Bty, 1 x Artillery Bty, 1 x Signals Sqn, 1 x Engineer Field Troop, 1 x Army Air Corps Flight, 1 x Transport Sqn, 1 x Ordnance Company, REME Workshop, Field Ambulance detachment and an Intelligence section. The overall personnel total was probably in the region of 1,500 men.

Northern Ireland
The military presence in support of the civilian authorities in Northern Ireland is controlled by HQ Northern Ireland (HQNI) which is located at Lisburn, just outside Belfast.

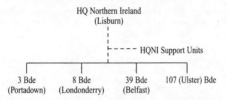

HQ Northern Ireland
(Lisburn)

HQNI Support Units

3 Bde
(Portadown)

8 Bde
(Londonderry)

39 Bde
(Belfast)

107 (Ulster) Bde

HQNI is responsible for counter terrorist operations in support of the Royal Ulster Constabulary (RUC). Under the operational command of these (during late 1999) brigades were:

    5 x Resident Infantry Battalions
    4 x Infantry Battalions on short 6 month tours
    1 x RA/RAC Regiments on short 6 month tours
    1 x Engineer Regiment
    1 x Royal Signals Regiment
    1 x Army Air Corps Regiment
    6 x Home Service Battalions of the Royal Irish Regiment
    1 x RLC Logistic Support Regiment
    1 x REME Workshop
    1 x Military Hospital manned by the Army Medical Services
    1 x RMP Regiment

RAF:
    1 x Wessex Squadron
    1 x Puma Squadron
    1 x Detachment of Chinook
    1 x RAF Regiment Squadron

Navy:
    4 x Ships
    2 x Launches
    1 x Detachment of Sea King helicopters.

During late 1999 it is believed that there were approximately 11,000 regular soldiers and around 4,100 Royal Irish Regiment Home Service soldiers stationed in the Province (a high percentage of the regular soldiers on detachment from units either permanently stationed in Germany or the remainder of the UK Military Districts) making a total of approximately 15,100 soldiers available for security duties. In addition there are approximately 200 Royal Naval and about 900 Royal Air Force personnel stationed in the Province.

Ulster Statistics
The last year for which comprehensive statistics are available was 1998.

	1998	1980
Deaths (Regular Army)	2	8
Deaths (Royal Irish)	0	8
Bombs neutralised	127	120
Explosives neutralised	1,340 kg	2,905 kg

Used in explosions	2,593 kg (est)	4,108 kg
Explosives found	883 kg	821 kg
Weapons found	108	203
Ammunition found	12,189 rounds	28,078 rounds

Overseas Garrisons

Brunei:	853 personnel
	1 x Gurkha Infantry Battalion
	Jungle Warfare Training School
	1 x Helicopter Flight

(Possibly 250 personnel on detachment to East Timor in November 1999)

Cyprus:	2,331 personnel
	2 x Infantry Battalions
	1 x Engineer Support Squadron
	1 x Helicopter Flight
	1 x Signals Regiment
	With UNFICYP (United Nations Force in Cyprus)
	1 Roulement Regiment - Infantry Role.

Falkland Islands:	800 men & women (approx)
	1 Infantry Company Group
	1 Engineer Squadron
	1 Signals Unit
	1 Logistics Group
	Plus RAF and RN Units.

Gibraltar:	72 regular soldiers (approx)
	The Gibraltar Regiment (Reserve Unit)

Bosnia (SFOR) Yugoslavia:	3,500 (Approx - late 1999)
	1 x Brigade Headquarters
	1 x Battlegroup plus supporting elements.

Kosovo (KFOR):	5,000 (Approx - early 2000)
	1 x Brigade HQ and subordinate units.

Other Locations:	Approx 2,767 personnel in about 26 countries including Brunei, Botswana, Egypt, Gambia, Ghana, Mauritius, Namibia, Nigeria, Oman, Qatar, Saudi Arabia, Sudan, Swaziland, United Arab Emirates, Uganda, Zimbabwe, Kenya and Canada.

CHAPTER 3 - NATO

Background

The United Kingdom is a member of the NATO (North Atlantic Treaty Organisation) and the majority of military operations are expected to be conducted in concert with the forces of NATO allies.

Following reorganisations that took effect from 1 July 1993, NATO was realigned from three into two major Commands. The first of these new commands is ACLANT (Allied Command Atlantic with headquarters at Norfolk, Virginia (USA) and the second is ACE (Allied Command Europe), with its headquarters at Mons in Belgium.

Future operations in the NATO area in which the United Kingdom was a participant would almost certainly be as part of a NATO force under the command and control of Allied Command Europe (ACE). From May 2000 the Supreme Allied Commander Europe will be General Joseph W. Ralston, US Air Force.

SACEUR - General Ralston

General Joseph W. Ralston entered the US Air Force in 1965 through the Reserve Officer Training Corps programme. His career includes operational command at squadron, wing, numbered air force and major command, as well as a variety of influential staff and management positions at every level. He has been closely involved with building the U.S. Air Force for the 21st century, holding a variety of positions related to the requirements and acquisition process. Prior to assuming his current position, he was the vice chairman of the Joint Chiefs of Staff Committee, at the Pentagon, Washington, D.C. In this capacity, he was the second highest ranking military officer in the US defence establishment. Prior to becoming vice chairman of the Joint Chiefs of Staff Committee he was the commander of US Air Force, Air Combat Command with headquarters at Langley Air Force Base, Virginia. He is a command pilot with more than 2,500 flying hours, including 147 combat missions over Laos and North Vietnam.

The current organisation of Allied Command Europe is as follows:

Allied Command Europe (ACE)

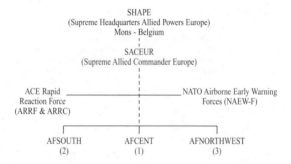

SHAPE
(Supreme Headquarters Allied Powers Europe)
Mons - Belgium

SACEUR
(Supreme Allied Commander Europe)

ACE Rapid Reaction Force (ARRF & ARRC) — NATO Airborne Early Warning Forces (NAEW-F)

AFSOUTH (2)   AFCENT (1)   AFNORTHWEST (3)

Notes:

(1) AFCENT - Allied Forces Central European Theatre with headquarters at Brunssum in the Netherlands and with overall responsibility for military operations in Central Europe. AFCENT is further sub-divided into three subordinate commands - see next diagram.

(2) AFSOUTH - Allied Forces Southern Europe, with headquarters at Naples in Italy and responsible for military operations in the area of Turkey, Greece, Italy and is responsible for some aspects of operations in the Former Yugoslavia.

(3) AFNORTHWEST - Allied Forces North-western Europe, with headquarters at High Wycombe in the UK. This new headquarters, was operational as from 1 July 1994 and is responsible for operations in Norway, the UK, and the maritime area between the two countries.

HQ AFNORTHWEST claims to be leaner and more efficient than its predecessor AFNORTH at Oslo in Norway, and became operational in July 1994. The headquarters is staffed by about 300 personnel, the majority of whom are British, American and Norwegians, but Belgium, Canada, Denmark, Germany and the Netherlands are all represented.

Following re-organisation the composition of AFCENT is as follows:

Allied Forces Central European Theatre

Notes:
(1) AIRCENT is now responsible for all air forces in the AFCENT region.
(2) As an example, the LANDCENT HQ Staff consists of 159 Officers, 149 Non-commissioned Officers and Other Ranks and 15 NATO civilians - a total of 323 headquarters personnel. With Direct Support Units included the total is 744, and with the supporting Signal Unit the personnel figure approximately 1,500.
(3) The AFCENT operational area includes Northern Germany and Denmark, extending 800 kms to the south as far as the Swiss and Austrian borders.

NATO Reaction Forces
In addition to the forces committed to NATO by the participating countries SACEUR has reaction forces available for crisis response. These reaction forces are multinational, held on a permanent state of readiness and allocated to major NATO commanders as authorised by the North Atlantic Council. They are sub-divided into Immediate Reaction Forces (IRF - capable of deployment within

3 to 7 days) and Rapid Reaction Forces (RRF - capable of deployment within 7 to 15 days), and have employment options covering all regions of the Alliance. They may be employed either alone, as part of "joint operations" (with one or more components such as Maritime, Land or Air forces), in "combined operations" (in conjunction with other national, NATO or international forces in the theatre of operations), or with a mixture of both in "combined joint operations".

Allied Command Europe (ACE) reaction forces have the following configuration:

The Allied Rapid Reaction Corps (ARRC)

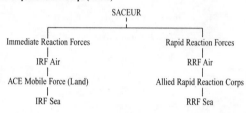

The concept of the Allied Rapid Reaction Corps was initiated by the NATO Defence Planning Committee in May 1991 and confirmed during November 1991. The concept called for the creation of Rapid Reaction Forces to meet the requirements of future challenges within the alliance. The ARRC provides the Supreme Allied Commander Europe with a multinational corps in which forward elements can be ready to deploy in Western Europe within 14 days.

Currently the ARRC trains for missions across the spectrum of operations from deterrence and crisis management to regional conflict. The formation has to be prepared to undertake Peace Support Operations - both peacekeeping and peacemaking. Belgium, Canada, Denmark, Germany, Greece, Italy, The Netherlands, Norway, Portugal, Spain, Turkey, the United Kingdom and the United States all contribute to the Corps. Ten divisions are assigned to the ARRC and up to four of them could be placed under command for any specific operation. These divisions range from heavily armoured formations to lighter air-portable units more suited to mountainous or difficult terrain. Some of these formations are National Divisions, some are Framework Divisions, where one nation takes the lead and another contributes, and two are Multinational Divisions where the member nations provide an equal share of the command, staff and combat forces.

The headquarters of the ARRC is fully multinational and is based at Rheindahlen, near Monchengladbach in Germany. The ARRC Commander (COMARRC) is a British 3 Star General, the Deputy Commander is an Italian 2 Star General and the Chief of Staff is a British 2 Star General. The Headquarters is approximately 1,000 strong, of which British personnel comprise about 50%.

During early 1996 HQ ARRC deployed to Sarajevo in Bosnia to command the NATO Implementation Force (IFOR) for six months. Of late the HQ of the ARRC was responsible for commanding the NATO force in Kosovo (KFOR) from June 1999.

Outline Composition of the ARRC (ACE Rapid Reaction Corps)

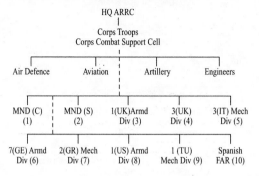

Notes: (1) MND (C) - Multinational Division - Central; (2) Multinational Division - South (3) Resident in Germany (4) Resident in the UK (5) IT - Italy (6) GE - Germany (7) GR - Greece (8) US - United States (9) TU - Turkish (10) FAR - Rapid Action Force.

In peace, the headquarters of the ARRC and the two Multinational Divisions are under the command and control of SACEUR, but the remaining divisions and units only come under SACEUR's operational control after being deployed.

The operational organisation, composition and size of the ARRC would depend on the type of crisis, area of crisis, its political significance, and the capabilities and availability of lift assets, the distances to be covered and the infrastructure capabilities of the nation receiving assistance. It is considered that a four-division ARRC would be the maximum employment structure.

The main British contribution to the ARRC is 1 (UK) Armoured Division that is stationed in Germany and there is also a considerable number of British personnel in both the ARRC Corps HQ and Corps Troops. In addition, in times of tension 3(UK) Div and 16 Air Assault Brigade could move to the European mainland to take their place in the ARRC's order of battle. In total, we believe that if the need arises some 55,000 British Regular soldiers could be assigned to the ARRC (17,800 resident in Germany) together with a substantial number of Regular Army Reservists and formed TA Units. This almost happened in mid 1999 when preliminary plans were made for a ground invasion of Kosovo that was to have taken place in October 1999. However, the Yugoslav's acceptance of NATO's demands for a withdrawal from Kosovo meant that the requirement for what would have been a partial mobilisation was averted.

ARRC Groupings

Composition of the Multinational Division (Central) - MND (C)

Div HQ
Rheindahlen - Germany

| 16(UK) Air Assault Bde (Colchester) | 31 (GE) Airborne Bde (Oldenburg) | Belgian Airborne Bde (Eversberg) | 11 (NE) Airmobile Bde (Arnhem) |

Composition of the Multinational Division (South) - MND (S)

Div HQ

| Italian Airborne Bde (Livorno) | Greek Infantry Bde (St Chalkis) | Turkish Commando Bde (Bolu) |

Composition of the 1st (UK) Armoured Division

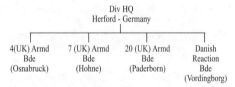

Div HQ
Herford - Germany

| 4(UK) Armd Bde (Osnabruck) | 7 (UK) Armd Bde (Hohne) | 20 (UK) Armd Bde (Paderborn) | Danish Reaction Bde (Vordingborg) |

Composition of the 3rd (UK) Mechanised Division

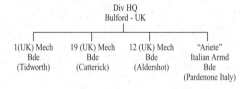

Div HQ
Bulford - UK

| 1(UK) Mech Bde (Tidworth) | 19 (UK) Mech Bde (Catterick) | 12 (UK) Mech Bde (Aldershot) | "Ariete" Italian Armd Bde (Pardenone Italy) |

Composition of the 3rd Italian Mechanised Division

```
                        Div HQ
                      Milan - Italy
        ┌──────────────────┼──────────────────┐
    "Garibaldi"         "Julia"          Portuguese
     Mech Bde          Mech Bde         Airborne Bde
     (Caserta)         (Udine)            (Tancos)
```

Composition of the 7th German Panzer Division

```
                          Div HQ
                   Dusseldorf - Germany
    ┌───────────┬───────────┼───────────┬───────────┐
  21 (GE)     19 (GE)      30 Engr     7 Arty    7 Armd Cav
  Armd Bde    Armd Inf Bde   Bde       Regt         Bn
 (Augustdorf)  (Ahlen)     (Hilden)   (Dulmen)  (Augustdorf)
```

Composition of the 2nd Greek Mechanised Division

```
                         Div HQ
                 Edessa - Northern Greece
        ┌──────────────────┼──────────────────┐
     33 (GR)            34 Greek             Bde
     Mech Bde           Mech Bde         to be allocated as
    (Polikastru)     (Thessaloniki)        required.
```

Note: Other NATO nations could be invited to contribute a similar brigade to act as the third brigade within this divisional framework structure.

Composition of the 1st United States Armoured Division

```
                          Div HQ
                  Bad Kreuznach - Germany
        ┌──────────────────┼──────────────────┐
     1 (US)              2 (US)            Aviation Bde
    Armd Bde            Armd Bde             (Hanau)
   (Friedberg)        (Baumholder)
```

Composition of the 1st Turkish Mechanised Division

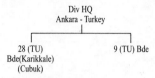

Composition of the Spanish FAR Contingent

Note: The Spanish FAR equates roughly to the size of a conventional division.

Note: 1st (UK) Armoured Division is earmarked for operations within the NATO ARRC (Allied Rapid Reaction Corps), and in an emergency both 3 (UK) Mechanised Division and 24 Airmobile Brigade would be expected to move from their bases in the UK to the European mainland, to reinforce the NATO formations of which they are a part.

British Forces in Bosnia

UK Forces have been deployed in the Former Yugoslavia since 1992. Initially these forces were under command of the United Nations Protection Force (UNPROFOR) and from 20th December 1995 these forces have been under the command of the NATO Implementation Force (initially IFOR and then SFOR). At the height of the UNPROFOR commitment there were approximately 5,000 British troops serving with the force. Towards the end of 1996 British Forces committed to IFOR numbered just over 10,000 - approximately 10 per cent of the army's effective strength.

Since the first deployment to the Former Yugoslavia in 1992 eleven members of the British forces have been killed as a result of hostile action and a further 17 have died as a result of gunshot wounds or vehicle accidents (figure correct up to April 1999).

The IFOR mandate agreed at Dayton, Ohio on the 21st November 1995 included:

(1) Boundary demarcation between the Federation of Bosnian Croats and Muslims and the Republika Srpska (including areas to be transferred from one entity to another).

(2) Separation of the forces of the former warring factions and the supervision of their withdrawal to barracks.

(3) Deployment of a multi-national force to implement the military aspects of the above arrangements.

(4) To implement confidence and security building measures to promote regional stability.

(5) To establish a constitution for Bosnia & Herzegovinia with a central government but separate administrations for the Federation and the Republika Srpska.

(6) Ensuring elections throughout Bosnia under the supervision of the OSCE (Organisation for Security and Co-operation in Europe).

(7) Observance of the rights of refugees and displaced persons and the maintenance of human rights in general.

(8) Implementation of the non-military aspects of the Peace Agreement.

(9) Establishment by the UN of an International Police Task Force.

Between December 1995 and January 1996 approximately 55,000 IFOR (now changed to SFOR) personnel deployed to the Former Yugoslavia.These forces were under the command of three multi-national divisions.

SFOR Command Structure (as of mid 1999)

On the 18th November 1996 NATO Foreign Ministers meeting in Brussels decided that after December 1996 a new NATO "Stabilisation Force" (SFOR) of approximately 30,000 personnel, roughly half of the strength of IFOR, would remain in the Former Yugoslavia until 1988. The command arrangements for the force are similar to the previous arrangements but divisional commands have been replaced by large brigades each of which is commanded by a two star general (in the case of the UK a major general).

Following a further reduction, by the end of 1999, there will be approximately 20,000 troops in Bosnia under the following SFOR command arrangements.

SACEUR
(SHAPE - Belgium)
|
SFOR HQ
(Tito Barracks -Sarajevo)

| HQ Multi-National Group (North) (Tuzla) US Command Group | HQ Multi-National Group (South-East) (Mostar) French Command Group | HQ Multi-National Group (South West) (Banja Luka) UK Command Group |

Notes:

(1) HQ MNG (N) or HQ Multi-National Group (North) is commanded by a US General and includes US, Russian, Turkish and Nordic units.
(2) HQ MNG(SE) or HQ Multi-National Group (South East) is commanded by a French General and includes French, Spanish and Italian Units.
(3) HQ MNG(SW) or HQ Multi-National Group (South West) is commanded by a British General.

Outline Organisation - HQ Multi-National Group (South West)

The Multi National Group (South West) is commanded by the a UK Brigade Headquarters. These brigade headquarters rotate from their locations in UK/Germany at 6 monthly intervals.

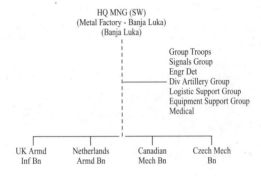

HQ MNG (SW)
(Metal Factory - Banja Luka)
(Banja Luka)

Group Troops
Signals Group
Engr Det
Div Artillery Group
Logistic Support Group
Equipment Support Group
Medical

| UK Armd Inf Bn | Netherlands Armd Bn | Canadian Mech Bn | Czech Mech Bn |

Following late 1999 withdrawals from Bosnia, the UK contribution will probably fall to around 3,500 with the major combat unit being an armoured infantry battalion.

Logistic Support

National SFOR contingents provide their own logistic support and, by late 1999 about 30% of the British troops in SFOR will be providing logistic support. The major support base is on the Adriatic coast at the port of Split in Croatia and, at the height of the operation the Royal Logistic Corps (RLC) were handling about 1,000 requests for supplies per day. Delivery of supplies from Split to the forward UK units had accounted for almost 5 million kilometres of road distance run by RLC vehicles by mid 1999.

KFOR

In early June 1999, NATO troops, led by soldiers from the British Army entered Kosovo under the terms of the Military-Technical agreement with the Yugoslav Army who then withdrew to bases in Serbia. To maintain peace in Kosovo NATO has divided the country into five multinational brigades areas with each brigade having one lead nation (France, Germany, Italy, United Kingdom and the United States). In total, at the end of October 1999 there were just over 46,000 troops in Kosovo and

KFOR expected the total to be approximately 50,000 troops by the end of December. Included in these figures are almost 6,000 troops deployed in FYROM (Former Yugoslav Republic of Macedonia) and Greece which are mainly support units.

The KFOR manning situation at 31 October 1999 was:

Austria	28
Canada	1,242
Denmark	895
France	6,291
Greece	525
Ireland	36
Netherlands	1,700
Poland	755
Russia	3,320
Sweden	8
United Arab Emirates	981
United States	7,119
HQ KFOR (Mixed)	455
Belgium	507
Czech Republic	122
Finland	181
Germany	6,239
Hungary	322
Italy	5,193
Norway	81
Portugal	329
Spain	1,231
Turkey	978
United Kingdom	7,401
Ukraine	54

Note:
We would expect the UK contribution to have fallen to around 5,000 personnel by 1 Jan 2000. The latest 1999 estimate for keeping a NATO soldier in Kosovo for one year is £44,125 (US$70,600). KFOR was expected to cost around £6.25 billion (US$10 billion) during 1999.

KFOR Brigades

MULTINATIONAL BRIGADE NORTH
Lead Nation: France
HQ Mitropvica
Contributing nations:
> Belgium
> Denmark
> Russia
> United Arab Emirates

MULTINATIONAL BRIGADE WEST
Lead nation: Italy
HQ: Pec
Contributing Nations:
- Portugal
- Spain

MULTINATIONAL BRIGADE CENTRAL
Lead Nation: UK
HQ: Pristina
Contributing nations:
- Canada
- Czech Republic
- Finland
- Norway
- Sweden

MULTINATIONAL BRIGADE EAST
Lead Nation: USA
HQ: Urosevac
Contributing nations:
- Greece
- Poland
- Russia

MULTINATIONAL BRIGADE SOUTH
Lead Nation: Germany
HQ: Prizren
Contributing nations:
- Austria
- Netherlands
- Russia
- Turkey

NATO Reorganisation

There are longer term plans for a post 2000 NATO reorganisation along the following lines:

Strategic Command Europe
(Mons - Belgium)

Regional Command North
(Brunssum-Netherlands)

Regional Command South
(Naples-Italy)

These major Regional Commands may be further sub-divided as follows:

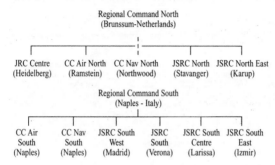

Regional Command North
(Brunssum-Netherlands)

JRC Centre	CC Air North	CC Nav North	JSRC North	JSRC North East
(Heidelberg)	(Ramstein)	(Northwood)	(Stavanger)	(Karup)

Regional Command South
(Naples - Italy)

CC Air South	CC Nav South	JSRC South West	JSRC South	JSRC South Centre	JSRC South East
(Naples)	(Naples)	(Madrid)	(Verona)	(Larissa)	(Izmir)

Note: A Component Command (CC) provides air or sea assets and support to other commands. Joint Sub-Regional Commands (JSRC) have a defined focus to their primary mission. For example JSRC South in Verona will be focused on operations in the area of the Balkans.

The Future

One of the reasons why "peacekeeping/peacemaking will almost certainly continue to be necessary:

"There are five Great National Delusions. The first is that there are solutions to all the problems. The second is that only a strong centre can solve the problems. The third is that the strong centre must embody one's own views exclusively. The fourth Great Delusion is that heroic surgery is required, and the fifth, that the heroic surgeons must be oneself and once's cronies armed with scalpels as big as machettes."

Louis de Bernieres - The Troublesome Offspring of Cardinal Guzman.

CHAPTER 4 - The Household Cavalry and the Royal Armoured Corps

Background

The Household Cavalry and The Royal Armoured Corps (RAC) traditionally provide the tank force and armoured reconnaissance component of the British Army. More recently they have also acquired the responsibility for the UK element of the Joint NBC Regiment.

Armour has represented battle winning shock action and firepower since the earliest tanks broke the stalemate of the Western Front during the First World War. In the same way, armoured reconnaissance, with the ability to penetrate the enemy's forward defences and gain information by using stealth and firepower, has shaped the way in which armour has been used to its best advantage.

Defence represents the best use of ground features in conjunction with engineering and concealed firepower. The ability of armour to ignore all but the heaviest defences, and deliver a group of highly capable armoured fighting platforms into a combat area remains a battle winning capability embraced by all major armies.

The modern main battle tank weighs over 50 tons, can move at up to 60 kph and can almost guarantee a first round hit with its main armament out to 2,000 m. Last tested in combat in the Gulf War of 1990, the tanks of the UK and US demonstrated the full range of advantage of armour in a desert landscape. Amongst these were the ability to cover rough terrain quickly and by the use of superior concentrated firepower create operational level, rather than simple local tactical, advantage. These tanks used the most up to date information equipment and state of the art imaging and sighting systems to locate, close with and destroy the enemy. The Gulf War experience underlined the need for all elements of large manoeuvre forces to be able to move swiftly and securely with protection and firepower to maintain a high "operational tempo". This includes infantry, artillery and of course the massive logistic supply required.

However, since the earliest discovery of the power of the tank, military planners and scientists have sought ways of negating its power and defeating its protection to reduce its advantage. To counter these enhancements, in turn, the tank has repeatedly been adapted and improved to maintain an its advantage. A tank now carries thermal imaging sights capable of acquiring a target and identifying it at any time day or night. It can carry explosive reactive armour, which detonates on contact with an incoming round disrupting its destructive power. More sophisticated anti tank weapons, mines, missiles and indeed helicopters, have created a new battlefield environment of sensing and counter sensing while trying to manoeuvre to exercise firepower advantage.

The UK armoured regiments are equipped with Challenger 2 built by Vickers and the reconnaissance regiments are equipped with Scimitar tracked reconnaissance vehicles built by Alvis. The planned replacement of these systems is integrated into future UK defence planning. The Scimitar replacement will be a concept vehicle called Tracer/Future Scout and Cavalry Vehicle to be produced under a joint UK/US programme and due in service in 2007. The Challenger 2 is due for replacement around 2020/2025 so the future developments likely to be experienced by this vehicle are likely to be those that enhance its protection in the face of more capable and accurate detectors and weapons, while maintaining its ability to strike at the enemy. What is most likely is the application of improvement through a number of technological "insertion packages" which will be designed to enhance both battlefield survivability but also its essential lethality. The replacement reconnaissance vehicle will embody as many interim capability enhancements as possible and experience in this field will to some extent shape the ultimate replacement for the tank itself.

While the future of the MBT may be overtaken by alternative technologies such as surveillance from space, and attack from complex unseen helicopter mounted or seeker weapons, the military will continue to require a mechanism to verify and occupy territory. This force, however small or specialised will require personnel who will need the protection, lethality and mobility which we have come to look upon as the role of the cavalry in both attack and reconnaissance. This assumption until history proves it wrong, suggests that the spirit and elan we have come to expect of the Armoured Corps will still have a major role in the Army of the 21st Century

The Household Cavalry consists of two regiments, the first of these being the Household Cavalry Mounted Regiment, stationed in London and with a primary task as a ceremonial unit providing escorts etc for state occasions. The second is the Household Cavalry Regiment currently employed as an armoured reconnaissance regiment in Windsor, but in the longer term could be equipped as a main battle tank regiment as units are rotated through different roles.

The RAC is composed of 11 regular regiments and four TA yeomanry regiments. Apart from the Royal Tank Regiment, which was formed in the First World War with the specific task of fighting in armoured vehicles, the regular element of the RAC is provided by the regiments which formed the cavalry element of the pre-mechanised era. Of the four TA yeomanry regiments one is roled to provide War Emergency Reserves to Regular Army Recce regiments. The remaining three are equipped to provide reserve reinforcements to Regular Army armoured regiments, an armoured delivery squadron to bring forward battlefield replacement tanks, and two additional NBC reconnaissance squadrons.

Of the 11 regular armour roled units remaining in the British Army post SDR there are to be; four in Germany, three MBT regiments equipped with Challenger 2 and a Recce regiment. In the UK there will be the remaining three MBT regiments equipped with Challenger 2, three Recce Regiments and the Joint NBC Regt. Current locations and roles of the Regiments are as follows:-

Germany

(1) Scots Dragoon Guards	MBT	Fallingbostel
(2) Queens Royal Hussars	MBT	Sennelager
(3) Kings Royal Hussars	MBT	Munster
(4) 2nd Royal Tank Regt	MBT	Fallingbostel
(5) Queens Royal Lancers	MBT	Osnabruck
(6) Light Dragoons	Recce	Hohne

UK

(1) Queens Dragoon Guards	MBT	Catterick
(2) Royal Dragoon Guards	MBT	Tidworth
(3) Household Cavalry Regt	Recce	Windsor
(4) 9th 12th Lancers	Recce	Swanton Morely
(5) 1 Royal Tank Regt	JNBC Regt	Honnington

Note: In addition the Household Cavalry Mounted Regiment carry out ceremonial duties in London.

Post SDR 99 Deployments will be completed between 2001 and 2005 when 2 RTR will move to a newly constructed barracks at Tidworth in Hampshire. Post SDR 99 deployment of armoured and cavalry regiments will be:-

Germany

(1) Scots Dragoon Guards	MBT	Fallingbostel	
(2) Queens Royal Hussars	MBT	Sennelager	
(3) Royal Dragoon Guards	MBT	Munster	(early 2000)
(4) Light Dragoons	Recce	Hohne	

UK

(1) Queens Royal Lancers	MBT	Catterick	(by 2001)
(2) Kings Royal Hussars	MBT	Tidworth	(early 2000)
(3) 2nd Royal Tank Regt	MBT	Tidworth	(2003/5)
(4) Household Cavalry Regt	Recce	Windsor	
(5) 9th 12th Lancers	Recce	Swanton Morely	
(6) Queens Dragoon Guards	Recce	Bovington	(early 2001)
(7) 1 Royal Tank Regt	JNBC Regt	Honnington	

Note: In addition the Household Cavalry Mounted Regiment carry out ceremonial duties in London.

With the change of deployment, post SDR, 1 RTR will become the first UK element of a new Joint NBC Regt. This role will be a two squadron task and a third squadron will remain in the armoured role and support the Combined Arms Training Centre at Warminster. This new Joint NBC Regt will support all existing plans for NBC defence throughout any future joint force actions, as well as for the British Army. In peace this regiment could be used to support action following radiological accidents and chemical spills. The core element of this new regiment is the 11 x NBC Fuchs reconnaissance vehicles that were supplied to the British Army during the Gulf War. These specialist vehicles are divided into reconnaissance and detection troops across three small squadrons and are equipped with the joint US/UK Interim Biological Detection System (IBDS), the British version of which was developed at the Chemical Defence Establishment at Porton Down in Wiltshire.

Challenger 2

In July 1991, the UK MOD announced the purchase of 127 Vickers Defence Systems (VDS) Challenger 2 main battle tanks. Vickers Defence Systems won the contract against intense competition from the French Leclerc, German Leopard 2 (Improved) and the US M1A2 Abrams. The Challenger 2 MBT unit price is believed to have been in the region of £4 million pounds and defence industry sources suggest that this price was considerably cheaper than that of the French Leclerc or the German Leopard 2. In July 1994, the UK Secretary of State for Defence announced the purchase of a further 259 Challenger 2 bringing the total to 386, and allowing for the complete UK MBT fleet to be upgraded to the Challenger 2 standard. The total bill for the Challenger 2 contract is believed to be £1.63 billion.

Following the Strategic Defence Review of 1999 all six MBT regiments will be equipped with 58 Challenger 2 in four squadrons with a war maintenance reserve (WMR) of approximately 30+ tanks. The Royal Scots Dragoon Guards took delivery of the first production models of the Challenger 2 in July 1994 and by mid 2000 our estimate is that all 386 Challenger will have been delivered.

In early 1996, VDS announced that problems had been identified in the Challenger 2 turret systems and that these problems were responsible for a delay in the tank's full commissioning into service. The company stated that there had been some integration and quality control problems with turret subsystems, 80 per cent of which had been purchased from outside contractors. The exact details of these problems were not revealed, but VDS has recently stated that the problems had been overcome, tested on the vehicles and implemented. Unlike many other MBT programmes, no software problems have been reported on Challenger 2 and the chassis and 120 mm L30 rifled gun are believed to be problem free.

The Future

British armoured forces appear to be emerging from a period where their utility has been questioned and although the value of armour has once again been proven during the Gulf War and recent operations in Bosnia, at the time of writing the long term future of the MBT in its present form remains uncertain, and although the most dedicated armoured soldier will still insist that the tank is the most effective anti-tank weapon on the battlefield, others would disagree. The supremacy of armour on the modern battlefield continues to be challenged by anti-tank helicopters such as the Russian Havoc and US Apache. Helicopters which travel at speeds of up to 300 kph, carrying missiles with ranges of up to 5,000+ metres, threaten the flanks of armoured formations that might have a top speed of 80 kph and effective gun ranges of 2,000 metres. On the ground the infantry can defend themselves with portable missile systems such as the Soviet Spigot , European Milan and US TOW, while third generation "fire and forget" weapons such as Trigat that will shortly enter service will further enhance defences. Missiles such as these, with ranges in excess of 2,000 metres, and the ability to penetrate over 350 mm of armour, contribute to making the modern battlefield a more lethal environment for armour.

Syrian experience in the Lebanon during the 1982 war, when over 400 Soviet manufactured Syrian T-62 and T-72's were destroyed by the Israelis using a combination of aircraft, attack helicopters and ground based TOW missiles, would serve to underline this belief. We feel that experience in the Gulf in 1991 has added more weight to the argument in favour of the attack helicopter and believe that the current trend in up-armouring main battle tanks will obtain a short breathing space for armour, before the next round of improvements in anti-tank weapons appear.

We predict that during the early part of the next century armoured formations will remain an essential part of any military force. We are at the beginning of a time of great military change, and the only military certainty that we can see on the horizon is for the continuing need to hold or capture ground. This requirement will ensure the survival of armoured formations, but the size of these formations will almost certainly be greatly reduced, and armoured organisations and tactics could be very different from those in use today. It must also be said that although main battle tanks are slow in comparison with attack helicopters and lack the range of Trigat or hellfire missiles, when the weather is bad and attack helicopters cannot fly, armoured vehicles such as main battle tanks will continue to be available and capable of carrying out their mission. Recent defensive measures such as lasers that destroy "incoming missiles", multi-spectral smoke that confuses missile guidance systems and "goalkeeper" type machine guns linked to close radar systems, capable of destroying anti-tank missiles during the last 5 seconds of flight may well provide a significant defensive boost for the tank of the future.

For the longer term the "crystal ball" appears to be clearing a little. While we are reasonably certain of a reduction in the numbers of main battle tanks in most national inventories, the manoeuvrable light armoured vehicle, capable of operating in a 24 hour battlefield scenario and possibly acting as a command and control unit (electronic mother station/digital relay) for smaller mobile sub units is beginning to look like a priority option. The UK Tracer programmes appears to be coming together in a joint venture US/UK initiative to provide such an option.

Digitisation of the future battlefield has been identified as essential, but base architecture programmes essential for the target data transmission through battlefield management systems is currently running some ten to fifteen years behind schedule. This time lag may enable the tank in its present form to survive for much longer than many analysts had previously predicted.

Therefore, as we enter the 21st Century, we see the major defence orientated countries of the world experiencing a massive doctrinal rethink based on new IT and digital technology capabilities. The future, however, always has its roots in the present and while the large fleets of tanks we now have may be more visible from space, and more difficult to protect from remotely fired missiles and guns, the armies who have them will continue to explore and exploit armoured "stretch" technologies to ensure their armoured capability is credible until successor technologies appear in service.

Armoured Reconnaissance Regiment

Post SDR 99 there are four Regular armoured reconnaissance regiments each of three squadrons in the British Order of Battle. This format favours "peace time" liabilities which include short duration tours in OOTW theatres such as Bosnia, Kosovo and Northern Ireland. In war however the number of regiments would be reduced to three and one squadron of the disbanded regiment posted to each of the other three to make up a war time scale of four recce squadrons per regiment. The current Recce Regiment formation affiliations are;

a.	1 UK Div Germany	Light Dragoons
b.	3 UK Div England	9/12 Lancers (until 2001)
c.	3 UK Div England	QDG on return from Germany in 2001
d.	16 Air Assault Bde	Household Cavalry Regt

Armoured reconnaissance regiments are usually under the direct command of a divisional headquarters and their more usual task in a defensive scenario is to identify the direction and strength of the enemy thrusts, impose maximum delay and damage while allowing main forces to manoeuvre to combat the threat. They would be assisted in such a task by anti-tank helicopters, long range anti-tank missile systems such as Swingfire, TOW and MR Trigat and for the action to be successful every engagement will need to be planned as an ambush. In support will be the indirect fire guns of the divisional artillery, and an air defended area (ADA) maintained by Rapier and Javelin or HVM air defence missiles.

The basic task of all of these recce regiments is to obtain accurate information about the enemy and ensure that it is passed back through the chain of command as quickly as possible.

Reconnaissance Regiment Wiring Diagram

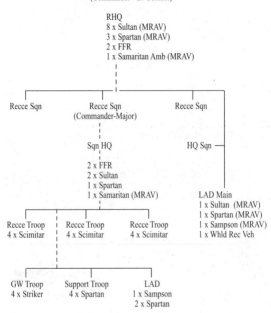

Armoured Reconnaissance Regiment
(Commander - Lt-Colonel)

RHQ
8 x Sultan (MRAV)
3 x Spartan (MRAV)
2 x FFR
1 x Samaritan Amb (MRAV)

Recce Sqn

Recce Sqn
(Commander-Major)

Recce Sqn

Sqn HQ

2 x FFR
2 x Sultan
1 x Spartan
1 x Samaritan (MRAV)

HQ Sqn

LAD Main
1 x Sultan (MRAV)
1 x Spartan (MRAV)
1 x Sampson (MRAV)
1 x Whld Rec Veh

Recce Troop
4 x Scimitar

Recce Troop
4 x Scimitar

Recce Troop
4 x Scimitar

GW Troop
4 x Striker

Support Troop
4 x Spartan

LAD
1 x Sampson
2 x Spartan

Totals: 48 x Scimitar, 16 x Striker, 20 x Spartan, Approx 600 men.

Armoured Regiment Wiring Diagram

The following diagram shows the current structure of an Armoured Regiment equipped with Challenger 2. Regiments equipped with Challenger 2 will have four "sabre" squadrons and a total of 58 tanks.

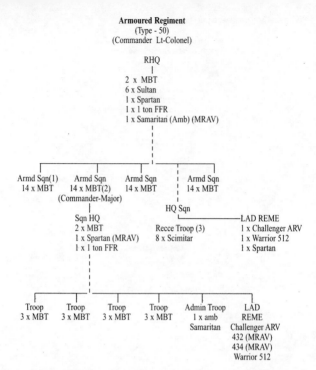

Armoured Regiment
(Type - 50)
(Commander Lt-Colonel)

RHQ

2 x MBT
6 x Sultan
1 x Spartan
1 x 1 ton FFR
1 x Samaritan (Amb) (MRAV)

Armd Sqn(1)
14 x MBT

Armd Sqn
14 x MBT(2)
(Commander-Major)

Armd Sqn
14 x MBT

Armd Sqn
14 x MBT

HQ Sqn

Sqn HQ
2 x MBT
1 x Spartan (MRAV)
1 x 1 ton FFR

Recce Troop (3)
8 x Scimitar

LAD REME
1 x Challenger ARV
1 x Warrior 512
1 x Spartan

Troop
3 x MBT

Troop
3 x MBT

Troop
3 x MBT

Troop
3 x MBT

Admin Troop
1 x amb
Samaritan

LAD REME
Challenger ARV
432 (MRAV)
434 (MRAV)
Warrior 512

Totals: 58 x MBT (Challenger 1), 8 x Scimitar, 5 x ARV, 558 men.

Notes: (1) Armoured Squadron; (2) Main Battle Tank; (3) We believe that this recce troop of 8 x Scimitar is normally held in HQ Sqn but on operations comes under the direct control of the commanding officer; (4) The basic building brick of the Tank Regiment is the Tank Troop of 12 men and three tanks. The commander of this troop will probably be a Lt or 2/Lt aged between 20 or 23 and the second-in-command will usually be a sergeant who commands his own tank. The remaining tanks in the troop will be commanded by a senior corporal; (5) A Challenger tank has a crew of 4 - Commander, Driver, Gunner and Loader/Operator.

Joint NBC Reconnaissance Regiment Wiring Diagram

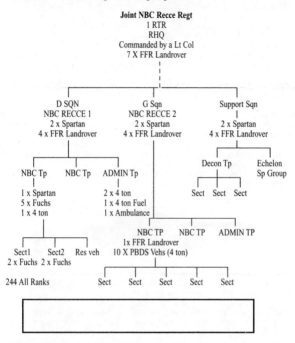

The Joint NBC Regiment is the UK component of any future coalition force Nuclear Biological or Chemical defence system. Currently provided by 1 Royal Tank Regiment, the JNBC Regt is based at Honnington.

The Biological and Chemical threat of the Gulf War resulted in the UK buying a small number of German Fuchs amphibious recce vehicles to serve as NBC detector assets. The Regiment consists of 2 NBC squadrons equipped to detect and measure NBC hazards. One Squadron is equipped with two troops of Fuchs armoured amphibious NBC recce vehicles and the second squadron with the latest "Provisional Biological Detector System" (PBDS).

The wide range of biological agents which can be used to manufacture biological weapons makes it difficult to design and produce a comprehensive detector defence system. It is likely that the biological detection element will require constant updating to keep pace with biological warfare development, not all of which is taking place within military circles.

In addition the Joint NBC Regt has, within its support squadron, a decontamination troop equipped to wash and scrub down regimental vehicles returning from contaminated task areas.

The NBC Recce troop and squadron commanders are mounted in Spartan armoured personnel carriers, this will enable them, and the Fuchs detector vehicles to keep pace with armoured formations in future manoeuvre battle situations. All UK armoured vehicles, APCs, tanks and artillery, are capable of operating for long periods in hostile NBC environments. The Fuchs troop elements of the JNBC Regt will be fully compatible with lead elements in any future conflict.

In peace the JNBC Regiment may also be called upon by the police and Home Office to deal with radiation or biological hazards or spillages.

Challenger 2

386 Challenger 2 in service Crew 4; Length Gun Forward 11.55m; Hull Length 8.32 m; Height to Turret Roof 2.49 m; Width 3.52 m; Ground Clearance 0.50 m; Combat Weight 62,500 kgs; Main Armament 1 x 120 mm L30 CHARM Gun; Ammunition Carried 52 rounds - APFSDS, HESH, Smoke, DU; Secondary Armament Co-axial 7.62 mm MG; Ammunition Carried 4,000 rounds 7.62 mm; Engine CV12TCA 12 cylinder - Auxiliary Engine Perkins 4.108 4 - stroke diesel; Gearbox TN54 epicyclic - 6 forward gears and 2 reverse; Road Speed 56 kph; Cross Country Speed 40 kph; Fuel Capacity 1,797 litres.

Challenger 2 is manufactured by Vickers Defence Systems and production undertaken at their factories in Newcastle-Upon-Tyne at a costing of £4 million per vehicle.

Challenger 2 completed its Reliability Growth Trial (RGT) in 1994 and during these trials 3 vehicles were tested over a total of about 285 battlefield days. For the purposes of the trial a battlefield day consisted of:

- 27 kms of Road Travel
- 33 kms of Cross Country Travel
- Firing 34 Main Armament Rounds
- Firing 1,000 7.62 mm MG rounds
- 16 Hours of Weapon Systems Operation
- 10 Hours of Main Engine Idling
- 3.5 Hours of Main Engine Running - Mobile

Although the hull and automotive parts of the Challenger 2 are based upon that of its predecessor Challenger 1, the new tank incorporates over 150 improvements aimed at increasing reliability and maintainability. The whole of the Challenger 2 turret is of a totally new design and the vehicle has a crew of four - commander, gunner, loader/signaller and driver. The 120 mm rifled Royal Ordnance L30 gun fires all current tank ammunition plus the new depleted uranium (DU) round with a stick charge propellant system.

The design of the turret incorporates several of the significant features that Vickers had developed for its Mk 7 MBT (a Vickers turret on a Leopard 2 chassis). The central feature is an entirely new fire control system based on the Ballistic Control System developed by Computing Devices Company (Canada) for the US Army's M1A1 MBT. This second generation computer incorporates dual 32-bit processors with a MIL STD 1553B databus and has sufficient growth potential to accept Battlefield Information Control System (BICS) functions and navigation aids (a GPS satnav system). The armour is an uprated version of Challenger 1's Chobham armour.

The only export order so far is an Omani order for 18 x Challenger 2 MBTs, 2 x Driver Training Vehicles and 4 x Challenger Armoured Repair and Recovery Vehicles signed during 1993. However, Vickers Defence Systems have high hopes for the vehicle in the remainder of the world market during the next ten years. Possible customers include, Turkey, Greece and Qatar.

Fv 102 Striker

(Approx 48 in service) Armament 10 x Swingfire Missiles: 1 x 7.62mm Machine Gun: 2 x 4 barrel smoke dischargers: Engine Jaguar J 60 No.1 Mark 100B: Engine Power 190bhp: Fuel Capacity 350 litres: Max Road Speed 80kph: Road Range 483km: All Striker Vehicles in service are due to be refittted with Diesel engines by 2005: Length 4.8m: Height 2.2m: Width 2.2m: Ground Clearance 0.35m: Ammunition Capacity 3,000 rounds 7.62: Main Armament Traverse 53 degrees left, 55 degrees right.

Striker is one of the family of the CVR(T) vehicles (Combat Vehicle Reconnaissance Tracked) which includes Spartan, Sultan, Samaritan and Scorpion. Striker carries 10 Swingfire anti-tank missiles with a range of up to 4,000 metres. Five of these missiles are carried in bins on top of the vehicle, which can be lowered when the system is not expected to be in action. One significant drawback to the system is the reload operation, which requires a crewman to reload the missile bins from outside the vehicle. There is also a separated sight available which enables the launch vehicle to be hidden in dead ground, and the operator to fire and control the flight of the missile from a position up to 100 m away from the launch vehicle.

Swingfire (cost per missile £7,500) is due for replacement possibly by MR Trigat early in the next decade. Plans to fit a vehicle with a longer range LR Trigat have not been funded.

The striker system enables a fast, hard hitting anti-tank missile launch platform to keep up with the latest MBTs. Striker is to be found in the armoured reconnaissance regiment which has a troop of four vehicles in each of its three recce squadrons. The Striker vehicle is likely to be replaced by an MRAV variant in due course.

Swingfire Data

Type - Anti Tank Guided Missile; Wire Guided; Command to line of sight: Length of Missile 1.06m: Body Diameter 37.3cm: Warhead Hollow Charge HE: Propellant Solid Fuel: Weight of Missile 37kg: Minimum Range 150m: Maximum Range 4,000m.

Fv 107 Scimitar

(192 in service). Armament 1 x 30mm Rarden L21 Gun: 1 x 7.62mm Machine Gun: 2 x 4 barrel smoke dischargers: Engine Jaguar J60 No.1 Mark 100B: Engine Power 190bhp: Fuel Capacity 423 litres: Max Road Speed 80kph: Weight loaded 7,750kg: Length 4.9m: Height 2.096m: Width 2.2m: Ground Clearance 0.35m: Road Range 644km: Crew 3: Ammunition Capacity 30mm - 160 rounds; 7.62mm - 3,000 rounds: Main Armament Elevation - 10 degrees to + 35 degrees.

he Scimitar is the mainstay of the Armoured Recce Regiment. The Scimitar is an ideal reconnaissance vehicle, mobile and fast with good communications and excellent viewing equipment. Recce Platoons belonging to Armoured Infantry Battalions stationed in Germany are also equipped with Scimitar.

Fuchs

(10 In Service) Road Range 800 kms; Crew 2; Operational Weight 17,000 kg; Length 6.83m; Width 2.98m; Height 2.30m; Road Speed 105 kph; Engine Mercedes-Benz Model OM-402A V-8 liquid cooled diesel; Armament 1 x 7.62mm MG; 6 x Smoke Dischargers.

Manufactured by the German company Thyssen-Henschel as the Transporter Panzer 1 this is an amphibious vehicle with a water speed of 10 kph. During the Gulf War the UK purchased 10 of the NBC Reconnaissance version of this vehicle and they will now become the core element of the UKs Nuclear, Biological and Chemical Defence. For NBC Defence work the vehicles will be equipped with the joint US/UK Provisional Biological Detection System (PBDS).

Approximately 1,000 Transporter Panzer 1 vehicles are in service with the German Army in seven basic roles. The NBC version is also in service with the USA (60), Israel (8), Turkey (4) and the Netherlands (6).

Challenger Repair and Recovery Vehicle (CRARV)

(80 In Service) Crew 3; Length 9.59m; Operating Width 3.62m; Height 3.005m; Ground Clearance 0.5m; Combat Weight 62,000kg; Max Road Speed 59 kph; Cross Country Speed 35 kph; Fording 1.07m; Trench Crossing 2.3m; Crane - Max Lift 6,500kg at 4.9m reach; Engine Perkins CV12 TCA 1200 26.1 V-12 direct injection 4-stroke diesel.

Between 1988 and 1990 the British Army ordered 80 Challenger CRARV in two batches and the contract was completed with the last vehicles bought into service during 1993. A 58 tank Challenger 2 Regiment has 5 x ARRV, one with each sabre squadron and one with the REME Light Aid Detachment (LAD).

The vehicle has a crew of three plus additional space in a separate compartment for another two REME fitters. The vehicle is fitted with two winches (main and auxiliary) plus an Atlas hydraulically operated crane capable of lifting a complete Challenger 2 powerpack. The front dozer blade can be used as a stabiliser blade for the crane or as a simple earth anchor.

TRACER

An explosion in sensor technologies and the expansion of exploitation in the electro magnetic spectrum has created delay and confusion in development of a successor vehicle for the UK Armoured Infantry and Recce Regiments. The concept vehicle named Tracer has reached prototype design sketch level several times in recent years. While the final vehicle build is certain to be a joint national venture project the most vital recent factor in the Tracer programme is the US participation which is likely to drive through an industry specification for an ISD (in service date) 0f 2007. This merging of requirements for Tracer and the US Future Scout Cavalry Recce Vehicle will provide a viable manufacture quantity to provide an interim high capability armoured reconnaissance vehicle to lead the way into 21st Century armoured warfare.

This vehicle will carry more advanced sensors and defensive suites than ever before, but will certainly be armoured and carry a gun to enable it to fight for information and extricate itself from hostile contacts when necessary. Like the MBT it may be overtaken by the pace of technological change on the battlefield in the new century. However, being produced in the first decade of the 21st Century alongside the majority of other vehicles that will be due for replacement between 2020 and 2030, the Tracer/FCSV programme provides an exciting opportunity to explore a new trend in armoured warfare.

Trigat LR

Range 5000+ metres: Missile Weight 20 kgs:

Trigat is a European collaborative programme which is designed to produce a family of medium and long range, anti tank missiles for the new century. Trigat LR (Long Range) could possibly be the missile that replaces Swingfire in British Service.

Trigat LR is believed to be designed for heliborne or tank destroyer type launch platforms and will have a fully "fire and forget" capability. Present plans are thought to include a launch platform with a raised gantry, which could be elevated to a height of about 6 metres and produce a dramatic increase in the operators field of fire.

We believe that Trigat LR will cost over £50,000 per missile and if this initial estimate is correct, there is little doubt that practice firings will not be an everyday occurrence. There is much confusion regarding the UK's future involvement in the Trigat LR programme. The UK MOD state that the development programme is continuing on a revised basis, consistent with the UK's priorities. At present an in service Trigat LR remains an unfunded UK aspiration.

The three partners in the Trigat LR project are France, Germany and the UK with the manufacturer being the Euromissile Dynamics Group. A number of other European Union nations are showing interest in the system.

CHAPTER 5 - INFANTRY

At the end of the day it is the individual fighting soldier who carries the battle to the enemy; Sir Andrew Agnew commanding Campbell's Regiment (Royal Scots Fusiliers), giving orders to his infantrymen before the Battle of Dettingen in 1743 shouted; "Do you see yon loons on yon grey hill? Well, if ye dinna kill them, they'll kill you!"

Regiments and Battalions

The British Infantry is based on the well tried and tested Regimental System, which has proved to be successful on operations over the years. It is based on Regiments, some which are comprised of one regular battalion and one TA battalion, and others that have two or three battalions and a corresponding number of TA battalions. The esprit de corps of the Regimental system is maintained in the names and titles of British Infantry Regiments handed down through history, with a tradition of courage in battle. The repeated changing size of the British Army, dictated by history and politics, is reflected in the fact that many of the most illustrious Regiments still have a number of Regular and Territorial Reserve battalions. For manning purposes Infantry Regiments are grouped within administrative "Divisions" These are no longer field formations but represent original historical groupings based on recruiting geography.

The "Division" of Infantry is an organisation that is responsible for all aspects of military administration, from recruiting, manning and promotions for individuals in the regiments under its wing, to the longer term planning required to ensure continuity and cohesion. Divisions of Infantry have no operational command over their regiments, and should not be confused with the two remaining operational divisions such as 1(UK) Armoured Division and 3(UK) Division.

The Administrative "Divisions" of Infantry are as follows:

The Guards Division	- 5 regular battalions
The Scottish Division	- 6 regular battalions
The Queen's Division	- 6 regular battalions
The King's Division	- 6 regular battalions
The Prince of Wales Division	- 7 regular battalions
The Light Division	- 4 regular battalions

Not administered by "Divisions" of Infantry but operating under their own similar administrative arrangements are the following:

The Parachute Regiment	- 3 regular battalions
The Brigade of Gurkhas	- 2 regular battalions
The Royal Irish Regiment	- 1 regular battalion

TA battalions are under the administrative command (from mid 1999) of the following:

The Guards Division	- Nil
The Scottish Division	- 2 TA battalions
The Queen's Division	- 3 TA battalions
The King's Division	- 3 TA battalions
The Prince of Wales Division	- 3 TA battalions
The Light Division	- 2 TA battalions

| The Parachute Regiment | - 1 TA battalion |
| The Royal Irish Regiment | - 1 TA battalion |

In total the British Army has 40 regular battalions available for service and this total combined with the 15 TA battalions could give a mobilisation strength of 55 infantry battalions.

Outside the above listed Regiments are three companies of guardsmen each of 110 men, who are provided to supplement the Household Division Regiments while on public duties in London, to allow them to continue to carry out normal training on roulement from guard duties. Gibraltar also has it's own single battalion of the Gibraltar Regiment comprising one Regular and two volunteer companies.

At the beginning of 2000 the infantry will be located as follows:

United Kingdom	31 battalions (5 Resident in Northern Ireland)
Germany	6 battalions
Cyprus	2 battalions
Falkland Islands	1 company group on detachment
Bosnia	1 composite battalion on detachment
Kosovo	1 composite battalion on detachment
Brunei	1 battalion (Gurkha - detached reinforced company In East Timor)

As explained previously it would be unusual for the Infantry to fight as battalion units especially in armoured or mechanised formations. If the task is appropriate, the HQ of an infantry battalion will become the HQ of a "battle group", and be provided with armour, artillery, engineers and possibly aviation to enable it to become a balanced Infantry Battle Group. Similarly, Infantry companies can be detached to HQs of Armoured Regiments to make up Armoured Battle Groups.

Types of Infantry Battalions

Infantry Battalion Armoured	- Equipped with Warrior AFV.
Infantry Battalion Mechanised	- Equipped with Saxon APC.
Infantry Battalion Light Role	- Equipped for General Service.
Infantry Battalion Air Assault	- Equipped for Air Mobile Operations

The other types of battalion are:

Parachute Battalion - There are three parachute battalions of which two serve with 16 Air Assault Brigade (as Air Assault battalions) at any one time. Total battalion strength is 687 men.

Gurkha Infantry Battalion - Equipped as a light role Battalion.

TA General Reserve Infantry Battalion - Scaled and equipped to suit the special requirements of the Territorial Army, generally speaking these battalions have three rifle companies.

Numbers of Battalions in Specific Roles

Infantry Battalions (Armoured)   - 9
Infantry Battalions (Mechanised)   - 6
Infantry Battalions (Light Role)   - 16
Infantry Battalions (Parachute)   - 2 (Air Assault)
Infantry Battalions (Northern Ireland) - 5 (Resident in Ulster)
Infantry Battalions (Gurkha)   - 2
Infantry Battalions (TA)   - 15

Armoured Infantry Battalion
(Commander - Lt Colonel)

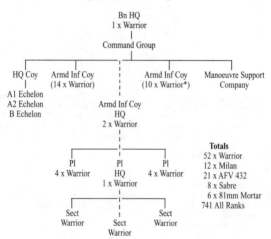

Bn HQ
1 x Warrior

Command Group

HQ Coy
A1 Echelon
A2 Echelon
B Echelon

Armd Inf Coy
(14 x Warrior)

Armd Inf Coy
(10 x Warrior*)

Manoeuvre Support
Company

Armd Inf Coy
HQ
2 x Warrior

Pl
4 x Warrior

Pl
HQ
1 x Warrior

Pl
4 x Warrior

Sect
Warrior

Sect
Warrior

Sect
Warrior

Totals
52 x Warrior
12 x Milan
21 x AFV 432
8 x Sabre
6 x 81mm Mortar
741 All Ranks

* In response to recent pressure for formation of Assault Pioneer Platoons, the third rifle platoon in the third rifle coy has been moved to Manoeuvre Support Company and trained as Assault Pioneers.

Armoured Infantry Battalion - Manoeuvre Support Company

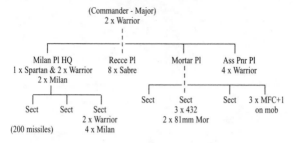

(Commander - Major)
2 x Warrior

Milan Pl HQ	Recce Pl	Mortar Pl	Ass Pnr Pl
1 x Spartan & 2 x Warrior	8 x Sabre		4 x Warrior
2 x Milan			

Milan Pl HQ sections:
Sect | Sect | Sect
2 x Warrior
4 x Milan
(200 missiles)

Mortar Pl:
Sect | Sect | Sect | 3 x MFC+1
3 x 432 | | | on mob
2 x 81mm Mor

Note: (1) There are 9 x Armoured Infantry Battalions, 6 of which are in Germany with 1 (UK) Armoured Division and the remaining 3 in the UK with 3 (UK) Division. (2) There are plans are to replace the remaining AFV 432's on issue to armoured infantry battalions with a new Multi role Armoured Vehicle (MRAV) by the year 2005. (3) Another 4 Milan firing posts are held by the mobilisation section that is only activated in time of deployment for war.

Mechanised Infantry Battalion

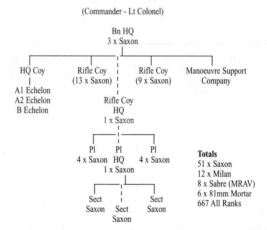

(Commander - Lt Colonel)

Bn HQ
3 x Saxon

| HQ Coy | Rifle Coy | Rifle Coy | Manoeuvre Support |
| | (13 x Saxon) | (9 x Saxon) | Company |

HQ Coy:
A1 Echelon
A2 Echelon
B Echelon

Rifle Coy
HQ
1 x Saxon

Pl	Pl	Pl
4 x Saxon	HQ	4 x Saxon
	1 x Saxon	

Sect | Sect | Sect
Saxon | Saxon | Saxon

Totals
51 x Saxon
12 x Milan
8 x Sabre (MRAV)
6 x 81mm Mortar
667 All Ranks

Once again the third rifle company has lost one platoon to the Manoeuvre Support Company as assault pioneers.

Mechanised Infantry Battalion - Manoeuvre Support Company

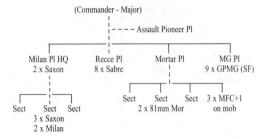

(Commander - Major)

- - - - Assault Pioneer Pl

| Milan Pl HQ | Recce Pl | Mortar Pl | MG Pl |
| 2 x Saxon | 8 x Sabre | | 9 x GPMG (SF) |

Sect Sect Sect
3 x Saxon
2 x Milan

Sect Sect Sect 3 x MFC+1
2 x 81mm Mor   on mob

Note: (1) Sabre is a vehicle that has been created by taking a Fox turret, mounting it on a Scorpion chassis and replacing the GPMG with a Chain Gun.

Light Role Infantry Battalion

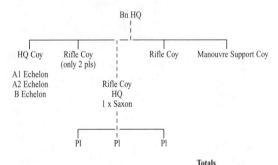

(Commander - Lt Colonel)

Bn HQ

| HQ Coy | Rifle Coy | Rifle Coy | Manouvre Support Coy |
| | (only 2 pls) | | |

A1 Echelon
A2 Echelon
B Echelon

Rifle Coy
HQ
1 x Saxon

Pl   Pl   Pl

Totals
12 x Milan
6 x 81mm Mortars
620 All Ranks

Light Role Infantry Battalion - Manoeuvre Support Company

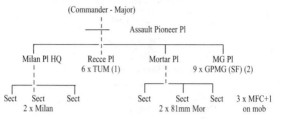

(Commander - Major)

Assault Pioneer Pl

| Milan Pl HQ | Recce Pl
6 x TUM (1) | Mortar Pl | MG Pl
9 x GPMG (SF) (2) |

Sect — Sect — Sect
2 x Milan

Sect — Sect — Sect   3 x MFC+1
2 x 81mm Mor   on mob

Notes: (1) TUM is the abbreviation for Truck-Utility-Medium; (2) General Purpose Machine Guns mounted on tripods with a range of up to 1,800 metres.

Territorial Army Infantry Battalion

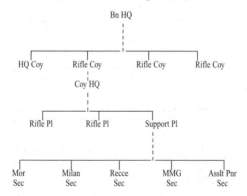

(Commander Lt Col TA or Regular officer)

Bn HQ

HQ Coy — Rifle Coy — Rifle Coy — Rifle Coy

Coy HQ

Rifle Pl — Rifle Pl — Support Pl

| Mor
Sec | Milan
Sec | Recce
Sec | MMG
Sec | Asslt Pnr
Sec |

Platoon Organisation

The basic building bricks of the Infantry Battalion are the platoon and the section. Under normal circumstances expect a British infantry platoon to resemble the organisation in the following diagram:

63

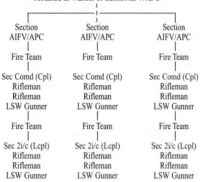

Armoured or Mechanised Infantry Platoon
Platoon Commander (2/Lt or Lt)
Platoon Sergeant
Radio Operator
|
51mm Mortar Team
No 1
No 2
Mounted in Warrior or Saxon AIFV/APC

Section AIFV/APC	Section AIFV/APC	Section AIFV/APC
Fire Team	Fire Team	Fire Team
Sec Comd (Cpl)	Sec Comd (Cpl)	Sec Comd (Cpl)
Rifleman	Rifleman	Rifleman
Rifleman	Rifleman	Rifleman
LSW Gunner	LSW Gunner	LSW Gunner
Fire Team	Fire Team	Fire Team
Sec 2i/c (Lcpl)	Sec 2i/c (Lcpl)	Sec 2i/c (Lcpl)
Rifleman	Rifleman	Rifleman
Rifleman	Rifleman	Rifleman
LSW Gunner	LSW Gunner	LSW Gunner

Notes:

(1) In Mechanised & Light Bns a fourth "Support Section" with 2 GPMGs in the light role is carried in the existing platoon transport. The 51mm Mortar men from Pl HQ are grouped with this fourth section which is commanded by a Corporal but controlled by the Pl HQ .

(2) The platoon could be reinforced by a two man team armed with the GPMG in the Sustained Fire (SF) Role. In most regular battalions the GPMG SF gunners are concentrated in the Manoeuvre Support Company.

(3) The whole platoon with the exception of the LSW (Light Support Weapon) gunners are armed with IW - SA80 (Individual Weapon).

(4) The APC could be either Warrior or Saxon and possibly AFV 432.

(5) Platoons in armoured or mechanised infantry battalions are armed with the LAW 80 for anti-tank operations. The LAW 80 is issued to other types of infantry battalion when a tank threat exists.

(6) All riflemen in the Pl carry a rifle grenade sight which can be attached to the SA80. In combat each SA80 user is also issued with two "Bullet Catcher" rifle grenades. This grenade is simply pushed onto the end of the barrel and an ordinary 5.56 mm round fired into it. The grenade absorbs the bullet without damage and is projected towards the target up to 150 m away.

The Royal Irish Regiment

The Royal Irish Regiment was formed in July 1992 following the merger of the Ulster Defence Regiment and the Royal Irish Rangers. The Royal Irish Regiment is comprised of 1 x General Service, 1 x TA and 6 x Home Service Battalions.

The soldiers of the General Service Battalion (1 Royal Irish) operate as does any other unit of the Regular Army and in mid 1999 the battalion was amongst the first British troops that entered Kosovo. The Home Service battalions serve only in Northern Ireland except for occasional training overseas and include both full time and part time soldiers.

Royal Irish Regiment (Home Service) Strength (1 April 1999)

Males	2,361	(Full Time)
Females	244	(Full Time)
Males	1,698	(Part Time)
Females	208	(Part Time)
Total	4,511	

General Service	-	1 R Irish
Home Service	-	3 R Irish (Co Down & Co Armagh)
		4 R Irish (Co Fermanagh & Co Tyrone)
		5 R Irish (Co Londonderry)
		7 R Irish (City of Belfast)
		8 R Irish (Co Tyrone)
		9 R Irish (Co Antrim)
		4/5th Rangers (V)

The Special Air Service

The SAS (Special Air Service) is considered as part of the Infantry and the single regular battalion is established to carry out special operations. SAS soldiers are selected from other branches of the Army after exhaustive selection tests. There are two regiments of TA SAS.

AFV 432

(Approx 1,600 in service as Command Vehicles, Ambulances, and 81 mm mortar carriers). Crew 2 (Commander and Driver): Weight loaded 15,280 kg: Length 5.25 m: Width 2.8 m: Height 2.28 m: Ground Pressure 0.78 kg km squared: Armament 1 x 7.62 mm Machine Gun; 2 x 3 barrel smoke dischargers: Engine Rolls Royce K60 No.4 Mark 1-4: Engine Power 240 bhp: Fuel Capacity 454 litres: Max Road Speed 52 kph: Road Range 580 km: Vertical Obstacle 0.9 m: Trench Crossing 2.05 m: Gradient 60 degrees: Carries up to 10 men: Armour 12.7 mm max.

With the approach of MRAV and the "Future Infantry Fighting Vehicle" replacement planned for WARRIOR, the FV 432 is obsolescent and the remaining few still operating in Infantry Battalions Armoured or Mechanised will be replaced as soon as an MRAV or other alternative becomes available. However, the vehicle is still to be found in a variety of battlefield roles especially with the support arms.

The vehicle is NBC proof and when necessary can be converted for swimming when it has a water speed of 6kph. Properly maintained it is a rugged and reliable vehicle with a good cross country performance. The most serious drawback is the lack of vision ports for the crew and their subsequent disorientation after dismounting.

MCV - 80 Fv 510 (Warrior)

(497 in Service). Weight loaded 24,500 kg: Length 6.34 m: Height to turret top 2.78 m: Width 3.0 m: Ground Clearance 0.5 m: Max Road Speed 75 kph: Road Range 500 km: Engine Rolls Royce CV8 diesel: Horsepower 550 hp: Crew 2 (carries 8 infantry soldiers): Armament L21 30 mm Rarden Cannon: Coaxial EX-34 7.62 mm Hughes Helicopter Chain Gun: Smoke Dischargers Royal Ordnance Visual and Infra Red Screening Smoke (VIRSS).

Warrior is an armoured infantry fighting vehicle (AIFV) that replaced the AFV 432 in the armoured infantry battalions. The original buy of Warrior was reduced to 789 units. Of this total the vast majority had been delivered by early 1995 and the vehicle is in service with 3 armoured infantry battalions in the UK (with 3 (UK) Div) and 6 armoured infantry battalions in Germany with 1 (UK) Armd Div).

Warrior armed with the 30 mm Rarden cannon gives the crew a good chance of destroying enemy APC's at ranges of up to 1,500 m and the vehicle carries an infantry section of eight men.

The vehicle is NBC proof, and a full range of night vision equipment is included as standard.

The vehicle has seen successful operational service in the Gulf (1991) and with the British contingent serving with the UN in Bosnia. The vehicle has proven protection against mines, and there is dramatic BBC TV footage of a Warrior running over a Serbian anti tank mine with little or no serious damage to the vehicle or crew .

The Kuwait MOD has signed a contract for the purchase of warrior vehicles some of which are Recce vehicles armed with a 90 mm Cockerill gun. Industry sources suggest that the Kuwait contract is for 230 vehicles.

The process to update Warrior to hold its place on the future battlefield up to the year 2015 is under way but a Mid Life Improvement (MLI) programme is planned to begin in 2001/3 has been shelved. The next generation FIFV programme cannot be completed without the inclusion of digitisation components.

The future digitisation programme in service date (ISD) has slid to to around 2017. Current thinking suggests that the British Army may replace existing rifle platoon Warriors with the improved Warrior 2000. This would release existing Warriors to be refitted to fulfil roles currently carried out by ageing and obsolescent FV 432s. This plan would create a new Battalion Assault Support Vehicle (BASV) which can carry Manoeuvre Support elements, principally 81 mm mortars, at the same pace as the Warrior fighting vehicles. This was a major failing of the FV 432 Mortar Vehicles in the 1991 Gulf War.

This solution would be cheaper than developing a new FIFV concept vehicle and then having to adapt it for digitisation and on board IT components. The scheme would also carry the Warrior through to its original replacement date of 2020 without the expense of planning and engineering a mid-life improvement which could have included the fitting of a new larger calibre cannon and turret.

AFV 103 Spartan

(450 in service) Crew 3: Weight 8,172 kg: Length 5.12 m: Height 2.26 m: Width 2.26 m: Ground Clearance 0.35 m: Max Road Speed 80 kph: Road Range 483 kms: Engine Jaguar J60 No.1 Mark 100B: Engine Power 190 bhp: Fuel Capacity 386 litres: Ammunition Carried 3,000 rounds of 7.62 mm: Armament 1 x 7.62 mm Machine Gun.

Spartan is the APC of the Combat Vehicle Reconnaissance Tracked (CVRT) series of vehicles, which included Fv 101 Scorpion, Fv 102 Striker, Fv 104 Samaritan, Fv 105 Sultan, Fv 106 Sampson and Fv 107 Scimitar. Spartan is a very small APC that can only carry 4 men in addition to the crew of 3. It is therefore used to carry small specialised groups such as the reconnaissance teams, air defence sections, mortar fire controllers and ambush parties.

Samaritan, Sultan and Sampson are also APC type vehicles, Samaritan is the CVRT ambulance vehicle, Sultan is the armoured command vehicle and Sampson is an armoured recovery vehicle.

Spartan, like FV 432 is likely to be replaced by the future Multi Role Armoured Vehicle (MRAV) by the year 2005. In some cases Spartan may be replaced by another future concept vehicle, the Future Command Liaison Vehicle (FCLV).

Spartan is in service with the following nations: Belgium - 266: Oman - 6: Philippines - 7.

Sabre

As part of the UK MoDs CVR(T) rationalisation programme both the tracked
Scorpion with its 76mm gun and the wheeled Fox with its 30mm Rarden Cannon were withdrawn
from service and a hybrid vehicle - Sabre produced. Essentially Sabre consists of the Scorpion chassis fitted with the turret of a Fox.

In addition to the installation of the manually operated two man Fox turret, extensive modifications have been carried out by 34 Base Workshops at Donnington. These modifications include redesigned smoke grenade dischargers, replacement of the 7.62 MG with a 7.62mm Chain Gun, new light clusters and additional side bins. Domed hatches have also improved headroom for both commander and gunner.

We believe that about 104 Sabre vehicle will be introduced into service and that the vehicle has is now on issue to the Reconnaissance Platoons or Armoured and Mechanised Infantry Battalions.

AT - 105 Saxon

(550 in service) Weight 10,670 kg: Length 5.16 m: Width 2.48 m: Height 2.63 m: Ground Clearance (axles) 0.33 m: Max Road Speed 96 kph: Max Road Range 510 km: Fuel Capacity 160 litres: Fording 1.12 m: Gradient 60 degrees: Engine Bedford 600 6-cylinder diesel developing 164 bhp at 2,800 rpm: Armour proof against 7.62 mm rounds fired at point blank range: Crew 2 + 10 max.

The Saxon was manufactured by GKN Defence and the first units for the British Army were delivered in late 1983. The vehicle, which can be best described as a battlefield taxi is designed around truck parts and does not require the enormous maintenance of track and running gear normally associated with APC/AIFVs.

As a vehicle capable of protecting infantry from shell splinters and machine gun fire in Europe during the Cold War years Saxon was a useful addition to the formerly larger Army. It does not, however, have the speed and agility which the lessons of recent mobile combat suggest will be necessary for infantry to survive in the assault in the future. The vehicle is fitted with a 7.62 mm Machine Gun for LLAD.

Each vehicle cost over £100,000 at 1984 prices and they are on issue to 4 mechanised infantry battalions assigned to 3 (UK) Division infantry battalions.

Essentially a mine proof lorry rather than an armoured personnel carrier, the vehicle has been used very successfully by British mechanised battalions serving with the UN in Bosnia.

The Army holds a number of Saxon IS (Patrol) vehicle for service in Northern Ireland. In the recent more peaceful period in the province this vehicle seldom leaves its storage areas The IS equipped vehicle has a Cummins BT 5.1 engine instead of the Bedford 6 cylinder installed on the APC version and other enhancements for internal security operations such as roof mounted searchlights, improved armour, a barricade removal device and an anti-wire device.

Saxon Patrol comes in two versions, troop carrier and ambulance. The troop carrier carries ten men and the ambulance 2 stretcher cases. Industry sources suggest that this latest contract was for 137 vehicles at a cost of some £20 million resulting in a unit cost per vehicle of approximately £145,000.

Some vehicles in the Saxon Battalion are likely to be replaced by the future Multi Role Armoured Vehicle (MRAV).

Saxon is in service with the following overseas customers: Bahrain - 10: Brunei - 24: Hong Kong - 6: Malaysia - 40: Oman - 15.

Milan 2

Missile - Max Range 2,000 m; Mix Range 25 m; Length 918 mm; Weight 6.73 Kg; Diameter 125 mm; Wing Span 267 mm; Rate of Fire 3-4rpm; Warhead - Weight 2.70kg; Diameter 115mm; Explosive Content 1.79kg; Firing Post- Weight 16.4kg; Length 900mm; Height 650mm; Width 420mm; Armour Penetration 352mm; Time of Flight to Max Range 12.5 secs; Missile Speed 720kph; Guidance Semi-Automatic command to line of sight by means of wires:

Milan is a second generation anti-tank weapon, the result of a joint development project between France and West Germany with British Milan launchers and missiles built under licence in the UK by British Aerospace Dynamics. We believe that the cost of a Milan missile is currently in the region of £9,000 and that to date the UK MOD has purchased over 50,000 missiles.

The Milan comes in two main portable components which are the launcher and the missile, it then being a simple matter to clip both items together and prepare the system for use. On firing the operator has only to keep his aiming mark on the target and the SACLOS guidance system will do the rest.

Milan was the first of a series of infantry anti-tank weapons that seriously started to challenge the supremacy of the main battle tank on the battlefield. During fighting in Chad in 1987 it appears that 12 Chadian Milan post mounted on Toyota Light Trucks were able to account for over 60 Libyan T-55's and T-62's. Reports from other conflicts suggest similar results.

Milan is on issue throughout the British Army and an armoured infantry battalion could be expected to be equipped with up to 20 firing posts and 200 missiles. In the longer term we expect to see Milan replaced by MR Trigat in the first decade of the new century. Milan is in service with 36 nations world-wide

MR TRIGAT

Range 2,000 m: Missile Weight 16 kg: Firing Post Weight 20 kg.

MR TRIGAT (Medium Range) is a manportable or vehicle borne, third generation anti-tank missile system designed to replace Milan in service with the British Army by the year 2010. MR TRIGAT is a medium range missile (2,000 m) with SACLOS beam riding guidance. Launch will be low velocity, with thrust vectoring keeping the missile airborne as the aerodynamic surfaces come into effect.

The missile is the result of a European collaborative project with the three main partners being France, Germany and the UK. The manufacturer is Euromissile Dynamics Group (EDMG). Current predictions are that the missiles may cost as much as £25,000 each by the time that the system is accepted into service. The MR Trigat is scheduled to enter service with a single battalion equipped in 2005 and a first Brigade equipped by 2007. Issues may be complete by 2010.

The longer range version LR Trigat with an anti tank battle range out to 4,000 m remains an unfunded aspiration.

LAW 80

Effective Range, Up to 500 m: Armour Penetration, Up to 650 mm: Impact Sensor - Scrub and Foliage Proof: Launcher Length (Firing Mode) 1.5m: Launcher Length (Carrying Mode) 1 m: Carrying Weight 10 kg: Projectile Diameter 94 mm: Temperature Range -46 to +65 degrees C: Rear Danger Area 20 m.

LAW 80 has replaced the 84 mm Carl Gustav and the US 66 mm in service with the British Army, and infantry units in armoured and mechanised battalions are equipped down to section level with this weapon. The latest materials and explosives technology have been utilised in this one-man portable weapon which is capable of destroying main battle tanks at ranges of up to 500 m. Outstanding accuracy against both static and moving targets is achieved by the use of a built-in semi-automatic spotting rifle which reduces aiming errors prior to firing the main projectile. This feature roughly doubles the first-shot kill probability and the shaped charge warhead penetrates armour in excess of 650 mm. In addition to the low light performance of the built in sight, full night capability is available using a night sight.

Hunting Engineering has also developed a range of systems to fire the weapon as a remotely fired anti tank mine. Each system utilises a standard LAW 80 with identical tripod and firing unit. Called ADDERMINE – it is suitable as an off-route mine and is fired when a trip or break wire is disturbed. ADDERMINE/ARGES- is a fully autonomous off-route mine system. The programmable sensor package is capable of selecting a particular target before firing. ADDERLAZE - provides the remote capability to engage single or multiple targets at ranges of up to 2 km by the use of a coded laser pulse to fire the weapon.

A replacement has been planned for Law 80 entitled NLAW. This weapon is intended to embody many of the features of Law 80 but have an increased range out to 600 m. There is also a possibility that the weapon will have an in-built bunker busting capability. There is a projected in service date of 2004 but this is unlikely to be met.

81 mm L16 Mortar

(500 in service) Max Range HE 5,650 m: Elevation 45 degrees to 80 degrees: Muzzle Velocity 255 m/s: Length of barrel 1,280 mm: Weight of barrel 12.7 kg: Weight of base plate 11.6 kg: In action Weight 35.3 kg: Bomb Weight HE L3682 4.2 kg: Rate of Fire 15 rpm: Calibre 81 mm.

The 81mm Mortar is on issue to all infantry battalions, with each battalion having a mortar platoon with 3 or 4 sections; and each section deploying 2 mortars. These mortars are the battalions organic Manoeuvre Support Firepower and can be used to put a heavy weight of fire down on an objective in an extremely short period. Mortar fire is particularly lethal to infantry in the open and in addition is very useful for neutralising dug in strongpoints or forcing armour to close down.

The fire of each mortar section is controlled by the MFC (Mortar Fire Controller) who is usually an NCO and generally positioned well forward with the troops being supported. Most MFCs will find themselves either very close to or co-located with a Task Group commander. The MFC informs the base plate (mortar position) by radio of the location of the target and then corrects the fall of the bombs, directing them onto the target.

Mortar fire can be used to suppress enemy positions until assaulting troops arrive within 200-300 m of the position. The mortar fire then lifts onto enemy counter attack and supporting positions while the assault goes in. The 81mm Mortar can also assist with smoke and illuminating rounds.

The mortar is carried in an AFV432 or a Truck Utility Light or Medium and if necessary can be carried in two man portable loads of 11.35 kg and one 12.28 kg respectively. In the past, infantry companies working in close country have carried one 81mm round per man when operating in areas such as Borneo where wheeled or tracked transport was not available. For Air mobile and Air Assault operations mortar rounds are issued in twin packs of two rounds per man on initial deployment. These are used as initial ammunition resources until palletted ammunition loads can be flown in.

With a strong post Gulf War demand for longer range from the 81 mm Mortar whose 432 vehicles could not keep up with the tanks and Warrior a Mortar Mid-Life Improvement (MLI) programme is under way. The intention is to increase the performance of the barrel, with a minimum increase in weight. There will also eventually be a new digitised fire control system incorporating a global positioning system or GPS.

The 81 mm mortar mid life improvement will inevitably involve digitisation, but as this is slipping in time towards 2015-20 measures have been taken in the interim to enhance the performance of the existing mortar.

Early in 2000 a new compass and GPS Automatic Gun Laying System (AGLS) will be brought into service. Also in 2000 a laser range finder with integrated GPS a Target Locating System (TLE) will come into use which will speed up the identification of precise target Grid locations.
The long awaited replacement Fire Control System, hand held computer has been shelved pending

full digitisation but an Interim Mortar Fire Control System (IMFC) which is a PC based uprate of the existing system should be in service by 2002.

Moves to lighten the barrel and baseplate while achieving greater range using ceramic or other modern materials has been shelved pending full mid life improvement and examination of the emerging possibility of breech loading vehicle borne mortars. There is no UK project funding to examine these innovations at present.

Improved Performance ammunition with greater lethality against buildings, armour and equipment is expected to be in service by 2005.

51 mm Light Mortar

(2093 in service) Range 750 m: Bomb Weight 800 gms (illum), 900 gms (smk), 920 gms (HE): Rapid Rate of Fire 8 rpm: Length of barrel 750 mm: Weight Complete 6.275 kg: Calibre 51.25 mm

The 51 mm Light Mortar is a weapon that can be carried and fired by one man, and is found in the HQ of an infantry platoon. The mortar is used to fire smoke, illuminating and HE rounds out to a range of approximately 750 m; a short range insert device enables the weapon to be used in close quarter battle situations with some accuracy. The 51 mm Light Mortar has replaced the older 1940s 2" mortar.

5.56 mm Individual Weapon (IW) (SA 80)

Effective Range 400 m: Muzzle Velocity 940 m/s: Rate of Fire from 610-775 rpm: Weight 4.98 kg (with 30 round magazine): Length Overall 785 mm: Barrel Length 518 mm: Trigger Pull 3.12-4.5 kg:

Designed to fire the standard NATO 5.56 mm x 45 mm round the SA 80 is fitted with an X4 telescopic (SUSAT) sight as standard. The total buy for SA 80 was for 332,092 weapons. Issues of the weapon are believed to have been made as follows:

Royal Navy	7,864
Royal Marines	8,350
Royal Air Force	42,221
MOD Police	1,878
Army	271,779

At 1991/92 prices the total cost of the SA80 Contract was in the order of £384.16 million. By late 1994 some 10,000 SA 80 Night Sights and 3rd Generation Image Intensifier Tubes for use with SA80 had been delivered.

Since the introduction of the SA 80 the trials carried out during development have borne fruit. In 1993, the Infantry Trials and Development Unit (ITDU) at Warminster in Wiltshire conducted comparative tests on both the SA80 and the SLR using the old SLR APWT (Annual Personal Weapons Test) for both weapons. The results were as follows:

Results	SLR	SA80 with SUSAT
Passes	72%	100%
Marksmanship Standard	17%	51%
Average Score	53	60

There is no doubt that today British Army rifle shooting across the board represents a degree of accuracy previously considered unachievable.

Note: In the trial, based on the Annual Personal Weapons Test, which every soldier is measured by, the highest possible score was 70; the pass mark 49 and the marksmanship standard was 60 out of a possible 70. The APWT has since been amended to take into account the greater accuracy of the SA 80.

The weapon has had a mixed press and much has been made of the 32 modifications that have been made to the SA80 since 1983. Further modifications have recently had to be made to enable the weapon to be more reliable when firing 5.56 ammunition supplied by other NATO countries. Although there are many critics outside of the services, in the main the serving soldiers that we have spoken to have praised the weapon, and those that have had experience on both the SLR and SA80 are unstinting in their praise for the newer system.

Our own enquiries suggest that the SA 80 is highly accurate, it is easily handled and comfortable to use. The weapon is finely engineered and perhaps lacks the robust operational durability of some of its predecessors. It is intolerant of dust and dirt and is inclined to stoppages in dry dusty conditions. It is the first British short assault carbine into service, it will not be the last. It compares favourably with anything else of its type available on the current world market.

The weapon capability has also been extended by the introduction into service of a bullet catcher rifle grenade used in conjunction with a sight fitting issued to individual riflemen and section commanders. Once pulled down over the barrel of the SA80 the grenade is launched by firing a bullet into it which projects it accurately up to 150 m and provides an area suppression capability out to 300 m.

5.56 mm Light Support Weapon (LSW)

Range 1,000 m: Muzzle Velocity 970 m/s: Length 900 mm: Barrel Length 646 mm: Weight Loaded with 30 round magazine 6.58 kg: Rate of Fire 610-775 rpm.

The LSW has been developed to replace the GPMG in the light role and about 80% of the parts are interchangeable with the 5.56 IW (SA 80). A great advantage for the infantryman is the ability of both weapons to take the same magazines. A rifle section will have two 4 man fire teams and each fire team 1 x LSW.

Like the SA 80 the LSW is currently experiencing some difficulty in firing 5.56 mm ammunition supplied by other NATO countries. This problem is under review.

An Image Intensifier night sight, the CWS, has been produced for LSW which gives excellent night vision out to 400 m.

7.62 mm General Purpose Machine Gun (GPMG)

Range 800 (Light Role), 1,800 m (Sustained Fire Role): Muzzle Velocity 538 m/s: Length 1.23 m: Weight loaded 13.85 kg (gun + 50 rounds); Belt Fed: Rate of Fire up to 750 rpm: Rate of Fire Light Role 100 rpm: Rate of Fire Sustained Fire Role 200 rpm.

An infantry machine gun which has been in service since the early 1960s, the GPMG can be used in the light role fired from a bipod or can be fitted to a tripod for use in the sustained fire role. The gun is also found pintle mounted on many armoured vehicles. Used on a tripod the gun is effective out to 1,800 m although it is difficult to spot strike at this range because the tracer rounds in the ammunition belt burns out at 1,100 m.

The GPMG in the light role was the principal manoeuvre support weapon for the section and platoon. It has been replaced by the 5.56mm Light Support Weapon (LSW). The LSW weighs approximately half as much as the GPMG.

1999 SDR cuts in the TA and Regular Army have now made it possible for Light Role and Mechanised Infantry battalions to have 2 light role GPMGs in a fourth Manoeuvre Support Section in each platoon. This additional heavy, long range, firepower, while less accurate than the LSW provides an excellent depth suppression area beaten zone of fire.

Machine Gun platoons in infantry battalions remain equipped with the GPMG in the sustained fire role.

A new heavy machine gun, is planned to come into service by the year 2004. In the meantime the GPMG performance is being enhanced by the issue of a Maxi Kite night image intensification sight giving excellent visibility out to 600 m.

Long Range - Large Calibre rifle (LCR)

The SA 80 is designed to shoot accurately out to 300 m and be easily handled in combat situations. With the disappearance of the .303 the skill of shooting accurately above 400 m has largely died away. The 7.62 mm Sniper Rifle filled the gap for a while but the vulnerability of the round to wind deflection over longer ranges made it desirable to come up with a weapon which could be fired with some precision in all phases of modern warfare.

The result has been the development by Accuracy International UK of the .338 Long Range Large Calibre Rifle. Capable of shooting accurately out to 1,100 m the LCR is due to come into service in early 2000. The weapon will be issued to JRRF (Joint Rapid Reaction Force) units on the basis of 14 per battalion, with one per platoon and a small pool for snipers in the battalion recce platoons.

CHAPTER 6 - ARTILLERY

Background

The Royal Regiment of Artillery (RA) provides the battlefield fire support and air defence for the British Army in the field. Its various regiments are equipped for conventional fire support using field guns, for area and point air defence using air defence missiles and for specialised artillery locating tasks. There are now three Regiments equipped with the Multiple Launch Rocket System (MLRS) which have now taken their place in the Order of Battle and these weapons were used to great effect during the 1991 war in the Gulf. In October 1993 1st Royal Horse Artillery became the first regiment to be equipped with the AS 90 self propelled howitzer.By 1999 the AS 90 self propelled howitzer is the primary 155 mm artillery weapon of the British Army and the towed 155 mm FH 70 has been retired from service.

Following the Strategic Defence Review of 1990, the RA remains one of the larger organisations in the British Army with 17 Regiments included in its regular Order of Battle. It has the following structure in both the UK and Germany (ARRC).

	UK	Germany
Field Regiments (AS 90 SP Guns)	3	3
Field Regiments (Light Gun)	2 (1)	-
Depth Fire Regiments (MLRS)	2 (2)	-
Air Defence Regiments (Rapier)	2	-
Air Defence Regiment (Javelin)	1	- HVM from 2001
Air Defence Regiment (HVM)	-	1
Training Regiment (School Assets Regt)	1	-
The Kings Troop (Ceremonial)	1	-

Note:

(1) Of these 2 Regiments one is a Commando Regiment (29 Cdo Regt) and the other is an Air Assault Regiment (7 PARA RHA*). This Regt has one battery in the Parachute role but the Regt is assigned to the 16th Air Assault Bde at Colchester. Both of these regiments are equipped with the Light Gun. Either of these Regiments can be called upon to provide Manoeuvre Support Artillery to the AMF. On deployment of the AMF it is 29 Cdo Regt RA which forms the AMF Arty HQ and the Commanding Officer is CO Force Arty.

* 7 RHA will, incidentally, keep the designation "PARA" as well as the word "Horse" in their title. 7 RHA Battery titles are those of the famous horse drawn batteries at Waterloo,

(2)The third MLRS Regiment is now a TA Regt with 12 Launch vehicles in peace uprateable to 18 in war.

(3) Although the artillery is organised into Regiments, much of a "Gunner's" loyalty is directed towards the battery in which they serve. The guns represent the Regimental Colours of the Artillery and it is around the batteries where the guns are held that history has gathered. A Regiment will generally have three or four gun batterys under command.

(4) The Schools Asset Regiment is not included in the totals given for artillery in Chapter 1.

The Royal Horse Artillery (RHA) is also part of the Royal Regiment of Artillery and its three regiments have been included in the totals above. There is considerable cross posting of officers and soldiers from the RA to the RHA, and some consider service with the RHA to be a career advancement.

At the turn of the century The Royal Artillery is undergoing a transformation. As when gunpowder lifted the range of the bow and arrow to that of the cannon, currently modern technology both in space and on the ground is showing signs of yielding ever greater range and accuracy to the artillery.

Greater ability to fix locations in depth and the ability to fire projectiles accurately over longer distances is transforming the horizons for modern artillery. Base bleed ammunition reduces drag by burning chemical compounds at the rear of the projectile and results in greatly increased range. Similarly, technology has discovered that there is an optimum relationship between projectile range, diameter and barrel length. Longer ranges used to mean greater beaten zone or dispersion of the fall of shot.

Micro technology now makes it possible for on board computers and navigation systems to provide a long range shell with a once only correction, which brings the round back onto a more precise route to the target. Re-barrelled British Artillery will enter the next decade capable of firing accurately to double their present range.

Rocket artillery is reaching ever further towards the enemy rear areas. The next generation of rocket artillery rounds is looking beyond a range of 80 kms and designers are also looking at precision guided terminal sub munitions. In addition, unmanned aerial vehicles (UAVs) are flying deeper into enemy territory and sending back ever more accurate target data which will be used by the artillery of the future.

The manned aircraft could carry a man and weapons with pinpoint accuracy far beyond the range of an artillery observer. This situation is about to be reversed, and there will probably be little support for sending a man where an artillery observation vehicle can go for a fraction of the cost and a guaranteed target strike. This is likely to happen in the first two decades of the next century. The term "Depth Battle" will have real meaning for the Artillery, they will have an increasingly important part in shaping the future battlefield. Attacking an enemy with ground troops in the field will be less costly if all his command and control headquarters up to 100 km behind the lines have already been identified and destroyed.

Artillery recruits spend the first period of recruit training (Phase 1 Training, Common Military Syllabus) at the Army Training Regiment - Pirbright. Artillery training (Phase 2) is carried out at the Royal School of Artillery (RSA) at Larkhill in Wiltshire. After Phase 2 training, officers and gunners will be posted to RA units world-wide, but soldiers will return to the RSA for frequent career and (Phase 3) employment courses.

The current (1 Jan 2000) permanent locations of the Regular Regiments of the Royal Artillery are as follows:

United Kingdom

1 Regiment RHA	Tidworth	155 mm AS 90
3 Regiment RHA	Hohne	155 mm AS 90
5 Regiment RA	Catterick	STA (3) & Special Ops
7 Parachute Regiment RHA	Colchester (2000)	105 mm Lt Gun

14 Regiment RA	Larkhill	All School Equipments
19 Regiment RA	Colchester	AS 90 (from early 2000)
22 Regiment RA	Kirton-in-Lindsey	Rapier
29 Commando Regiment RA (1)	Plymouth	105 mm Light Gun (2)
47 Regiment RA	Thorney Island	Javelin (HVM 2001)
32 Regiment RA	Larkhill	MLRS & Phoenix UAV
16 Regiment RA	Woolwich	Rapier FSC
39 Regiment RA	Harlow Hill	MLRS & Phoenix UAV
The King's Troop RHA	London	13 Pounders (Ceremonial)

Notes:

(1) The Regimental HQ of 29 Commando Regiment with one battery is at Plymouth. The other two batterys are at Arbroath and Poole. Those at Poole provide the amphibious warfare Naval Gunfire Support Officers (NGFSO).

(2) This Regiment has Cymbeline Locating Radar that is due to be replaced by a new Mobile Artillery Monitoring Battlefield Radar designated "MAMBA", by 2004.

(3) The Surveillance and Target Acquisition (STA) Battery is now equipped with a new Counter Battery Radar designated COBRA.

Germany

4 Regiment RA	Osnabruck	155 mm AS 90
12 Regiment RA	Sennelager	SP HVM on Stormer (1)
26 Regiment RA	Gutersloh	155 mm AS 90
40 Regiment RA	Hohne	155 mm AS 90

(1) Stormer is a tracked vehicle HVM carrier manufactured by ALVIS with 6 road wheels. Very similar in shape to the CVRT Spartan, it is slightly longer and can accommodate the HVM and its guidance equipment.

TA Artillery Regiments

The Honourable Artillery Coy	London	STA and Special Ops
100 Fd Regt RA (V)	Luton	Reinforcement Regt
101 Fd Regt RA (V)	Newcastle	MLRS (12 in peace)
103 Fd Regt RA (V)	Liverpool	Javelin
104 Fd Regt RA (V)	Newport	Javelin
105 Fd Regt RA (V)	Edinburgh	Javelin
106 Fd Regt RA (V)	London	Individual Reinforcements

The diverse equipment available to artillery and the computerised locating and fire control systems now coming into service, combined with "intelligent" munitions and long range weapon platforms are creating another revolution in tactical thinking. In the longer term these developments may have the same effect on land warfare as the emergence of the tank.

Artillery has always been a cost effective way of destroying or neutralising targets. When the cost of a battery of guns, (approx £15 million) is compared with the cost of a close air support aircraft, (£25 million) and the cost of training each pilot, (£4 million +) the way ahead for governments with less and less to spend on defence is clear.

Air Defence is a vital part of the role of the Royal Artillery and updates to the Rapier system continue, and batterys have been upgraded to Field Standard B2 with radar target tracking and Field Standard C which has uprated technology and the ability to carry out dual simultaneous target engagement.

By 2001 there will be two Regiments equipped with HVM, one in the UK and one in Germany. The Germany based Regiment has SP HVM mounted on Stormer tracked vehicles.

In addition, the close air defence systems have been enhanced by the Air Defence Alerting Device (ADAD) for Javelin and HVM, and the Air Defence Command, Control and Information System (ADCIS) which first entered service in late 1994.

The Royal Artillery provides the modern British armoured formation with a protective covering. The close air defence assets covers the immediate airspace above and around the formation, with the field artillery reaching out to 30 kms in front, and 60 kms across the flanks of the formation being supported. An armoured formation that moves out of this protective covering is open to immediate destruction by an intelligent enemy.

Divisional Artillery Group (DAG)

An armoured or mechanised division has it own artillery under command. This artillery usually consists of 3 Close Support Regiments, with a number of units detached from the Corps Artillery and could include TA reinforcements from the UK. In war the composition of the DAG will vary from division to division according to the task.

Armoured Divisional Artillery Group (DAG) - Organisation for War

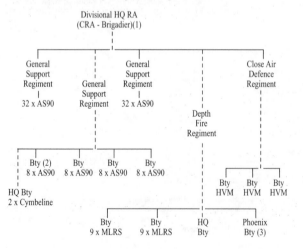

Notes:

(1) This is a diagram of the artillery support which may typically be available to an Armd Div deployed with the ARRC. Expect each brigade in the division to have one Close Support Regiment with AS 90. Artillery regiments are commanded by a Lieutenant Colonel and a battery is commanded by a Major.

(2) The number of batterys and guns per battery in an AS90 Close Support Regiment has changed post SDR 1999 at 4 batterys of six guns per battery in the UK Regiments, and 3 batteries of 6 in the Germany Regiments. In war all batteries will have eight guns each. These additional guns are currently in the training inventory at The School of Artillery and at BATUS in Canada where regular field training takes place

(3) The Locating Battery in the Depth Fire Regiment will have the following configuration:

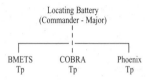

(3) Area Air Defence (AAD) is provided by Rapier.

(4) The staff of an armoured or mechanised division includes a Brigadier of Artillery known as the Commander Royal Artillery (CRA). The CRA acts as the Offensive Support Advisor to the Divisional Commander, and could normally assign one of his Close Support Regiments to support each of the Brigades in the division. These regiments would be situated in positions that would allow all of their batteries to fire across the complete divisional front. Therefore, in the very best case, a battlegroup under extreme threat could be supported by the fire of more than 128 guns.

Artillery Fire Support

A square brigade (of two infantry battalions and two armoured regiments) will probably have a Close Support Regiment of 4 Batterys in support, and the CO of this regiment will act as the Offensive Support Aviser to the Brigade Commander.

It would be usual to expect that each of the 4 battlegroups in the brigade would have a Battery Commander acting as the Offensive Support Adviser to the Battlegroup Commander. Squadron/Company Groups in the Battlegroup would each be provided with a Forward Observation Officer (FOO), who is responsible for fire planning and directing the fire of the guns onto the target. The FOO and his party travel in equivalent vehicles to the supported troops to enable them to keep up with the formation being supported and are usually in contact with:

    (a) The Gun Positions
    (b) The Battery Commander at BGHQ
    (c) The Regimental Fire Direction Centre
    (d) The Company Group being supported.

Having identified and applied prioritisation of targets, the FOO will call for fire from the guns, and he will then adjust the fall of shot to cover the target area. The FOO will be assisted in this task by the use of a Warrior FCLV or future, MRAV OP vehicle containing the computerised fire control equipment which provides accurate data of the target location.

Given a vehicle with its surveillance and target acquisition suite the FOO can almost instantly obtain the correct grid of the target and without calling for corrections, order 1 round fire for effect.

Field Artillery

AS 90

179 in Service: Crew 5: Length 9.07 m: Width 3.3 m: Height 3.0 m overall: Ground Clearance 0.41 m: Turret Ring Diamet er 2.7 m: Armour 17 mm: Calibre 155 mm: Range (39 cal) 24.7 kms (52 cal) 30kms: Recoil Length 780 mm: Rate of Fire 3 rounds in 10 secs (burst) 6 rounds per minute (intense) 2 rounds per minute (sustained): Secondary Armament 7.62 mm MG: Traverse 6,400 mills: Elevation -89/+1.244 mills: Ammunition Carried 48 x 155 mm projectiles and charges (31 turret & 17 hull): Engine Cummins VTA903T turbo-charged V8 diesel 660hp: Max Speed 53 kph: Gradient 60%: Vertical Obstacle 0.75 m: Trench Crossing 2.8 m: Fording Depth 1.5 m: Road Range 420kms.

AS 90 was manufactured by Vickers Shipbuilding and Engineering (VSEL) at Barrow in Furness. 179 Guns have been delivered under a fixed price contract for £300 million. These 179 guns have completely equipped 6 field regiments replacing the older 120 mm Abbot and 155 mm M109 in British service. Three of these Regiments are under the command of 1(UK) Armoured Division in Germany and three under the command of 3 (UK) Division in the United Kingdom.

AS 90 is currently equipped with a 39 calibre gun which fires the NATO L15 unassisted projectile out to a range of 24.7kms (Base Bleed ERA range is 30kms). Funding is available for the rebarrelling of 96 x AS 90 with a 52 calibre gun with ranges of 30kms (unassisted) and 60 t0 80 kms with improved accuracy and long range ERA ammunition. The current in service date for the 52 calibre gun is 2002/3 based on a firm programme which will fit 50% of the guns by November 2002 and up to 90% of them by April 2003.

AS 90 has been fitted with an autonomous navigation and gun laying system (AGLS), enabling it to work independently of external sighting references. Central to the system is an inertial dynamic reference unit (DRU) taken from the US Army's MAPS (Modular Azimuth Positioning System). The bulk of the turret electronics are housed in the Turret Control Computer (TCC) which controls the main turret functions, including gunlaying, magazine control, loading systems control, power distribution and testing.

227mm MLRS

63 launchers in service - 54 operational in 3 Regiments: Crew 3: Weight loaded 24,756 kg: Weight Unloaded 19,573 kg: Length 7.167 m: Width 2.97 m: Height (stowed) 2.57m: Height (max elevation) 5.92m: Ground Clearance 0.43 m: Max Road Speed 64 kph: Road Range 480 km: Fuel Capacity 617 litres: Fording 1.02 m: Vertical Obstacle 0.76 m: Engine Cummings VTA-903 turbo-charged 8 cylinder diesel developing 500 bhp at 2,300 rpm: Rocket Diameter 227 mm: Rocket Length 3.93 m: M77 Bomblet Rocket Weight 302.5 kg: AT2 SCATMIN Rocket Weight 254.46 kg: M77 Bomblet Range 11.5 –32 kms: AT2 SCATMIN Rocket Range 39 kms: One round "Fire for Effect" equals one launcher firing 12 rockets: Ammunition Carried 12 rounds (ready to fire).

The MLRS is based on the US M2 Bradley chassis and the system is self loaded with 2 x rocket pod containers, each containing 6 x rockets. The whole loading sequence is power assisted and loading takes between 20 and 40 minutes. There is no manual procedure.

A single round "Fire for Effect" (12 rockets) delivers 7728 bomblets or 336 scatterable mines and the coverage achieved is considered sufficient to neutralise a 500m x 500m target or produce a minefield of a similar size. Currently the weapon system accuracy is range dependent and therefore more rounds will be required to guarantee the effect as the range to the target increases. Future smart warhead sub munitions currently under development will enable pinpoint accuracy to considerably extended ranges. Ammunition for the MLRS is carried on the DROPS vehicle which is a Medium Mobility Load Carrier. Each DROPS vehicle with a trailer can carry 8 x Rocket Pod Containers and there are 15 x DROPS vehicles supporting the 9 x M270 Launcher vehicles within each MLRS battery.

The handling of MLRS is almost a military "art form" and is an excellent example of the dependence of modern artillery on high technology. Getting the best out of the system is more than just parking the tubes and firing in the direction of the enemy. MLRS is the final link in a chain that includes almost everything available on the modern battlefield, from high speed communications, collation of intelligence, logistics and a multitude of high technology artillery skills and drills. Unmanned aerial vehicles (UAVs)can be used to acquire targets, real time TV and data links are used to move information from target areas to formation commanders and onward to the firing positions. Helicopters can be used to dump ammunition and in some cases to move firing platforms. The refining of this capability is an interesting and dynamic future development area in which available technologies are currently being harnessed and applied.

MLRS is deployed as independent launcher units, using "shoot-and-scoot" techniques. A battery of nine launchers will be given a battery manoeuvre area (BMA), within which are allocated three troop manoeuvre areas (TMA). These TMAs will contain close hides, survey points and reload points. In a typical engagement, a single launcher will be given its fire mission orders using burst data transmission.

An important initial piece of information received is the "drive on angle"; the crew will drive the launcher out of the hide (usually less than 100m) and align it with this angle. Using the navigation equipment, its location is fed into the ballistic computer which already has the full fire mission details. The launcher is then elevated and fired and the process can take as little as a few minutes to complete.

As soon as possible after firing, the vehicle will leave the firing location and go to a reload point where it will unload the empty rocket pods and pick up a full one; this can be done in less than five minutes. It will then go to a new hide within the TMA via a survey point to check the accuracy of the navigation system (upon which the accuracy of fire is entirely dependent). The whole of this cycle is co-ordinated centrally, and details of the new hide and reload point are received as part of the fire mission orders. The complete cycle from firing to being in a new hide ready for action might take half an hour.

In a typical day, a battery could move once or twice to a new BMA but this could impose a strain upon the resupply system unless well planned (bearing in mind the need for the ammunition to be in position before the launcher vehicle arrives in a new BMA). The frequent moves are a result of security problems inherent in MLRS's use. In addition to attack by radar-controlled counterbattery fire, its effectiveness as an interdiction weapon makes it a valuable target for special-forces units. Although MLRS will be hidden amongst friendly forces up to 15km behind the FEBA, its firing signature and small crew (three) will force it to move continually to avoid an actual confrontation with enemy troops.

There are currently two Regular and one TA MLRS Regiments. The Regular Regiment operates 18 launcher vehicles and the TA Regiment 12 in peace and 18 in war.

The US Army is currently operating 857 MLRS, the French have 58, the Germans 154 and the Italians 21.

105 mm Light Gun
(72 in service). Crew 6: Weight 1,858 kg: Length 8.8 m: Width 1.78 m: Height 21.3 m: Ammunition HE, HEAT, WP, Smoke, Illuminating, Target Marking: Maximum Range (HE) 17.2 kms: Anti Tank Range 800 m: Muzzle Velocity 709m/s: Shell Weight HE 15.1 kg: Rate of Fire 6 rounds per minute.

The 105 mm Light Gun has been in service with the Royal Artillery for 25 years and is about to receive its first and only major upgrade in that time. The enhancement is an Auto Pointing System (APS) which performs the same function as the DRU on the AS 90. The APS is based on an inertial navigation system which enables it to be unhooked and into action in 30 seconds. The APS replaces the traditional dial sight and takes into account trunnion tilt without the requirement to level any spirit level bubbles as before.

A touch screen display tells the gun controller when his gun is laid onto the correct target data provided. This enhancement improves the accuracy of the fall of shot to a greater degree of accuracy than possible with the dial sight. User trials will begin in early 2000 with a proposed in service date across all Light Gun Batteries of May 2001.

The Light Gun is in service with the UK Parachute/Air Assault and Commando Field Artillery Regiments as a go-anywhere, airportable weapon which can be carried around the battlefield underslung on a Puma or Chinook.

The gun was first delivered to the British Army in 1975 when it replaced the 105mm Pack Howitzer. A robust, reliable system, the Light Gun proved its worth in the Falklands, where guns were sometimes firing up to 400 rounds per day.

The Light Gun has been extremely successful in the international market with sales to Australia (59), Botswana (6), Brunei (6), Ireland (12), Kenya (40), Malawi (12), Malaysia (20), Morocco (36), New Zealand (34), Oman (39), Switzerland (6), UAE (50), United States (548) and Zimbabwe (12).

Air Defence Artillery

Javelin

(240 Fire Units in Service) Length 1.4 m: Missile Diameter 76 cm: Missile Weight 11.1 kgs: Max Range 5.5 kms: Warhead Weight 2.72 kgs: Max Altitude 3,000 feet: Max Speed Mach 1.7+: Fuse Proximity or Impact: Guidance SACLOSBR; Mount Man-Portable.

Javelin , soon to be fully replaced in Regular units by HVM was the British Army's successor to Blowpipe and is currently in service with one regular regiment and 3 TA regiments in the UK. 47 AD Regt batterys support UK brigades as follows:-

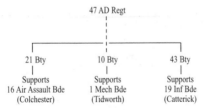

47 AD Regt is due to re-equip with HVM by 2001.

Javelin is an electronically more sophisticated system than Blowpipe with a greater range and a night sight. The greatest advantage is that it is now SACLOSBR guided, and all the operator has to do is keep the aiming mark on the target, leaving the guidance system to do the rest.

Javelin is a highly accurate system. Target practice during Javelin testing in 1985 presented the British Army with a problem regarding the numbers of available target drones. So many target drones were being destroyed during training that testing had to be slowed down until the manufacture of target drones caught up.

Javelin is deployed in armoured vehicles (Spartan or AFV 432) or wheeled vehicles to provide point air defence for troops in the forward areas of the battlefield. A Javelin battery normally has 36 launchers.

There has been considerable overseas interest in Javelin which was believed to cost about £60,000 per missile at 1990 prices. Sales have already been made to Jordan and South Korea with potential customers believed to be Malaysia, Chile, Oman and Zimbabwe.

Javelin's predecessor Blowpipe achieved considerable success in the world market and we believe that over 30,000 missiles had been manufactured by 1990, with sales being made to the following - Canada, Chile, Ecuador, Malawi, Nigeria, Oman, Portugal, Qatar, and Thailand. Guerrilla forces in both Angola and Afghanistan are known to have acquired Blowpipe missiles.

Starstreak HVM
(108 Fire Units In Service) Missile Length 1.39m: Missile Diameter 0.27m: Missile Speed Mach 3+: Maximum Range 5.5 kms:

Short Missile Systems of Belfast are the prime contractors for the HVM (High Velocity Missile) which continues along the development path of both Blowpipe and Javelin. The system can be shoulder launched or mounted on the LML (lightweight multiple launcher) or vehicle borne on the Alvis Stormer APC. The Stormer APC has an eight round launcher and twelve reload missiles can be carried inside the vehicle.

HVM has been optimised to counter threats from fast pop-up type strikes by attack helicopters. The missile employs a system of three dart type projectiles which can make multiple hits on the target. Each of these darts has an explosive warhead. It is believed that the HVM has an SSK (single shot to kill) probability of over 95%.

12 Regiment RA stationed at Sennelager in German is equipped with HVM and supports 1 (UK) Division. This regiment is configured as follows:

12 Regiment RA

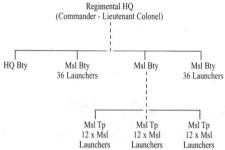

84

Note: The Regiment has 108 launchers divided amongst the three missile batteries. An HVM detachment of 4 is carried in a Stormer armoured vehicle and in each vehicle there are 4 personnel.

Rapier
(64 fire units in service) Guidance Semi Automatic to Line of Sight (SACLOS): Missile Diameter 13.3 cm: Missile Length 2.35 m: Rocket Solid Fuelled: Warhead High Explosive: Launch Weight 42 kg: Speed Mach 2+: Ceiling 3,000 m: Maximum Range 6,800 m: Fire Unit Height 2.13 m: Fire Unit Weight 1,227 kg: Radar Height (in action) 3.37 m: Radar Weight 1,186 kg: Optical Tracker Height 1.54 m: Optical Tracker Weight 119 kg: Generator Weight 243 kg: Generator Height 0.91 m.

The Rapier system provides area 24 hour through cloud, Low Level Air Defence (LLAD) over the battlefield. The two forms of Rapier in service are as follows:-
Rapier Field Standard B2 consists of an Optical Tracker, a launcher, a Radar and a Generator. The into-action time of the system is thought to be about 15 minutes and the surveillance radar is believed to scan out to 15 km. Each fire unit can therefore cover an Air Defence Area (ADA) of about 100 square kms. Having discharged the 6 missiles on a Fire Unit, 2 men are thought to be able to carry out a reload in about 3 minutes.

Rapier Field Standard C (FSC) incorporates a range of technological improvements including an advanced 3 dimensional radar tracker acquisition system designed by Plessey. The towed system launcher will mount eight missiles (able to fire two simultaneously) which will be manufactured in two warhead versions. One of these will be a proximity explosive round and the other a kinetic energy round. The total cost of the Rapier FS "C" programme is £1,886 million.

The Royal Artillery has two regiments equipped with Rapier and both are in the UK. In the Falklands Campaign, Rapier was credited with 14 kills and 6 probables from a total of 24 missiles fired.

Rapier has now been sold to the armed forces of at least 14 nations. We believe that sales have amounted to over 25,000 missiles, 600 launchers and 350 Blindfire radars.

Artillery Locating Devices

Sound Ranging
Sound Ranging is now obsolescent in all but one or two situations. Sound Ranging (SR) locates the positions of enemy artillery from the sound of their guns firing. Microphones are positioned on a line extending over a couple of kilometres to approximately 12 kilometres. As each microphone detects the sound of enemy guns firing the information is relayed to a Command Post which computes the location of the enemy battery. Enemy locations are then passed to Artillery Intelligence and counter battery tasks fired as necessary. Sound Ranging can identify an enemy position to within 50 metres at 10 kms. The only Sound ranging assets remaining in the Royal Artillery are those with 5 Regt RA at Catterick.

The UK has one battery equipped with HALO 2A, an accoustic weapons locating equipment specifically for use in out of area or sensitive operations where flying UAVs might be sensitive. Consideration is being given to providing a Sound Ranging troop to 29 Cdo Regt RA.

MSTAR

Weight 30 kg: Wavelength J - Band: Range in excess of 20 kms.

MSTAR is a Lightweight Pulse Doppler J - Band All Weather Radar that has replaced the ZB 298 in the detection of helicopters, vehicles and infantry. Powered by a standard army field battery this radar will also assist the artillery observer in detecting the fall of shot. The electroluminescent display that shows dead ground relief and target track history, also has the ability to superimpose a map grid at the 1:50,000 scale to ease transfer to military maps. MSTAR can be vehicle borne or broken down into three easily transportable loads for manpacking purposes.

MSTAR has been delivered to the Royal Artillery and will be used by Forward Observation Officers. In time there should be over 100 MAOV (Warrior Mechanised Artillery Observation Vehicles) equipped with MSTAR. MSTAR is believed to cost about, 50,000 pounds per unit at 1993 prices, and, by the late 1990s we see a requirement for over 250 MSTAR equipments for use throughout the British Army.

COBRA

Cobra (Counter Battery Radar)is a 3-D Phased Array Radar that has been developed for West Germany, France and the UK. Cobra came into service with 5 Regt RA in mid 1999. The dominant cost element of the Cobra Radar is the antenna, which probably accounts for about 70% of the unit price. There are believed to be about 20,000 Gallium Arsenide integrated circuits in each antenna. This will enable the equipment to produce the locations of multiple enemy artillery at extremely long ranges, and the radar will be able to cope with saturation type bombardments. In addition there will be a high degree of automated software, with high speed circuitry and secure data transmission to escape detection from enemy electronic countermeasures.

Cobra therefore appears to be an ideal equipment for operation in conjunction with MLRS. 5 Regt will field three Cobra Troops, each Troop consisting of three radars.

Cymbeline Mortar Locating Radar
(10 in service) Range 20 kms: Weight of Radar 390 kgs: Frequency I/J Band:

Cymbeline is the mortar locating radar which is currently under the command of the General Support Regiments in both Germany and the UK. Cymbeline is mounted on an AFV 432.

Cymbeline detects the flight path of a mortar bomb at two points in the trajectory as it passes through the radar beam(s); rapid computing then enables the grid reference of the enemy base plate to be identified and engaged with artillery. An 81 mm mortar bomb can be detected at a range of about 10 kms while a 120mm bomb is detectable at about 14 kms.

Cymbeline first came into service with the British Army in 1973 and will probably stay in service for some time to come, with the possibility of a further Mark 4 upgrade to the present Mark 3 systems.

In 1994, Cymbeline was deployed by the British Army in support of United Nations operations in the Sarajevo area of the Former Yugoslavia to identify gun and mortar positions around the city. The equipment appears to have been extremely successful in this role and provided much valuable intelligence for the UN Command Staff. The equipment was used extensively during the late 1995 UN bombardment of Serb artillery positions.

At the beginning of 1999 we believe that there were over 325 Cymbeline in service with 18 nations, including Singapore, Norway, Denmark, Finland, Oman, Saudi Arabia, Egypt, Kuwait, Nigeria, South Africa, Malawi, Switzerland and New Zealand.

Phoenix

Phoenix is an all weather, day or night, real time surveillance system which consists of a variety of elements. The twin boom UAV (unmanned air vehicle) provides surveillance through its surveillance pod, the imagery from which is datalinked via a ground data terminal (GDT) to a ground control station (GCS). This controls the overall Phoenix mission and is used to distribute the UAV provided intelligence direct to artillery forces, to command level, or to a Phoenix troop command post (TCP). The principal method of communication from the GCS to artillery on the ground is via the battlefield artillery engagement system (BATES).

Powered by a 19kW (25hp) Target Technology 342 two stroke flat twin engine, the Phoenix air vehicle (with a centrally mounted fuel tank) is almost entirely manufactured from composites such as Kevlar, glass fibre, carbon reinforced plastics and Nomex honeycomb. The principal subcontractor is Flight Refuelling of Christchurch in Dorset.

The modular design UAV can be launched within one hour of reaching a launch site and a second UAV can be dispatched within 8 minutes from the same launcher. The wing span is 5.5m and the maximum launch weight 175kgs. The manufacturer, GEC states that "Flight endurance is in excess of 4 hours, radius of action 50kms and the maximum altitude 2,700m (9,000 feet).

A flight section consists of a launch and recovery detachment and a ground control detachment. The launch and recovery detachment consists of three vehicles; the launch support vehicle, with several UAVs and mission pods in separate battlefield containers, plus operational replacement spares and fuel; the launch vehicle, which features a pallet-mounted lifting crane, the hydraulic catapult and launch ramp, a pre-launch detonator device, built-in test equipment, and the Land Rover recovery vehicle which is fitted with cradles for the air vehicle and mission pod. The ground-control detachment consists of two vehicles, the ground control station and the Land Rover towed ground data terminal.

The British Army has two operational batterys of Phoenix (54 UAV) deployed to the two Regular MLRS Regts. The balance which make up the TA MLRS Regt allocation are in use for school and training purposes. A battery has 27 x UAV, with associated ground support equipment they have enough resources to launch 72 flights. There is sufficient Phoenix equipment to field 3 battereys in war two are operational now and the third, a reserve/training pool deployed to the TA MLRS Regt in war. The total cost of the programme is £227 million.

BMETS

The Battlefield Meteorological System (BMETS) came into service in 1999 and replaces AMETS which entered service in 1972 and provided met messages in NATO format. However, with AMETS there was only one system for each division resulting in a high radius of data application and the system was vulnerable because it used an active radar.

BMETS troops are generally 20 strong, and the troop is usually part of a larger Locating Battery that also has a Cymbeline counter battery radar. With the extreme range of modern artillery and battlefield missiles, very precise calculations regarding wind and air density are needed to ensure that the target is accurately engaged.

BMETS units can provide this information by releasing hydrogen filled balloons at regular intervals recording important information on weather conditions at various levels of the atmosphere.

To benefit from current technology BMETS uses commercially available equipment manufactured by VAISALA linked to the Bafflefield Artillery Target Engagement System (BATES). It is a two vehicle system with a detachment of 5 in peace, 6 in war. It will be deployed with all regular field artillery and MLRS regiments.

BMETS can operate in all possible theatres of conflict world wide where the Meteorological Datum Plan (MDP) varies from 90m below to 4,000m above sea level, and can be used with a variety of radiosonde types to sound the atmosphere to a height of up to 20 km. Measurements are made by an ascending radiosonde. This is tracked by a passive radiotheodolite which provides wind data, air temperature, atmospheric pressure and relative humidity from the datum plan for each sounding level, until flight termination. In addition, virtual temperature, ballistic temperature and ballistic density are calculated to a high degree of accuracy. Cloud base is estimated by observation. The data is then processed by receiver equipment in the troop vehicles to provide formatted messages to user fire units via the existing military battlefield computer network

Air Defence Alerting Device (ADAD)
An infra-red thermal imaging surveillance system that is used by close air defence units, to detect hostile aircraft and helicopter targets and directs weapon systems into the target area. The air defence missile operators can be alerted to up to four targets in a priority order. The passive system which is built by Thorn EMI, has an all weather, day and night capability.

Chapter 7 - Army Aviation

"Float like a butterfly - sting like a bee".

      Muhammad Ali.

Aviation Support

The Army obtains its aviation support from two agencies. The first is the Army Air Corps (AAC), which is an Army organisation with 6 separate regiments and a number of independent squadrons. The AAC also provides support for Northern Ireland on a mixed resident and roulement basis and the two squadrons concerned are sometimes referred to as the seventh AAC Regiment, although the units would disperse on mobilisation and have no regimental title.

By mid 1995 and following the "Options for Change" restructuring AAC regimental locations will be as follows:

1 Regiment - Germany	(651,652 & 661 Sqns)
3 Regiment - Wattisham	(653,662 & 663 Sqns)
4 Regiment - Wattisham	(654,659 & 669 Sqns)
Regiment - Aldergrove	(655 & 665 Sqns)
7 Regiment - Netheravon	(658 & 666(V) Sqns)
9 Regiment - Dishforth	(656, 657 & 664 Sqns)
2 (Trg) Regiment - Depot	

The HQ of 2 (Trg) Regiment is at Middle Wallop and there are TA Flights at Netheravon, Turnhouse and Shawbury.

In addition to the Regiments in the UK and Germany there are small flights in Cyprus, Bruggen (Germany), Brunei, Suffield (Canada) and the Falklands Islands.

The AAC Centre at Middle Wallop in Hampshire acts as a focal point for all Army Aviation, and it is here that the majority of corps training is carried out. From Mid 1997 elementary flying training for all three services has been taking place at RAF Shawbury in Shropshire.

Although the AAC operates some fixed wing aircraft for training, liaison flying and radar duties, the main effort goes into providing helicopter support for the ground forces. About 350 AAC helicopters are used for anti-tank operations, artillery fire control, reconnaissance, liaison flying and a limited troop lift. As of mid 1999 the Army Air Corps had approximately 3,200 personnel. There is an establishment figure for 544 trained pilots and at the beginning of 1999 there was a shortfall of 44.

Attack Helicopters

Army aviation is heavily involved in the battlefield revolution that was mentioned earlier in this publication. With the ability to move ground forces around the battlefield at speeds of up to 200 kph and the proven ability of anti-tank helicopters to defeat tanks at 5,000 m+, the helicopter has approached the point where it could be claimed to be one of the most important equipments on the battlefield.

All of the credible military nations have expressed their belief in the importance of the armed helicopter, and the United States lead the way with over 1,400 armed helicopters of which over 700 are AH-64 attack types. Many analysts believe that the armed helicopter has a superiority over the tank in the region of 20:1 and recent West German operational analysis figures suggest that this superiority may be even higher.

During the 1991 Gulf War the US Army deployed 288 x AH-64 Apache in 15 Army Aviation battalions. The US Army claim that these aircraft destroyed 120 x APCs, 500 x MBT, 120 x Artillery Guns, 10 Radar Installations, 10 x Helicopters, 30 x Air defence Units, about 300 soft skinned vehicles and 10 x fixed wing aircraft on the ground. A single Army Aviation AH-64 battalion is believed to have destroyed 40 x APCs and over 100 x MBT in an engagement that lasted over 3 hours, firing 107 Hellfire missiles and over 300 x 70 mm rockets.

At the very beginning of the war 8 x AH-64 each equipped with 8 x Hellfire, 76 x 70 mm rockets and 1,100 rounds of 30 mm ammunition attacked radar early warning installations about 80-100 kms inside Iraq. Their task was to open a 30 km wide sterilised air corridor through which allied aircraft could transit to targets deep inside enemy territory. During the operation the helicopters fired 27 x Hellfire missiles, 100 rockets and about 4,000 rounds of 30 mm ammunition, and achieving a very high success rate over a total distance of some 1,300 kms during the 15 hour mission.

What we are looking at is the natural progression of cavalry operations into another dimension. The 1980s aphorism "Rotors are to tracks as tracks were to horses" has not yet quite come to pass. Tracks, machine guns, and barbed wire drove horses from the modern battlefield. However, as the 20th century draws to a close, tanks, APCs, and other tracked vehicles are still very prominent and viable on that battlefield. Just as armour is most effective when supported by infantry, artillery, and even tactical air, helicopters are most effective when used in conjunction with, rather than in place of, armour and the other combat arms. However, helicopters so increase the range, mobility, reach, and vision of armoured forces, that they may be thought of as the latest manifestation of cavalry.

Cavalry operations used to be thought of as light or heavy. In classic cavalry operations, heavy cavalry, as manifested by the mounted man-at-arms or Murat's Cavalry Corps, delivered shock action and exploited penetrations. Confederate General JEB Stuart's operations in the first two years of the American Civil War typify light cavalry as a scouting and screening force.

Indeed, the division persisted into armoured operations. Heavy armour provided shock, penetration, and exploitation or pursuit, while scouting, screening, and the control of insurgents were the province of light armour. Attack or combat helicopters are roughly analogous to heavy cavalry. Their heavy armament provides shock and limits the enemy's freedom of operation, while their defensive and protective features enable them to operate in the thick of the modern battlefield or strike deep behind enemy lines. Lighter helicopters, while often armed, lack the survivability of their heavier brethren. Consequently, they must operate from concealment or from behind friendly lines. Thus, they inherit the light cavalry roles of scouting and observation.

However, it would be wise to take all of these recent changes in their turn and not "go overboard" on any one particular system. The attack helicopter is going to be an increasingly important battlefield system in the years to come, but it is part of an essential military "whole" and not a battle winner in isolation.

In its turn the helicopter is already threatened. To ensure survival helicopters fly close to the "nap of the earth" (NOE) and hide behind features such as woods and small hills. The race is on to produce effective anti-helicopter mines that recognise friend from foe, and either destroy low flying helicopters operating along likely transit routes, or force them to fly higher where they become vulnerable to missiles and anti-aircraft fire. Plans for large procurements of anti-helicopter mines have already been made in the US and many European Union (EU) nations.

We believe that there are approximately 11,000 helicopters, armed to some degree, in current world service. Of these, about 4,000 may be classed as attack helicopters.

AAC Attack Helicopter

The current attack helicopter in service with the AAC is Lynx with TOW, and will continue to be so until after about 2002 when a significant number of the British Army"s new attack helicopter will be in service.

During July 1995 the UK MoD announced the purchase of 67 x Westland WAH-64 Apaches at a cost of £2.5 billion. The WAH-64 was chosen in preference to the European Tiger alternative from British Aerospace and the lower-cost Cobra Venom offer from GEC-Marconi Avionics.

The aircraft, an improved McDonnel Douglas AH-64 is to be powered by Rolls-Royce Turbomeca RTM322 engines, giving commonality with the Royal Air Force and Royal Navy EH 101 helicopters.

It is believed that an air-to-air weapon capability will continue to be investigated and trials of the Shorts Starstreak missile onboard an AH-64 will continue in the US. Any longer term decision to proceed will be based on the results of these US Army trials.

The WAH-64 will be deployed with two AAC Regiments supporting two divisions, 16 Air Assault Brigade and the Royal Marines. It is probable that about 3,000 jobs will be created in the UK as a result of the purchase.

Support Helicopters

The majority of the troop lift and logistical support for military operations is provided by the RAF who currently operate approximately 75 support helicopters (Wessex, Puma, Chinook). This is a slightly unusual arrangement and there are excellent reasons to support proposals which suggest that these aircraft should be under AAC command and control. This system may not work as well as it might because of differences in operational procedures linked to traditional service attitudes and priorities. We firmly believe that an army commander on the ground should command all the battlefield assets at his disposal including troop lift helicopters and their crews. The British Army is the one remaining major NATO Army where the Army Commander does not have total command and control over his helicopter fleet. Allowing such a situation to continue to exist could invite confusion in a crisis situation. However, it should be said that the recent establishment of a Joint Helicopter Command (under PJHQ command) has gone some way to rectifying the situation.

AAC Regimental Organisation

Organisations for the individual AAC Regiments appear to have settled following the "Options for Change Review". The following wiring diagram outlines the organisation of a 3 Regiment AAC in early 1999. 3 Regiment supports the Colchester based 16 Air Assault Brigade. Various regimental organisations are a variation on this theme.

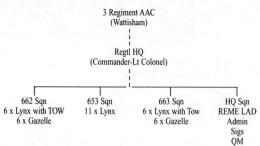

3 Regiment AAC
(Wattisham)

Regtl HQ
(Commander-Lt Colonel)

662 Sqn	653 Sqn	663 Sqn	HQ Sqn
6 x Lynx with TOW	11 x Lynx	6 x Lynx with Tow	REME LAD
6 x Gazelle		6 x Gazelle	Admin
			Sigs
			QM

Totals: Approx 450 personnel
35 Helicopters

Notes:

(1) A Regiment of this type could act as the core formation of an airborne battlegroup. If necessary an infantry aviation company consisting of 3 x rifle platoons and a Milan anti-tank platoon will be attached. The infantry could be moved in RAF Chinooks or Pumas.

(2) 4 Regiment AAC joined 3 Regiment in Wattisham during early 1995 and we believe that both regiments have a similar organisation. Wattisham is also the home of 7 Bn REME - a unit configured as an aircraft workshops. First indications are that the WAH-64D will be deployed with both of these regiments.

(3) Both 3 and 4 Regiments are set to be equipped with WAH-64 Apache and each regiment will probably have 24 aircraft (8 per squadron).

RAF Support

As previously mentioned the second agency that provides aviation support for the Army is the Royal Air Force. In general terms the RAF provides helicopters that are capable of moving troops and equipment around the battlefield, and fixed wing fighter ground attack (FGA) aircraft that provide close air support to the troops in the vicinity of the Forward Edge of the Battlefield Area (FEBA). The RAF also provides the heavy air transport aircraft that will move men and material from one theatre of operations to another.

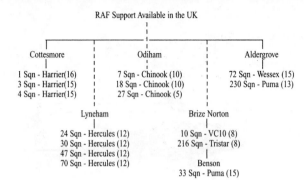

RAF Support Available in the UK

Cottesmore
1 Sqn - Harrier(16)
3 Sqn - Harrier(15)
4 Sqn - Harrier(15)

Odiham
7 Sqn - Chinook (10)
18 Sqn - Chinook (10)
27 Sqn - Chinook (5)

Aldergrove
72 Sqn - Wessex (15)
230 Sqn - Puma (13)

Lyneham
24 Sqn - Hercules (12)
30 Sqn - Hercules (12)
47 Sqn - Hercules (12)
70 Sqn - Hercules (12)

Brize Norton
10 Sqn - VC10 (8)
216 Sqn - Tristar (8)

Benson
33 Sqn - Puma (15)

(1) Figures in brackets are our estimate of the number of aircraft in each squadron during early 2000.

(2) A further 18 x Harrier are available with the Operational Conversion Unit (OCU) at RAF Cottesmore. This OCU has the mobilisation title of 20 (R) Sqn.

(3) Not shown on the above diagram but available for support if necessary are 24 x Tornado GR1A and 30 x Jaguar GR1A/B.

We would expect the AAC armed helicopter to deal with the localised armoured threats to a British force on operations, with RAF aircraft (such as the Harrier and Tornado) being used on targets of regimental size (90 tanks) and above. However, high performance modern aircraft are very expensive and fast jet pilots take up to 3 years to train. It would only be sensible to risk such valuable systems when all other options had failed. In addition, the strength of enemy air defences would probably allow only one pass to be made over the target area. A second pass by fixed wing aircraft after ground defences had been alerted would be almost suicidal.

AAC Aircraft

Longbow Apache (WAH-64)

(67 On Order) Gross Mission Weight 7,746 kgs (17,077 lb; Cruise Speed at 500 meters 272 kph; Maximum Range (Internal Fuel with 20 minute reserve) 462 kms; General Service Ceiling 3,505 meters (11,500 ft); Crew 2; Carries - 16 x Hellfire II missiles (range 6,000 meters approx); 76 x 2.75" rockets; 1,200 30 mm cannon rounds; 4 x Air to Air Missiles; Engines 2 x Rolls Royce RTM-332.

The UK MoD ordered 67 Longbow Apache from Westland during mid 1995 with the first aircraft being delivered to the Army Air Corps during 2000. From this figure of 67 aircraft we believe that there will be 48 aircraft in two regiments (each of 24 aircraft). The remaining 19 aircraft will be used for trials, training and a war maintenance reserve (WMR).

In September 1999, the first WAH-64 Apache made its first flight and was handed over to GKN Westland (the UK contractor) at the Boeing aircraft plant in Arizona. Boeing is building the first eight aircraft and will partially assemble the other 59. GKN Westland will undertake final assembly, flight testing and programme support at his Yeovil factory.

Lynx AH - Mark 7/9

(115 in service). Length Fuselage 12.06 m: Height 3.4 m: Rotor Diameter 12.8 m: Max Speed 330 kph: Cruising Speed 232 kph: Range 885 km: Engines 2 Rolls-Royce Gem 41: Power 2 x 850 bhp: Fuel Capacity 918 litres(internal): Weight (max take off) 4,763 kg: Crew one pilot, one air-gunner/observer: Armament 8 x TOW Anti-Tank Missiles: 2-4 7.62 mm machine guns: Passengers-able to carry 10 PAX: Combat radius approximately 100 kms with 2 hour loiter.

Lynx is the helicopter currently used by the British Army to counter the threat posed by enemy armoured formations. Armed with 8 x TOW missiles the Lynx is now the mainstay of the British armed helicopter fleet. However, in addition to its role as an anti-tank helicopter, Lynx can be used for fire support using machine guns, troop lifts, casualty evacuation and many more vital battlefield tasks.

During hostilities we would expect Lynx to operate on a section basis, with 2 or 3 Lynx aircraft armed with TOW directed by a Section Commander possibly flying in a Gazelle. The Section Commander would control what is in reality an airborne tank ambush and following an attack on enemy armour decide when to break contact. Having broken contact, the aircraft would return to a forward base to refuel and rearm. Working from forward bases, some of which are within 10 kms of the FEBA, it is suggested that a Lynx section could be "turned around" in less than 15 minutes. Lynx with TOW replaced SCOUT with SS11 as the British Army's anti-tank helicopter.

We believe the majority of Lynx in British service to be Lynx Mark 7 and that there are currently 24 Lynx Mark 9 (the latest version) in the inventory.
Lynx is known to be in service with France, Brazil, Argentina, The Netherlands, Qatar, Denmark, Norway, West Germany and Nigeria. The naval version carries anti-ship missiles.

TOW 2B
(Tube Launched, Optically Tracked, Wire Guided, Anti-Tank Missile). Length 1.17 m: Diameter 15 cm: Maximum Range 3,750 m: Speed 1,127 khp (200mps): Warhead 3.9 kg shaped charge high explosive HEAP : Missile Weight 28.1 kg: Guidance Automatic command to line of sight: Armour Penetration 800 mm.

TOW is the US system that has been adopted for use on the Lynx anti-tank helicopter. First seen in US service in 1965 TOW is a very powerful system that can defeat the armour on all conventional MBTs. It is also a second generation missile in that the operator no longer "flies" the missile to the target using a control stick. All the operator needs to do is keep the aiming mark on the target and the guidance system will do the rest. AAC Lynx are fitted with the roof-mounted stabilised M65 sight.

TOW 2B is the top attack version of the missile system and these systems in AAC service are being upgraded under the Further Improved Tow Programme which enhances both range (possibly 5,000 m) and armour penetration.

Gazelle
(154 in service). Fuselage Length 9.53 m: Height 3.18 m: Rotor Diameter 10.5 m: Maximum Speed 265 kph: Cruising Speed 233 kph: Range 670 km: Engine Turbomeca/Rolls-Royce Astazou 111N: Power 592 shp: Fuel Capacity 445 litres: Weight 1,800 kg (max take off): Armament 2 x 7.62 mm machine guns (not a standard fitting).

Gazelle is the general purpose helicopter in use by the AAC and it is capable of carrying out a variety of battlefield roles. Gazelle is a French design built under licence by Westland Aircraft. Over 1,000 Gazelles are in service with air forces and civil aviation organisations throughout the world.

A-109

(5 in service) Fuselage Length 10.7 m: Rotor Diameter 11.0 m: Cruising Speed 272 kph: Range 550 kms: Service Ceiling 4,570 m: Engines 2 x 420-shp Allison 250-C20B turboshafts: Fuel Capacity 560 litres: Weight 1,790 kg: Max Take Off Weight 2,600 kg: Crew Pilot plus observer + 7 pax:

The AAC has five of these light general purpose aircraft for liaison flying and special tasks. The aircraft are part of 8 Flight based at Netheravon in Wiltshire.

BN-2 Islander

(7 In Service) Crew 2; Length Overall 12.37 m; Max Take Off Weight 3,630 kg; Max Cruising Speed at 2,135 m (7,000 ft and 75% of power) 257 kph (154 mph); Ceiling 4,145 m (13,600 m); Range at 2,137 m (7,000 ft and 75% of power) 1,153 km (717 miles); Range with Optional Tanks 1,965 kms (1,221 miles).

The AAC's BN-2 Islanders carry the Thorn EMI CASTOR (Corps Airborne Stand Off Radar) that is designed to provide intelligence information in the forward edge of the battlefield (FEBA) and beyond while operating well within friendly territory. The radar, located in the nose cone of the aircraft has a 360 degree scan and offers wide coverage against moving and static targets.

Chipmunk T Mark 10

(21 In Service) Crew 2; Length 7.8 m; Span 10.3 m; Height 2.13 m; Max Speed 222 km/ph (138 mph); Engine 1 x 1DH Gipsy Major 8 Piston Engine.

The world famous Chipmunk is currently used to give air experience/basic flying training to potential AAC pilots. These aircraft were initially taken into service with the RAF in 1950 and we are sure that it will be some considerable time before they disappear from service. At the height of the "Cold War" the RAF's permanent presence in Berlin was a flight of 2 x Chipmunks, a presence that we are assured was not directly responsible for the collapse of the Warsaw Pact.

RAF Aircraft

Puma

In Service With:

33 Sqn	RAF Benson
230 Sqn	RAF Aldergrove

(33 in Service) Crew 2 or 3; Fuselage Length 14.06 m; Width 3.50 m; Height 4.38 m; Weight (empty) 3,615 kg; Maximum Take Off Weight 7,400 kgs; Cruising Speed 258 km/ph (192 mph); Service Ceiling 4,800 m; Range 550 kms; 2 x Turbomecca Turmo 111C4 turbines.

The "package deal" between the UK and France on helicopter collaboration dates back to February 1967 when Ministers of the two countries signed a Memorandum of Understanding (MOU). The programme covered the development of three helicopter types - the Puma, Gazelle and Lynx. The main contractors engaged on the programme were Westland and SNIAS for the airframe, and Rolls Royce and Turbomeca for the engines.

Development of the Puma was already well advanced in France when collaboration began. However, the flight control system has been developed jointly by the two countries, and a great deal of work done by Westland to adapt the helicopter for the particular operational requirements of the RAF. Production of the aircraft was shared between the two countries, the UK making about 20% by value of the airframe, slightly less for the engine as well as assembling the aircraft procured for the RAF. Deliveries of the RAF Pumas started in 1971.

The Puma is powered by 2 x Turbomeca Turmo 111C4 engines mounted side by side above the main cabin. Capable of many operational roles Puma can carry 16 fully equipped troops, or 20 at light scales. In the casualty evacuation role (CASEVAC), 6 stretchers and 6 sitting cases can be carried. Underslung loads of up to 3,200 kgs can be transported over short distances and an infantry battalion can be moved using 34 Puma lifts.

Chinook

In Service With:

7 Sqn	RAF Odiham
18 Sqn	RAF Odiham
27 Sqn (R) (OCU)	RAF Odiham
78 Sqn	RAF MPA (Falklands)

(29 in Service) Crew 3; Fuselage Length 15.54 m; Width 3.78 m; Height 5.68 m; Weight (empty) 10,814 kgs; Internal Payload 8,164 kgs; Rotor Diameter 18.29 m; Cruising Speed 270 km/ph (158

mph); Service Ceiling 4,270 m; Mission Radius(with internal and external load of 20,000 kgs including fuel and crew) 55 kms; Rear Loading Ramp Height 1.98 m; Rear Loading Ramp Width 2.31 m; Engines 2 x Avco Lycoming T55-L11E turboshafts.

The Chinook is a tandem-rotored, twin-engined medium lift helicopter. It has a crew of four (pilot, navigator and 2 x crewmen) and is capable of carrying 45 fully equipped troops or a variety of heavy loads up to approximately 10 tons. The first Chinooks entered service with the RAF in 1982. The triple hook system allows greater flexibility in load carrying and enables some loads to be carried faster and with greater stability. In the ferry configuration with internally mounted fuel tanks, the Chinook's range is over 1,600 kms (1,000 miles). In the medical evacuation role the aircraft can carry 24 x stretchers.

Chinook aircraft have been upgraded to the HC2 standard. The first of the 32 aircraft being upgraded was delivered to the RAF in the Spring of 1993, with the remaining aircraft modified by the end of 1995. The HC2 upgrade, for which a total of £145 million was allocated, allowed for the aircraft to be modified to the US CH-47D standard with some extra enhancements. These enhancements include fitting infra-red jammers, missile approach warning indicators, chaff and flare dispensers, a long range fuel system and machine gun mountings.

This is a rugged and reliable aircraft. During the Falklands War reports suggest that, at one stage 80 fully equipped troops were carried in one lift and, during a Gulf War mission a single Chinook carried 110 Iraqi POWs. The Chinook mid-life update significantly enhances the RAF's ability to support the land forces during the next 25 years.

Analysts suggest that since 1 April 1990 the RAF Chinook fleet has flown some 60,000 hours during which time the operating costs (personnel, fuel and maintenance) have been £310 million, a figure that results in a cost of about £5,200 per flying hour. On average, 27 of 32 aircraft have been available for front-line service at any one time, a figure reflecting the need for planned maintenance and servicing. On 9 March 1995, the UK MoD announced a purchase of a further 14 x Chinooks and a separate buy of 22 x EH 101 (Merlin) . The contract for the 14 x Chinooks was signed in early September 1995 at a price of £240 million (US$365), resulting in a possible unit cost of £17 million per aircraft.

Once the 14 new Chinooks are in service we believe that the RAF will be capable of operating a fleet of 38 Chinooks.

Westland Wessex Mark 2

(15 in service). Crew 1-3; Pax 16 in main cabin: Length 20.03 m: Main Rotor Diameter 17.07 m: Height 4.93 m: Cabin Door Size 1.22 m x 1.22 m: Operating Weight Mk2 3,767 kg: Payload Mk2 1,117 kg: Max Speed 212 kph: Cruising Speed 195 kph: Max Range 770 km.

The first production model of the Wessex Mk2 was delivered to the RAF in 1962, and until the introduction of Puma the Wessex Mk 2 was the most numerous transport helicopter in service with the British Forces. It is believed that the RAF now operates one Wessex Mk2 squadron which supports UKLF (72 Sqn - RAF Aldergrove - 15 aircraft), a Wessex squadron in service with the RAF in Cyprus (No 84 Sqn - RAF Akrotiri - possibly 5/6 aircraft). Other marks of Wessex are used by the RAF for Search and Rescue and by the Royal Navy for antisubmarine warfare.

Harrier

In Service With:

1 Sqn	RAF Cottesmore
3 Sqn	RAF Cottesmore
4 Sqn	RAF Cottesmore
20 Sqn (R) OCU*	RAF Wittering

(51 in service) Crew (GR7) 1; (T Mark 10) 2; Length (GR7) 14 m; Length (T10) 17 m; Wingspan (normal) 9.3 m; Height (GR7) 3.45 m; Height (T10) 4.17 m; Max Speed 1,083 kph (673 mph) at sea level; All Up Operational Weight approx 13,494 kg; Armament 2 x 30 mm Aden guns, 4 x wing weapon pylons and 1 x underfuselage weapon pylon, conventional or cluster bombs; Engine 1 x Rolls-Royce Pegasus 11-21; Ferry Range 5,382 kms (3,310 miles) with 4 x drop tanks.

Capable of taking off and landing vertically, the Harrier is not tied to airfields with long concrete runways but can be dispersed to sites in the field close to the forward edge of the battle area. The normal method of operation calls for a short take-off and vertical landing (STOVL), as a short ground roll on take-off enables a greater weapon load to be carried. The Harrier GR3 was the mark of the aircraft that was taken into service in large numbers starting in 1969.

The Harrier GR5 entered service in 1988 with the intention of replacing all of the RAF's GR3s on a one for one basis. However, the GR5 has been upgraded to the GR7 which, in turn, entered service in June 1990. All three of the operational Harrier squadrons have been equipped with the GR7 and all of the GR3s and GR5s have either been upgraded or withdrawn from service.

The differences in the GR5 and the GR7 are mainly in the avionics. The GR7 is equipped with the Forward Looking Infra-Red (FLIR) equipment which, when combined with the night vision goggles (NVGs) that the pilot will wear, gives the GR7 a night, low-level, poor-weather capability. There are small differences in the cockpits of the two aircraft including layout and internal lighting standards. In most other respects, the GR7 is similar to the GR5.

The GR7 offers many advantages over the older GR3. It possesses the capability to carry approximately twice the weapon load over the same radius of action, or the same weapon load over a much increased radius. In addition, it carries a comprehensive ECM (Electronic Counter Measures) suite which can operate in the passive or active MoDe and will greatly enhance the GR5/7s chances of survival in today's high threat environment. The GR7 also has an inertial navigation system that is significantly more effective than that of the GR3.

The cockpit of the GR7 has been completely revised. The raising of the cockpit in relation to the aircraft has vastly improved the pilot's outlook. Furthermore, the design has incorporated the principle of Hands-On-Throttle and Stick (HOTAS). To aid systems management Cathode Ray Tube (CRT) displays are much in evidence for the display of the FLIR image, moving map, systems status and flying instruments displays. Each CRT has numerous multi-function reprogrammable keys for each function selection, again aiding systems management.

The LRMTS of the GR3 has been replaced with the Angle Rate Bombing System (ARBS) as the primary weapon aiming system. The ARBS incorporates a Dual Mode Tracker, either TV colour contrasts or laser spot tracker. The GR7 has an increased wing area, improved aerodynamic qualities and the incorporation of Leading Edge Root Extensions which all combine to give the GR7 much improved manoeuvrability over that of the GR3. However, the GR7 maintains its ability to vector the engine's thrust in forward flight (VIFF), again increasing manoeuvrability.

The GR7 was derived from the McDonnell Douglas/British Aerospace AV-8B. Noteworthy changes include the addition of a moving map display, Martin Baker ejection seat, increased bird strike protection, a new Aden 25 mm cannon and additional electronic countermeasures equipment.

The T10 is an advanced trainer version of the aircraft. A total of 13 x Harrier T10 are available.

Expect a Harrier GR7 Squadron to have 17 established crews.

C-130 Hercules
In Service With:

24 Sqn	RAF Lyneham
30 Sqn	RAF Lyneham
47 Sqn	RAF Lyneham
70 Sqn	RAF Lyneham
57 Sqn (R) OCU	RAF Lyneham

Note: The LTW (Lyneham Transport Wing) appears to have a total of 54 aircraft.

Crew 5; Capacity 92 troops or 62 paratroops or 74 medical litters or 19,686 kgs of freight; Length 29.78 m; Span 40.41 m; Height 11.66 m; Weight Empty 34,287 kgs; Max Load 45,093 kgs; Max speed 618 km/ph (384 mph); Service Ceiling 13,075 m; Engines 4 x Allison T-56A-15 turboprops.

The C-130 Hercules C1 is the workhorse of the RAF transport fleet. Over the years it has proved to be a versatile and rugged aircraft, primarily intended for tactical operations including troop carrying, paratrooping, supply dropping and aeromedical duties. The Hercules can operate from short unprepared airstrips, but also possesses the endurance to mount-long range strategic lifts if required. The aircraft is a derivative of the C-130E used by the United States Air Force, but is fitted with British Avionic equipment, a roller-conveyor system for heavy air-drops and with more powerful engines. The crew of five includes, pilot, co-pilot, navigator, air engineer and air loadmaster.

As a troop carrier, the Hercules can carry 92 fully armed men, while for airborne operations 62 paratroops can be dispatched in two simultaneous "sticks" through the fuselage side doors. Alternatively, 40 paratroops can jump from the rear loading ramp. As an air ambulance the aircraft can accommodate 74 stretchers.

Freight loads that can be parachuted from the aircraft include: 16 x 1 ton containers or 4 x 8,000 pound platforms or 2 x 16,000 pound platforms or 1 x platform of 30,000 pounds plus. Amongst the many combinations of military loads that can be carried in an air-landed operation are: 3 x Ferret scout cars plus 30 passengers or 2 x Land Rovers and 30 passengers or 2 x Gazelle helicopters.

Of the original 66 C1 aircraft, some 31 have been given a fuselage stretch producing the Mark C3. The C3 "stretched version" provides an additional 37% more cargo space. Refuelling probes have been fitted above the cockpit of both variants and some have received radar warning pods under the wing tips. One aircraft, designated Mark W2, is a special weather version and is located at the DRA Farnborough.

RAF Hercules are often involved in humanitarian tasks in support of UN operations in many areas of the world. For example, working from a forward airhead at Ancona on the eastern coast of Italy, a detachment of 38 officers and men with a single Hercules from 47 Sqn, averaged almost three flights a day for the year 3 July 1992 - 3 July 1993. Over 900 sorties lifted more than 19 million pounds of freight into Sarajevo. The aircraft were flown by six crews on a two-week rotation from RAF Lyneham.

Current plans appear to be for the replacement of the RAF's ageing 1960s Hercules fleet during the next ten years and, in 1995, the UK MoD announced the purchase of 25 x C-130J from the US company Lockheed. This aircraft has improved engines, a new glass cockpit with flat screen displays and a two-man crew. After some delay with Lockheed admitting problems in getting demonstrator and production aircraft to the correct configuration the first aircraft should enter operational RAF service during late 1998.

101

The MoD is considering ordering a second batch of 30 transport aircraft and the contenders will probably be Lockheed once again, with a C-130 built to a new K standard and the FLA (Future Large Aircraft). The FLA which will be built by the Rome based Euroflag Consortium, will probably be ready for service from about 2004 and could be capable of carrying a maximum payload of 30 tons as opposed to the 20 tons of the C-130J. British Aerospace is a member of the Euroflag consortium.

The most commonly quoted argument in favour of the FLA is that this aircraft could carry a 25 ton payload over a distance of 4,000 km. Thus it is argued that a fleet of 40 x FLA could carry a UK Brigade to the Gulf within 11.5 days, as opposed to the 28.5 days required to make a similar deployment with 40 x C-130s.

Over 1,000 x C-130 have been manufactured and 467 are in service with the US Armed Forces.

Tristar

(9 in service) Crew 3; Passengers 265 and 35,000 pounds of freight; Length 50.05 m; Height 16.87 m; Span 47.35 m; Max Speed 964 km/ph (600 mph); Range 6,000 miles (9,600 kms); Engines 3 x 22,680 kgs thrust Rolls Royce RB 211-524B4 turbofans.

The Tristar K1 and KC1 are strategic tanker conversions of the Lockheed L-1011-500 Tristar commercial airliner. The Tristar K1 can also be fitted with up to 204 passenger seats for the trooping role. The Tristar KC1 tanker/freight aircraft have a large 140 x 102 inch, cargo door and a roller conveyer system capable of accepting up to 20 cargo pallets or seating for up to 196 passengers. Linked pallets can be used to permit the carriage of vehicles.

Also in service is the Tristar C2. This aircraft can carry 265 passengers and 35,000 pounds of freight over ranges in excess of 4,000 miles. It is planned to give these aircraft a tanker capability by fitting two wing refuelling pods.

The Tristar normally cruises at 525mph and with a payload of 50,000 pounds has a range in excess of 6,000 miles. The aircraft entered service in early 1986 with No 216 Sqn which reformed at RAF Brize Norton on 1 Nov 1984.

VC-10

(10 in service with 10 Sqn and 101 Sqn) Crew 4; Carries 150 passengers or 78 medical litters; Height 12.04 m; Span 44.55 m ; Length 48.36 m; Max Speed (425 mph); Range 7596 kms; All Up Operational Weight 146,513 kgs; Engines 4 x Rolls Royce Conway turbofans.

The VC-10 is a fast transport aircraft which is the backbone of Strike Command's long-range capability, providing flexibility and speed of deployment for British Forces. This multi-purpose aircraft can be operated in the troop transport, freight and aeromedical roles in addition to maintaining scheduled air services.

The VC-10 carries a flight deck crew of four - captain, co-pilot, navigator and engineer - and has a flight deck seat for an additional supernumerary crew member. Normal cabin staff are two air loadmasters and two air stewards. On scheduled services up to 126 passengers are carried. Under the floor of the aircraft are two large holds which can carry up to 8.5 tons of freight. If necessary, the aircraft can be converted for use as a freighter or an air ambulance when 78 stretcher cases can be carried. Five aircraft are used as airborne refuelling tankers.

Chapter 8 - Engineers

Background

The engineer support for the Army is provided by the Corps of Royal Engineers (RE). This large corps, currently composed of 12 regular regiments (including 2 training regiments) and 5 TA regiments filled with highly skilled tradesmen, is presently organised as follows:

	Germany	UK
Engineer Regiments	4	4
EOD Regiment	-	1
Resident N Ireland Regiment	-	1
Training Regiments	-	2
TA Engineer Regiments	-	5

There are also a number of independent engineer squadrons world-wide. The former Gurkha Engineer Regiment QGE (Queen's Gurkha Engineers) has now been reduced to a large squadron.

The Royal Engineers provide specialist support to the combat formations, and engineer detachments, can be found at all levels from the Combat Team/Company Group upwards. Combat Engineers could be expected to be involved in the following tasks during specific phases of warfare:

a. Defence: Construction of field defences; minelaying; improvement and construction of obstacles.

b. Attack: Obstacle crossing; demolition of enemy defences (bunkers etc);
mine clearance; bridge or ferry construction.

c. Advance: Building or strengthening roads and bridges; removal of booby
traps; mine clearance; airfield construction; supply of water; survey.

d. Withdrawal: Demolition - of airfields, roads and bridges, fuel ammunition and food dumps, railway tracks and rolling stock, industrial plant and facilities such as power stations; route clearance; minelaying; booby trapping likely enemy future positions and items that might be attractive to the enemy.

Some of the other tasks performed by the men of the RE include map making and survey, the disposal of unexploded munitions (enemy bombs etc), airfield damage repair and advice to other arms on camouflage and concealment. Often amongst the first soldiers into battle, and still involved in dangerous tasks such as Explosive Ordnance Disposal (EOD) and mine clearance in the former Yugoslavia, the Sappers can turn their hands to almost any engineering-related task.

Recent peacekeeping tasks have highlighted the importance of combat engineers in all spheres of military activity. During the period 1993-1997 the multitude of tasks for which engineer support was requested stretched the resources of the Corps to its limit. Engineers are almost always among the first priorities in any call for support: tracks must be improved, roads built, accommodation constructed for soldiers and refugees, and clean water provided. All of these are tasks that soak up large amounts of manpower and at the end of 1999 Engineer Regiments continue to be faced with an interval of about 10 months between operational tours - with some members of the Corps on their third or fourth operational tour in the Former Yugoslavia.

Organisations

The smallest engineer unit is the Field Troop which is usually commanded by a Lieutenant and consists of approximately 44 men. In an Armoured Division, a Field Troop will have up to four sections, each mounted in an APC. Engineer Regiments in UK may have only three sections and may be mounted in wheeled vehicles such as Land Rovers and 4 Ton Trucks. An engineer troop will deploy with most of its equipment scale (known as G1098), stores and explosives to enable it to carry out its immediate battlefield tasks.

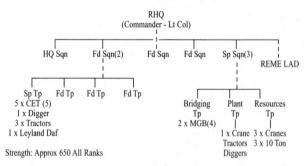

Armoured Divisional Engineer Regiment

RHQ
(Commander - Lt Col)

HQ Sqn   Fd Sqn(2)   Fd Sqn   Fd Sqn   Sp Sqn(3)
REME LAD

Sp Tp   Fd Tp   Fd Tp   Fd Tp
5 x CET (5)
1 x Digger
3 x Tractors
1 x Leyland Daf

Bridging   Plant   Resources
Tp   Tp   Tp
2 x MGB(4)

1 x Crane   3 x Cranes
Tractors   3 x 10 Ton
Diggers

Strength: Approx 650 All Ranks

(1) This Regiment would send most of its soldiers to man the engineer detachments that provide support for a Division's battlegroups; (2) Field Squadron (a Field Squadron will have approximately 68 vehicles and some 200 men; (3) Support Squadron; (4) Medium Girder Bridge; (5) Combat Engineer Tractor; (6) This whole organisation is highly mobile and built around the AFV 432 and Spartan series of vehicles; (7) In addition to the Regimental REME LAD, each squadron has its own REME section of approximately 12 - 15 men.

An Engineer Field Troop assigned to work in support of a Battlegroup operating in the area of the FEBA would normally resemble the following:-

Field Troop Organisation

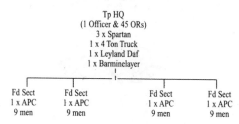

Tp HQ
(1 Officer & 45 ORs)
3 x Spartan
1 x 4 Ton Truck
1 x Leyland Daf
1 x Barminelayer

Fd Sect	Fd Sect	Fd Sect	Fd Sect
1 x APC	1 x APC	1 x APC	1 x APC
9 men	9 men	9 men	9 men

Engineer amphibious capability and specialist support is provided by elements of 28 Engineer Regiment in Germany and a TA Regiment with 227 Amph Engr Sqn in the UK. The current organisation of 28 Regiment resembles the following.

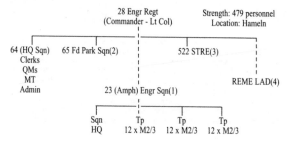

28 Engr Regt
(Commander - Lt Col)

Strength: 479 personnel
Location: Hameln

64 (HQ Sqn)
Clerks
QMs
MT
Admin

65 Fd Park Sqn(2)

522 STRE(3)

REME LAD(4)

23 (Amph) Engr Sqn(1)

Sqn HQ	Tp 12 x M2/3	Tp 12 x M2/3	Tp 12 x M2/3

(1) 23 Amphibious Engineer Squadron, with about 170 men, is believed to have 36 x M2 Ferries (to be replaced by M3 later in the decade); (2) 65 Field Park Squadron acts as the theatre engineering resource unit: as well as manufacturing and repairing equipment, it holds equipment required by all RE units in Germany. The Squadron has about 100 military and 150 civilian staff. (3) 522 Specialist Team Royal Engineers (STRE) is a small unit(approx 26 strong) which provides a "design consultancy" service for specific engineering tasks. (4) The REME LAD has three repair platoons and a strength of 152 personnel. (5) On mobilisation 28 Engineer Regiment would take 2 x Field Squadrons from 35 Engineer Regiment (also in Hameln) under command, and 21 Field Squadron (EOD) from 33 Engineer Regiment (EOD) in the UK.

The UK Engineer Field Regiment (Regular & TA) is generally a wheeled organisation that would normally have 2 Field Squadrons, a Support Squadron and possibly an Airfield Damage Repair

(ADR) Squadron. Engineer regiments supporting 3(UK) Division are likely to be structured along the lines of the Armoured Divisional Engineer Regiment.

Combat Engineer Tractor
(140 in service) Weight 17,010 kg: Length 7.54 m: Height 2.67 m: Road Speed 56 kph: Road Range 480 kms: Fuel Capacity 430 litres: Engine Rolls-Royce C6TCR: Engine Power 320 bhp: Crew 2: Armament 1 x 7.62 mm machine gun.

The Combat Engineer Tractor (CET), which entered service in 1977, is a versatile tracked AFV that can clear obstacles, dig pits, prepare barriers and recover other vehicles that become stuck or damaged. In short, it is an armoured vehicle that can assist in a variety of engineer battlefield tasks, and has an impressive amphibious capability. The 100 m winch cable can be fired from the CET by rocket and, using an anchor, can assist in dragging the vehicle up steep slopes and over river banks. CET is found mainly in the Divisional Engineer Regiments and the UK Engineer Regiments. India has 39 x CET in service and Singapore is believed to have another 18.

Replacement plans for the CET are already underway; during 1995 the UK MOD initiated a feasibility study for the next generation Armoured Combat Engineer Vehicle. The new vehicle will be called "Terrier" and indications are that some 100 vehicles could be required.

The key Terrier requirements are for a vehicle which could be tracked or wheeled, include the ability to dig, load, grab, lift, carry and winch with the crew under armour protection. The vehicle must also be able to tow a trailer carrying fascines, trackway, the GIAT Viper minefield breaching system; clear scatterable mines; remove or enhance obstacles, and establish routes while keeping pace with other armoured vehicles such as the Challenger 2 MBT and the Warrior MICV.

Project-definition contracts for the Terrier were awarded in mid 1999 to Marconi Marine, Land and Naval Systems and Vickers Defence Systems who are teamed with Caterpillar. One of these contractors will be awarded a production contract and the vehicle has in in-service date of 2008.

Chieftain Assault Vehicle Royal Engineers - CHAVRE
The CHAVRE has a crew of 4: the Chieftain gun turret has been removed and replaced by an armoured "penthouse" upon which the commanders cupola is situated. Mounted over the vehicle structure are two "hampers"; one at the front of the vehicle and one at the rear. These "hampers" carry engineer stores such as trackway, fascines or general equipment. A typical "hamper" load might be 4 x rolls of Class 60 trackway or 3 x fascines.

At the front of the vehicle is a dozer blade or mine plough (either can be used) and at the rear there is a hydraulic winch capable of pulling 10 tons. In the centre of the vehicle is a crane capable of lifting 3.5 tons, with a telescopic jib that extends to 5 metres. A Giant Viper mine clearance explosive hose system can be towed, and the vehicle is armed with an LSW for local defence.

The MOD ordered 48 vehicles, which were delivered by the end of 1995. CHAVRE replaces the Centurion Mk 5 Assault Vehicle Royal Engineers that had been in service since the early 1960s.

There are plans for a Future Engineer Tank (FET) which will replace the Chieftain AVRE and the Chieftain AVLB and the system will be deployed in both versions. The requirement is for between 80 and 102 vehicles that will probably use a Challenger chassis. AVRE Obstacle Breaching Vehicle will replace the AVRE, while the Future AVLB Gap Crossing vehicle will succeed the AVLB. This system will carry and launch the recently-introduced VDS BR-90 bridging system.

In mid 1999, three contractors won one-year feasibility study contracts for the FET: UK company Alvis Vehicles; OBRUM of Poland (teamed with Marconi Marine, Land and Naval Systems) and Vickers Defence Systems. One contractor will be selected for a development and production contract. The in-service date is probably around 2005.

Chieftain Bridgelayer (AVLB)
(49 in service) Weight 53,300 kg: Length 13.74 m: Height 3.92 m: Width 4.16 m: Max Road Speed 42 kph: Road Range 400 km: Engine L60 No4 Mark 7A: Engine Power 730 bhp: Fuel Capacity 886 litres: Bridge Length (No. 8 Bridge) 24.4 m: Bridge Width (No 8 Bridge) 4.16 m: Bridge Weight (No8 Bridge) 12,200 kg: Crew 3.

In service since 1974 the Chieftain AVLB can carry the No 8 Bridge (24.4m long) and the No 9 Bridge (13m long). A No 8 Bridge can normally be laid across a gap in about 5 minutes. The bridge can then be recovered from the far side of the gap and carried along behind the battlegroup being supported. The main holdings of AVLB are within 32 Engineer Regiment in Germany, with smaller numbers in the UK.

The replacement for this vehicle (Future AVLB Gap Crossing Vehicle) will be based on a Challenger chassis and has an in service date of 2001.

M2/3 Ferry
Weight 22,000 kg: Length 11.3 m: Height 3.58 m: Width 2.99 m: Width (bridge deployed) 1.42 m: Max Road Speed 60 kph: Water Speed 15 kph: Road Range 1,000 kms: Crew 4.

There are approximately 72 x M2 vehicles in British Army service; they are held in 28 Engineer Regiment in Germany and a TA Regiment in the UK. The M2 can be driven into a river and used as a ferry or, when bolted together, form a bridge capable of taking vehicles as heavy as the Challenger

MBT. The M2 is a German vehicle which first entered service in 1972 and it is currently being replaced by 34 M3 Bridge sets.

The M3 has three bridging ramps in place of the four on the M2, a length increase of 2.3 metres, increased buoyancy and can be driven in the water from either end. The vehicle is powered by marine jets instead of propellers and only 2 x ferries are required to carry an MBT (instead of the 5 x M2's needed for the same task). It is understood that the cost of the M3 is in the region of £1 million per vehicle.

Medium Girder Bridge (MGB)
The MGB is a simple system of lightweight components that can be easily manhandled to construct a bridge capable of taking the heaviest AFVs. Two MGBs are held by the Bridging Troop in the Support Squadron of a Divisional Engineer Regiment.

Single span bridge - 30 m long which can be built by about 25 men in 45 minutes.

Multi span bridge - a combination of 26.5 m spans: a 2 span bridge will cross a 51 m gap and a 3 span bridge a 76 m gap. If necessary, MGB pontoons can be also be joined together to form a ferry.

During late 1994 a team from 35 Engr Regt set a new world record by building a single storey 9 metre bridge in 10 minutes and 34 seconds. The manufacturer Williams Fairey claims that the MGB was in service with 35 nations world wide. MGB is due to be replaced by the BR90 system (although some MGB will be retained for certain operational requirements).

Class 16 Airportable Bridge
A much lighter bridge than the MGB, the Class 16 can be carried assembled under a Chinook helicopter or in 3 x 3/4 ton vehicles with trailers. A 15 m bridge can be constructed by 15 men in 20 minutes. The Class 16 can also be made into a ferry which is capable of carrying the heaviest AFVs.

Giant Viper
Trailer Weight 2,136 kgs; Hose Length 230 m; Cleared Zone 183 m x 7.3 m wide.

The Giant Viper is a system which is used for clearing lanes through a minefield. It consists of a rocket attached to an explosive-filled hose, which is carried in a special trailer. The trailer, containing rocket and hose, can be towed behind vehicles such as the CHAVRE, CET or FV 432.

The trailer is positioned 150m from the edge of the minefield and the rocket is fired, propelling the explosive-filled hose into, or right across, the minefield. The subsequent explosion of the hose will breach a lane 180 m long and 7.3 m wide. Trials and research suggest that in a "cleared" lane over 90% of anti-tank mines will have been destroyed.

Mine Warfare
Anti-tank minefields laid by the Royal Engineers will usually contain Barmines (anti-tank) or Mk. 7 (anti-tank) mines and anti-disturbance devices may be fitted to some Barmines. Minefields will always be recorded and marked; they should also be covered by artillery and mortar fire to delay enemy mine clearance operations and maximise the attrition of armour. ATGWs are often sited in positions covering the minefield that will give them flank shoots onto enemy armour; particularly the ploughs or rollers that might spearhead a minefield breaching operation.

Barmine (Anti-Tank)
Weight 11 kg: Length 1.2 m: Width 0.1 m: Explosive Weight 8.4 kg.

The Barmine is usually mechanically laid by a plough-type trailer that can be towed behind an AFV 432 or Warrior. The Barmines are manually placed onto a conveyor belt on the layer from inside the APC. The minelayer automatically digs a furrow, lays the mines into it at the correct spacing and closes the ground over them. Up to 600 mines can be laid in one hour by one vehicle with a 3-man crew. A full width attack (FWAM) fuze and an anti-disturbance fuze are available for Barmine; these are secured on the ends of the mine, adjacent to the pressure plate.

During early 1996 the British Army has announced that it has a requirement to refurbish up to 30,000 L9A1 anti-tank Barmines fitted with the L89A1 pressure fuze. In the longer term, the British Army has a requirement for a Barmine replacement system to meet Staff Requirement (Land) 4036.

This requirement includes both the Barmine and an associated command and control system, which could allow the minefield to be switched on and off according to operational requirements. There is an in service date of 2002 for the new system.

Volcano
To meet the British Army Staff Requirement (Land) 4020 for a vehicle-launched scattering anti-tank mine system, during late 1995 the UK MoD selected the Alliant Techsystems M163 Volcano system, with the Alvis Stormer flatbed as the carrier vehicle.

It is believed that the total value of the order is approximately £110 million for 29 x Volcano systems, anti-tank mines, training, spares and the Stormer flatbed carrier. The in service date for the system is 1999.

In British Army service Volcano will only lay anti-tank mines. These mines are carried in canisters, each of which hold six mines with up to up to 40 canisters are carried on a launcher rack. These are on the rear of the Stormer flatbed and discharge the anti-tank mines either side as the vehicle moves across the terrain. A dispenser control unit provides fire signals, testing and arming of the self-destruct mechanism.

Claymore Mine (Anti-Personnel)
Weight 1.58 kg: Length 210 mm: Width 30 mm: Charge Weight 0.68 kg.

The Claymore Mine has a curved oblong plastic casing mounted on a pair of bipod legs. The mine is positioned facing the enemy and fired electrically from distances up to 300 m away. On initiation, the mine scatters about 700 ball-bearings out to a range of 50 m across a 60 degree arc. First purchased from the US in 1963, the Claymore is an effective anti-infantry weapon that is likely to remain in service for many years to come.

Off-Route Mine (Anti-Tank)
Length 0.26 m: Weight 12 kg: Diameter 0.2 m: Range 75 m.

This French mine is designed for vehicle ambush. The mine is placed at the side of the road and a thin electric "breakwire" laid out across the vehicle's path. The mine is initiated when the vehicle breaks the wire; a shaped charge known as a "Misznay Schardin Plate" fires an explosively formed projectile into the side of the vehicle.

Mk. 7 Mine (Anti-Tank)
Charge Weight 8.89 kg: Mine Weight 13.6 kg: Diameter 0.13 m.

The Mk. 7 Mine is a large, round metal-cased blast mine which may be initiated by pressure or tilt-rod (to give it a full-width attack capability). It has been in service for many years and, when stocks are exhausted, will be replaced by the Barmine. The Mk. 7 mine can be mechanically laid from a large trailer, akin to a mobile assembly line. This obsolete piece of equipment has a very poor cross-country capability and no protection for the operators.

Mine Detectors

L77A1
Weight Packed with all accessories:	6.5 kg
Weight Deployed ready for use:	2.2 kg
Approximate Battery Life:	5 hrs
Detection Depth (metal AT mine):	0.6 - 0.7 m

The 4C, the standard mine detector of the British Army since 1968, has been replaced by the Ebinger EBEX-420PB. The Army have designated the detector L77A1 and assigned it the NATO Stock Number 6665-99-869-3649. The L77A1 is a lightweight modular design which uses pulse induction technology to locate the metallic content of mines. The battery compartment and electronics are built into the tubular structure, and an audible signal provided to the operator via a lightweight earpiece. The sensitivity is such that even modern plastic mines with a minimal metallic content can be detected to a depth of 15 cm.

BR90 Family of Bridges
In early 1994, the UK MOD announced that the production order had been placed for the BR90 family of bridges that should have entered service between January 1996 and June 1997 as follows:

January 1996	- General Support Bridge
November 1996	- Close Support Bridge
May 1997	- Two Span Bridge
June 1997	- Long Span Bridge

Reports during early 1999 indicate that, due to engineering problems the in service date for all four types have slipped and that only the General Support and Close Support Bridges are actually in service.

BR90 will be deployed with Royal Engineer units in both Germany and the UK. The production order, valued at approximately £140 million, was issued and accepted in October 1993.

The components of the system are:

Close Support Bridge - This consists of three tank-launched bridges capable of being carried on the in-service Chieftain bridgelayer and a TBT (Tank Bridge Transporter) truck.

	Weight	Length	Gap
No 10 Bridge	13 tons	26 m	24.5 m
No 11 Bridge	7.4 tons	16 m	14.5 m
No 12 Bridge	5.3 tons	13.5 m	12 m

The existing No 8 and No 9 bridges carried in the Chieftain AVLB will be retained in service.

The Unipower TBT 8 x 8 truck can carry 1 x No 1 Bridge, 1 x No 11 Bridge or 2 x No 12 Bridges. The TBT has an unladen weight of 21 tons and is also used to transport the General Support Bridge.

General Support Bridge - This system utilises the Automated Bridge Launching Equipment (ABLE) that is capable of launching bridges up to 44 metres in length. The ABLE vehicle is positioned with its rear pointing to the gap to be crossed and a lightweight launch rail extended across the gap. The bridge is then assembled and winched across the gap supported by the rail, with sections added until the gap is crossed. Once the bridge has crossed the gap the ABLE launch rail is recovered. A standard ABLE system set consists of an ABLE vehicle and 2 x TBT carrying a 32 metre bridge set. A 32m bridge can be built by 10 men in about 25 minutes.

Spanning Systems - There are two basic spanning systems. The long span systems allows for lengthening a 32 metre span to 44 metres using ABLE and the two span system allows 2 x 32 metre bridge sets to be constructed by ABLE and secured in the middle by piers or floating pontoons, crossing a gap of up to 60 metres.

Chapter 9 - Communications

"The Japanese airstrike at Pearl Harbour took about 2 hours and the Israeli airstrike in 1967 about 30 minutes to be effective. Some believe that a "first strike" in cyberspace could cripple a nation's defences in about five minutes. The "hackers" think otherwise. In the future it could take nano seconds. The hackers believe that in the short term they could be in and out of the C4I networks before current security systems can detect the intrusion.

In military terms the forward edge of the battlefield is known as the FEBA. This new FEBA is already being identified as the CEBA (Cyberic Edge of the Battlefield). If your communicators are not in control of the CEBA, all those billions spent on defence might well be totally wasted."

Defence Briefing in Washington DC - October 1996.

The Royal Corps of Signals

The Royal Corps of Signals (R Signals) provides the communications throughout the command system of the Army. Individual battlegroups are responsible for their own internal communications, but in general terms, all communications from Brigade level and above are the responsibility of the Royal Signals.

Information is the lifeblood of any military formation in battle and it is the responsibility of the Royal Signals to ensure the speedy and accurate passage of information that enables commanders to make informed and timely decisions, and to ensure that those decisions are passed to the fighting troops in contact with the enemy. The rapid, accurate and secure employment of command, control and communications systems maximises the effect of the military force available and consequently the Royal Signals acts as an extremely significant 'Force Multiplier'.

The Royal Corps of Signals provides about 9% of the Army's manpower with 10 Regular and 12 Territorial Army Regiments, each generally consisting of between 3 and up to 6 Sqns with between 600 and 1,000 personnel. In addition, there are 15 Regular and 4 Territorial Army Independent Squadrons, each of which has about 200 men, and 4 Independent Signal Troops of between 10 and 80 men each. Royal Signals personnel are found wherever the Army is deployed including every UK and NATO headquarters in the world. The Headquarters of the Corps is at the Royal School of Signals (RSS) located at Blandford in Dorset.

Royal Signals units based in the United Kingdom provide command and control communications for forces that have operational roles both in the UK itself, including Northern Ireland, and overseas including mainland Western Europe and further afield wherever the Army finds itself. There are a number of Royal Signals units permanently based in Germany, Holland and Belgium from where they provide the necessary command and control communications and Electronic Warfare (EW) support for both the British Army and other NATO forces based in Europe.

Royal Signals units are also based in Cyprus, the Falkland Islands, Belize and Gibraltar. Regular Army Royal Signals units based in the United Kingdom in support of NATO include:

UK Units Supporting NATO and JRRF Formations

2 Signal Regiment which provides command and Control communications for up to three Divisions in the ARRC including one multi-national Division.

3 (UK) Mechanised Division Headquarters and Signal Regiment. This Regiment provides the command and control communications for 3 (UK) Division that deploys as part of the Allied Command Europe (ACE) Rapid Reaction Corps or provides units to the RJDF.

1 (Mechanised) Brigade Signal Squadron. This unit provides communications for the UK Mobile Force (Land) which deploys to Northern Germany and Denmark.

209 Signal Squadron supports 19 (Mechanised) Brigade based in Catterick which is part of the ARRC.

210 (Airmobile) Brigade Signal Squadron provides communications for 24 (Airmobile) Brigade based in Colchester.

216 (Air Assault) Signal Squadron is part of 16 Air Assault Brigade which is able to operate either in the UK, within the NATO area of operations, or worldwide.

249 (AMF(L)) Signal Squadron provides communications for a multi-national NATO Brigade that deploys to Norway and Denmark or Turkey and Greece.

264 (SAS) Signal Squadron supports the Special Air Service Regiment.

UK Units - Supporting National Defence Formations

Regular Army Royal Signals units based in the UK which are not allocated to NATO include:

11 Signal Regiment stationed at Blandford in Dorset is the administrative unit for the Royal School of Signals (RSS) and carries out basic Trade Training, promotion courses for potential Non Commissioned Officers and basic training for the TA soldiers of the Royal Signals.

14 Signal Regiment (Electronic Warfare) provides the highly sophisticated electronic warfare support for 1st and 3rd (UK) Divisions. The Regiment is stationed at the former RAF base at Brawdy in Wales.

15 Signal Regiment provides command and control communications for the security forces in Northern Ireland. This Regiment has 3 Squadrons to support the 3 Brigades in the Province.

30 Signal Regiment which provides communications for all Army and RAF forces that deploy outside the NATO area of operations. This Regiment always maintains troops who are held on 24 hours notice to move to anywhere in the world. One Squadron of the Queen's Gurkha Signal Regiment is permanently attached to 30 Signal Regiment and serves in the United Kingdom.

Units Deployed Outside the UK

Royal Signals units that are permanently deployed in Europe in support of British and other NATO forces include:

1 (UK) Armoured Division Headquarters and Signal Regiment. This Regiment which has three Armoured Brigade Squadrons provides communications for the Divisional Headquarters and the three Brigades in the 1st (UK) Armoured Division.

7 (ARRC) Signal Regiment provides command and control communications for the ARRC headquarters which involves providing communications to the formation's multi-national Divisions.

16 Signal Regiment. This Regiment provides communication support for a number of multinational logistic organisations and fixed communications for British Forces Germany and RAF Germany.

A Royal Signals Regiment is based in Cyprus to support the Army and RAF forces in the Sovereign Base Areas and a Royal Signals Squadron supports the United Nations Force.

TA Units - At 1 June 1999

Royal Signals Territorial Army (TA) units include:

11 (ARRC) Signal Brigade based in Liverpool comprises the following units that all deploy to mainland Europe to provide communication for various headquarters in the ARRC.

33rd (Lancashire and Cheshire) Signal Regiment (V) based in Liverpool.
34th (Northern) Signal Regiment (V) based in Middlesbrough.
35th (South Midland) Signal Regiment (V) based in Coventry.
36th (Eastern) Signal Regiment (V) based in London

The Regular Army's 2 Signal Regiment also comes under the command of 11 Signal Brigade.

2nd (National Communications) Signal Brigade with its headquarters in Corsham is responsible for providing communication for Military Home Defence and operates the Army Fixed Telecommunications System (AFTS). Units include:

31 (Special Task) Signal Regiment (V) based in London.
32 (Scottish) Signal Regiment (V) based in Glasgow.
37 (Wessex and Welsh) Signal Regiment (V) based in Redditch.
38 Signal Regiment (V) based in Sheffield.
71 (Yeomanry) Signal Regiment (V) based in Bexleyheath.
56 Signal Squadron (V) based in Reading.

63 (V) SAS Signal Squadron is an independent unit that provides communication support for the Territorial Army Special Air Service Regiments.

In essence the 12 TA Signals Regiments provide:

3 x Ptarmigan Regiments
2 x Euromux Regiments
7 x National Communications Regiments
3 x Independent Signals Squadrons
2 x Special Communications Squadrons

The 2 (National Communications) Brigade units will be restructured to provide Regional and National Communications support to Land Command. An independent Combat Service Support Group Squadron will also be formed.

Armoured Divisional Signal Regiment Organisation

Notes: (1) SAN - Secondary Access Node (2) A Divisional HQ will have two HQs to allow for movement and possible destruction. The main HQ will be set up for approx 24 hrs with the alternative HQ (Alt HQ) set up 20-30 kms away on the proposed line of march of the division. When the Main HQ closes to move to a new location the Alt HQ becomes the Main HQ for another 24 hour period. (3) Expect a Brigade Sig Sqn to have a Radio Troop and a SAN Troop.

R Signals units are currently operating the following types of major equipment:

Mobile Satellite Terminals
HF, VHF and UHF Radios
Radio Relay (carrying telephone & teleprinter links)
Teleprinters, Fax, CCTV and ADP Equipment
Computers
Line

The communications systems used by the Royal Signals include:

Ptarmigan
Ptarmigan is a mobile, secure battlefield system that incorporates the latest technology and has been designed to improve communications reliability, capacity and interoperability.

Built by Siemens-Plessey Christchurch in the mid 1980s, Ptarmigan is a user-friendly, computer controlled communications system which was initially designed to meet the needs of the British Army in Germany. The system consists of a network of electronic exchanges or Trunk Switches that are connected by satellite and multichannel radio relay (TRIFFID) links that provide voice, data, telegraph and fax communications.

The Trunk Switch, radio and satellite relays together with their support vehicles comprise a 'Trunk Node' and all field headquarters include a group of communications vehicles that contain an Access Switch which can be connected to any Trunk Switch giving access to the system. This ensures that headquarters have exceptional flexibility in both siting and facilities and trunk communications then present no constraints on operations.

Additionally Ptarmigan has a mobile telephone or Single Channel Radio Access (SCRA) which gives isolated or mobile users an entry point into the entire system.

Triffid
Radio relay links within Ptarmigan are provided by TRIFFID which is a radio equipment that has 3 interchangeable radio frequency modules known as 'heads'. Each TRIFFID link carries the equivalent of up to 32 voice circuits at a data rate of 512 kb/s plus an engineering circuit.

Euromux
EUROMUX is a trunk system manufactured by Racal which is similar in principle to the PTARMIGAN system and is interoperable with the trunk systems of other NATO armies. TRIFFID is used to provide the relay links within the system.

Clansman
Is the name given to the in-service family of tactical radios with which the British Army is currently equipped to provide communications from formation headquarters forward to the fighting units. CLANSMAN is a lighter, far more reliable and adaptable system than the ageing LARKSPUR system that it replaced during the early 1980s. In its turn CLANSMAN will be replaced by BOWMAN.

Clansman Manpack Radios

	Used By	Weight	Range	Freq coverage
PRC 349	Inf Sec	1.5 kg	2km	37-46.975
PRC 350	Inf Pl or Sec	3.6 kg	5km	36-56.975
PRC 351	Coy/Sqn	6.3 kg	8km	30-75.975
PRC 352	Coy/Sqn	9.2 kg	16km	30-75.975
PRC 320	Coy/Pl	ll kg	50km	2-29.999

Clansman Vehicle Radios

	Used By	Weight	Range	Freq coverage
VRC 321	Command Nets	23 kg	60km	1.5-29.999
VRC-322	Command Nets	52 kg	80km	1.5-29.999
VRC-353	Bn/Coy/Sqn	22 kg	30km	30-75.975

On the FEBA these Clansman radios are operated by the Battlegroup Signal Platoons but further back (generally Brigade level and backwards towards Divisional, Corps and Army HQ) will be the responsibility of the Royal Signals.

Bowman
Bowman is a tactical communications system that has been designed to provide a replacement for the series of Clansman radios currently in service with the British Army. Bowman will almost cer-

tainly make use of the latest packet radio technology and an original project demonstrator contract for a 25 station system was awarded to Racal-BCC in 1988. Current plans are for an in service date for the first equipment in 2002.

The complete Bowman programme has been broken down into four phases, although any contracts awarded by the prime contractor Archer Communications Systems (ACS) include elements from each. They are:

Phase One - Bowman Risk Reduction: all aspects of development, certification and installation design and conversion (IDC) for vehicles, aircraft and ships. The contract, valued at £20 million was awarded to ACS in August 1998. This phase will ran until late 1999.

Phase Two - First Production Contract awarded in late 1999 and running for three and a half years. It will equip around eight British Army brigades and includes acceptance trials and first entry of Bowman into service in March 2002. Around 50 per cent of the armed forces will be converted to Bowman under Phase Two. Total contract value of this phase is around £900 million.

Phases Three and Four - Cover further production, including conversion and acceptance, and will be awarded in 2003/04 and 2005/06. Each of these contracts are worth around £500 million.

ACS will subcontract the armed forces' IDC process where the British Army vehicle conversion is the largest task. Six bidders, Alvis, Dytecna, GKN Defence, Hunting Engineering Ltd, Serco and Vickers Defence Systems have expressed interest in taking part in these contracts.

Satellite Communications (SATCOM)
The Royal Signals deploys transportable and manpack satellite ground stations to provide communications links for headquarters or small groups located in remote parts of the world via its SKYNET 4B system. Operations in the Falklands and Namibia proved the value of satellite communications and, during the Gulf war, there was an extensive use of SATCOM ground terminals particularly the Racal VSC501. It is expected that a new series of SKYNET 5 satellites will be introduced to enhance SATCOM facilities in the future.

Wavell
Wavell is a battlefield automatic data processing computer system, designed to accept information from all the battlefield intelligence agencies, and produce this information on request in hard copy or on a VDU. Information is then used to assist commanders and their staff with the analysis of intelligence and subsequent conduct of operations. Each headquarters from Corps down to Brigade level is equipped with its own Wavell computers that are linked to the PTARMIGAN system

Wavell was continually upgraded during the 1990s with interfaces planned for operation with BATES, ADCIS (Air Defence Command Information System) and Vixen. The integration of Wavell with the German HEROS, French SACRA and US MCS Command and Control system will probably be a high priority.

Slim
SLIM is a new system using the personal computer equipment used in the Gulf war which is being developed to complement WAVELL.

Bates

BATES is a battlefield artillery engagement system which has been designed to centralise the command and control of artillery, with all fire missions being routed through a central control cell and then passed on to the appropriate fire units. Access to the system is available down to the level of artillery FOOs (Forward Observation Officers) who have their own digital entry devices. BATES will eventually replace FACE (Forward Artillery Computing Equipment).

Artillery intelligence entered in the system is available for commanders and their staff through the Wavell interface and much of the routine and logistic tasks are processed by the equipment, thus freeing the staff for other tasks.

BATES is an important part of the MLRS - AS 90 - PHOENIX - COBRA series of battlefield fire support systems and when it is finally in service will provide valuable support to these equipments. However, there appear to have been serious delays in bringing BATES into service, and once in service there could be significant teething problems as BATES is integrated with other systems.

We believe that some £50 million has been spent on BATES and that there will eventually be up to 200 systems in operation with the British Army.

Vixen

Vixen has been designed to provide an automated system for processing of electronic intelligence. It will probably be mounted in soft skinned vehicles and deployed with the electronic warfare regiment which, amongst its many tasks, listens to enemy signal traffic and passes vital intelligence to the operational staff. Vixen became operational in late 1992 and it is probable that the system is linked to the existing electronic direction finding equipment subsequently feeding results into the BATES and Wavell ADP systems. The cost of the Vixen system was believed to be in the region of ,36.5 million.

Scimitar

Scimitar has been designed to provide a secure combat net communications system to include a frequency agile ability for use in areas where the ECM threat is high. Equipments are man portable or vehicle mounted and the system has three basic equipments:

Scimitar H (HF radio)

Freq 1.6 - 30MHz - 284,000 channels - Weight 4.0 kgs (manpack).

Scimitar V (VHF vehicle or man-pack radio)

Freq 30-88MHz - 2,320 channels - Weight 4.8 kgs (manpack)

Scimitar M (Pocket sized VHF radio)

Freq 68 - 88MHz - 800 channels - Weight 0.5 kg.

Some Scimitar units are in use with the British Army and it is known to be in use with Jordan, Portugal, Turkey and Sweden. Manufactured by Plessey the average cost of a Scimitar radio is probably in the area of £8,000.

Jaguar

Jaguar is manufactured by Racal Tacticom and is a similar system to Scimitar with the ability to frequency hop in ECM environments. The radio can be used in both the vehicle and manpack roles and the main characteristics are as follows:

Frequency Range	30-88MHz
Temperature Range	-40 to 70 degrees C
Weight	5 kgs
Channels	2,320
Spacing	25 kHz

Jaguar is in service with the British Army and US Navy. Over 30 nations are currently using this equipment and sales to date are believed to be in excess of £130 million.

Army Fixed Telecommunications System

The peacetime management of the Army depends heavily on effective communications . The Royal Signals Army Fixed Telecommunication System (AFTS) provides all the telephone, telegraph, facsimile, data systems and radio and line links for the Army in the United Kingdom. AFTS is operated and maintained by 2 (National Communications) Brigade and the system serves over 40,000 subscribers. The staff required to operate the AFTS is approximately 1,100 of whom 40% are military personnel who are located all over the UK in six (Fixed Service) Signal Squadrons supported by operational, engineering, planning and co-ordination staff at Headquarters 2 (NC) Brigade at Corsham in Wiltshire.

One of the ADP systems in the UK is MAPPER which stands for Maintenance, Preparation and Presentation of Executive Reports. This system is used both as a peacetime management aid to staffs in major headquarters and also for command and control of Military Home Defence and was expanded for use in the Gulf war when MAPPER stations were deployed to Saudi Arabia and linked back to the United Kingdom. Its success in the Gulf has led to the system being used in post Gulf war operations including the Balkans.

In Germany, the Telecommunications Group Headquarters based at Rheindahlen provides a sophisticated fixed communications system based on the Integrated Services Digital Network (ISDN). Project Rodin which is intended to modernise the fixed communications system for both the Army and the RAF in Germany will, when introduced, use state of the art digital technology and will be able to interact with other German and British military and civilian networks.

The Communications Projects Division (CPD) provides engineering support for military fixed communications systems worldwide. CPD is part of the Royal School of Signals at Blandford in Dorset.

Digitisation

Digitisation refers to putting the capabilities for digital communications into a platform. Digital modulation is the process of encoding a continuous analogue signal into a discontinuous signal. Then numerical codes consisting of discrete on (one) and off (zero) pulses are assigned to represent a measure of the basic signal. The measuring process involves sampling the amplitude of the continuous signal at intervals and transmitting a digital code to represent the amplitude. The same process can be used in data transmissions where digital codes represent letters and numbers. Linking platforms from aircraft to mines and sensors on the ground in an intelligent circuit allows these systems to interact automatically on a continual flow of information around the circuit.

Linked to digitisation, the next trend in communications is probably towards secure image transmission linking information from humans and sensors. For example, a platoon commander's sketch map of the current situation in his area can be transmitted simultaneously to the company, battalion, brigade and divisional headquarters and either modified or confirmed by sensor information. This map could then be scanned into the overall C3I system and both humans and sensors made aware of the results. Time spent in talking about the situation on the air and the possibility of confusion and misunderstandings are dramatically reduced.

Chapter 10 - Combat Service Support

"Wellington paid the greatest tribute to him (Sir William Beresford) when he declared that if he were removed by death or illness he would recommend Beresford to succeed him, not because he was a great general, but because he alone could 'feed an army'".

The Dictionary of National Biography

"It is more important to destroy those places that contain the elements of military power (the magazines and stores) than soldiers, who are nothing without their stores."

Systeme de Guerre moderne - General Comte de Cessac 1797

Logistic Support
In the wake of the 1990 Logistic Support Review the British Army decided that in the future logistic support will be based upon the twin pillars of service support (the supply chain) and equipment support (the maintenance of equipment).

Combat Service Support within the British Army is now provided by the Royal Logistic Corps (RLC), the Royal Electrical and Mechanical Engineers (REME) and the Royal Army Medical Corps (RAMC).

Within any fighting formation logistic units from these Corps typically represent about 30% of the manpower total of an Armoured Division and, with the exception of certain members of the RAMC all are fully trained fighting soldiers.

The task of the logistic units on operations is to maintain the combat units in the field which entails:

a. SUPPLY AND DISTRIBUTION   -   of ammunition, fuel, lubricants, rations and spare parts.

b. RECOVERY AND REPAIR   -   of battle damaged and unserviceable equipment.

c. TREATMENT AND EVACUATION   -   of casualties.

In a Division, the commanders of the logistic units all operate from a separate, self contained headquarters under the command of a Colonel who holds the appointment of the Division's Deputy Chief of Staff (DCOS). This headquarters, usually known as the Divisional Headquarters (Rear), co-ordinates the whole of the logistic support of the Division in battle.

Supplies, reinforcements and returning casualties pass through an area located to the rear of the Division where some of the less mobile logistic units are located. This area is known as the Divisional Admin Area (DAA) and its staff are responsible for co-ordinating the flow of all materiel and personnel into and out of the Divisional area.

The Royal Logistic Corps (RLC)
The RLC is the youngest Corps in the Army and was formed in April 1993 as a result of the recommendations of the Logistic Support Review. The RLC results from the amalgamation of the Royal Corps of Transport (RCT), the Royal Army Ordnance Corps (RAOC), the Army Catering

Corps (ACC), the Royal Pioneer Corps (RPC) and elements of the Royal Engineers (RE). The Corps makes up about 16% of the Army with about 16,800 Regular personnel and 10,000 Territorial Army soldiers wearing its cap badge.

The RLC has very broad responsibilities throughout the Army including the movement of personnel throughout the world, the Army's air dispatch service, maritime and rail transport, operational resupply, explosive ordnance disposal which includes the hazardous bomb disposal duties in Northern Ireland and in mainland Britain during the IRA terrorist campaign, the operation of numerous very large vehicle and stores depots both in the UK and overseas, the training and provision of cooks to virtually all units in the Army, the provision of pioneer labour and the Army's postal and courier service.

The principal field elements of the RLC are the Close Support and the General Support Regiments whose primary role is to supply the fighting units with ammunition, fuel and rations (Combat Supplies).

A division has an integral Close Support Regiment which is responsible for manning and operating the supply chain to Brigades and Divisional units.

Close Support Regiment (RLC)

Note:
(1) A regiment could have two or three brigade support squadrons depending upon the size of the division being supported.
(2) Some of these regiments may have a Postal and Courier Sqn.

Brigade Support Squadron

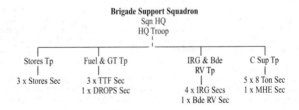

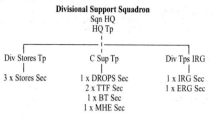

Divisional Support Squadron
Sqn HQ
HQ Tp

Div Stores Tp	C Sup Tp	Div Tps IRG
3 x Stores Sec	1 x DROPS Sec	1 x IRG Sec
	2 x TTF Sec	1 x ERG Sec
	1 x BT Sec	
	1 x MHE Sec	

The General Support Regiment's role is primarily to supply ammunition to the Royal Artillery using DROPS vehicles and to provide tank transporters that move armoured vehicles more rapidly and economically than moving them on their own tracks.

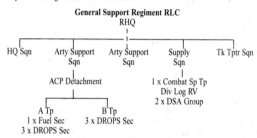

General Support Regiment RLC
RHQ

HQ Sqn	Arty Support Sqn	Arty Support Sqn	Supply Sqn	Tk Tptr Sqn
	ACP Detachment		1 x Combat Sp Tp	
			Div Log RV	
			2 x DSA Group	

A Tp
1 x Fuel Sec
3 x DROPS Sec

B Tp
3 x DROPS Sec

Both types of Regiment have large sections holding stores both on wheels and on the ground. A Division will typically require about 1,000 tons of Combat Supplies a day but demand can easily exceed that amount in high intensity operations.

Battlegroups in contact with the enemy can carry a limited amount of C Sups, particularly ammunition As ammunition is expended, it is replenished from RLC vehicles located immediately to the rear of battlegroups in an Immediate Replenishment Groups (IRGs) area. As the IRG vehicles are emptied they return to the RLC Squadron location and fully loaded replacements are automatically sent forward so that a constant supply is always available to the battlegroup.

Ammunition and spares are generally carried on NATO standard pallets which are loaded to meet the anticipated requirements of particular units and if required bulk consignments are broken down at the IRG location. Fuel is usually carried in bulk fuel tankers (TTFs) which top-up battlegroup vehicles direct. However, there is still a requirement for a large number of the traditional jerricans. Much of other fuel is delivered to the forward areas through the NATO Central European Pipeline System (CEPS).

Artillery ammunition constitutes by far the largest single element in the logistic pipeline and the bulk of it is delivered directly to the Royal Artillery guns, rocket and missile launchers by RLC Demountable Rack Off Loading and Pickup System (DROPS) vehicles from the General Support Regiment which are capable of meeting the requirement of even the highest intensity consumption.

Logistic Support in Bosnia

An excellent example of RLC operations is what happened in Bosnia between 1 Jan and 31 October 1996 following the entry of the NATO IFOR force into the area.

Ammunition

Tonnage held at 2nd Line	1,488 tons

Petrol, Oil and Lubricants

Litres Drawn	36 million
Disposal of waste oil/fuel	300,000 litres
LPG filled	518,000 kg

Rations

Total issued to units	£8.128 million
Fresh ration issues to units	15,479 pallets

Transport

Total kms travelled	7.050 million
DROPS movements	3,307 kms
TTF movement	448,000 kms
Tank transporter movement	942,000 kms
Armoured vehicle movements	1,608 kms

Movements

Containers received into theatre	1,194
Containers despatched out of theatre	543
Vehicle loads into theatre (40 ft vehicles)	1,170
Loaded rail wagons received	325
Loaded rail wagons dispatched	39
Flights to/from theatre	1,111
Equipment flown into theatre	1,259 million kgs

Materiel

Demands received from units	234,305
Receipts into theatre	5,155,227 kg

Postal

Receipts (surface)	96,000 kg
Receipts (air)	42,000 kg
Despatches (surface)	36,000 kg
Despatches (surface)	63,000 kg
Blueys (received)	2.572 million
Blueys (dispatched)	6.628 million

Laundry & Baths

Laundry washed	249,322 bags
Showers provided	98,582 personnel

There are some fascinating statistics included in the above list. Blueys are the name given to the lightweight, blue coloured forces airmail letters. The fact that about 2.6 times more letters were written by troops in Bosnia than were received will probably keep a horde of social scientists in employment for some considerable time.

RLC Miscellaneous

Apart from the RLC units that provide direct support to the operational formations the RLC is directly responsible for:

Army School of Mechanical Transport - Leconfield
Base Ordnance Depots (Bicester & Donnington)
Base Ammunition Depots (Longtown & Kineton)
Army School of Ammunition (Temple Herdwyke)
Petroleum Centre (West Moors)
Army Base Vehicle Organisation (Ashchurch)
Armoured Vehicle Sub Depot (Ludgershall)
Army School of Catering (Aldershot)
Royal Logistic Corps Training Centre (Deepcut)

Daily Messing Rates

The allowances per day for catering purposes are based on a ration scale costed at current prices and known as the daily messing rate (DMR). The ration scale is the same for all three services, and contrary to popular army belief, the RAF are not supplied with wine etc at public expense. The rate per day is the amount that the catering organisation has to feed each individual serviceman or servicewoman.

The scale is costed to the supply source of the food items. When the source of supply is more expensive due to local conditions the DMR is set higher to take account of local costs. A general overseas ration scale exists for overseas bases and attachments. This scale has a higher calorific value to take into account the conditions of heat, cold or humidity that can be encountered.

The UK ration scale is designed to provide 2,900 kilo calories nett- that is after loss through preparation and cooking. The general overseas ration scale includes an arduous duty allowance to allow for climate and provides some 3,400 kilo-calories nett. In field conditions where personnel are fed from operational ration packs 3,800 kilo calories are provided.

RLC Catering Units feed the Army generally using detachments of cooks attached to units.

At the beginning of 1999 the daily messing rates (DMR) was approximately £2.00 per day per soldier. With this amount RLC cooks, in barracks have to provide three meals per day.

The Central Army Post Office (APO) is located at Mill Hill in North London and there are individual British Forces Post Offices (BFPO) wherever British Forces are stationed.

The Royal Electrical & Mechanical Engineers - REME

The Logistic Support review of 1990 recommended that Equipment Support should remain separate from the other logistic pillar of Service Support and consequently the REME has retained not only its own identity but expanded its responsibilities. Equipment Support encompasses equipment management, engineering support, supply management, provisioning for vehicle and technical spares and financial management responsibilities for in-service equipment.

The aim of the REME is "To keep operationally fit equipment in the hands of the troops" and in the current financial environment it is important that this is carried out at the minimum possible cost. The equipment that REME is responsible for ranges from small arms and trucks to helicopters and main battle tanks. All field force units have some integral REME support (1st line support) which will vary, depending on the size of the unit and the equipment held, from a few attached tradesmen up to a large Regimental Workshop of over 200 men. In war, REME is responsible for the recovery and repair of battle damaged and unserviceable equipments.

The development of highly technical weapon systems and other equipment has meant that REME has had to balance engineering and tactical considerations. On the one hand the increased scope for forward repair of equipment reduces the time out of action, but, on the other hand engineering stability is required for the repair of complex systems.

The major changes which have resulted from the Options for Change and Logistic Support Reviews are that four REME Equipment Support Battalions were formed in 1993, to provide second line support for the British contribution to the ACE Rapid Reaction Corps (ARRC) and formations in the UK. Two battalions are based in the UK and three battalions are based in Germany to support 1(UK) Armoured Division.

There are four TA REME battalions.

REME Support Battalion

Battalion Headquarters

Close Sp Company	General Sp Company	Headquarters Company
FRGs & MRGs		Note: Approx 450 personnel.

The Close Support Company will normally deploy a number of FRG's (Forward Repair Groups) and MRGs (Medium Repair Groups) in support of brigades. The company is mobile with armoured repair and recovery vehicles able to operate in the forward areas, carrying out forward repair of key nominated equipment often by the exchange of major assemblies. It is also capable of carrying out field repairs on priority equipment including telecommunications equipment and the repair of damage sustained by critical battle winning equipments.

The role of the General Support Company is to support the Close Support Companies and Divisional Troops. Tasks include the regeneration of fit power packs for use in forward repair and the repair of equipment backloaded from Close Support Companies. The General Support Company will normally be located to the rear of the divisional area in order to maximise productivity and minimise vulnerability.

In manpower terms the REME support available to 1(UK) Armoured Division in the ARRC will be somewhere in the area of the following:

Armoured Regiment	120
Armoured Recce Regiment	90
Armoured Infantry Battalion	90
Close Support Engineer Regiment	85
General Support Engineer Regiment	110
Field Regiment Royal Artillery	115
Air Defence Regiment Royal Artillery	160
Army Air Corps Regiment	130
Signals Regiment	60
RLC Close Support Regiment	75
RLC General Support Regiment	95
REME Battalion	450

Medical Services

"Stop dying at once and when you get up, get your bloody hair cut".

> *Colonel AD Wintle (RAMC) to Trooper Cedric Mayes (Royal Dragoons)*
> *The patient lived for another 40 years.*

The Royal Army Medical Corps (RAMC)
In peace, the personnel of the RAMC are based at the various medical installations throughout the world or in field force units and they are responsible for the health of the Army.

On operations, the RAMC is responsible for the care of the sick and wounded, with the subsequent evacuation of the wounded to hospitals in the rear areas. Each Brigade has a field ambulance which is a regular unit that operates in direct support of the battlegroups. These units are either armoured, airmobile or parachute trained. In addition, each division has two field ambulance units that may be regular or TA. These units provide medical support for the divisional troops and can act as manoeuvre units for the forward brigades when required.

All field ambulance units have medical sections that consist of a medical officer and eight Combat Medical Technicians. These sub-units are located with the battlegroup or units being supported and they provide the necessary first line medical support. In addition, the field ambulance provides a dressing station where casualties are treated and may be resuscitated or stabilised before transfer to a field hospital. These units have the necessary integral ambulance support, both armoured and wheeled to transfer casualties from the first to second line medical units.

Field hospitals may be regular or TA and all are 200 bed facilities with a maximum of 8 surgical teams capable of carrying out life saving operations on some of the most difficult surgical cases. Since 1990, most regular medical units have been deployed on operations either in the Persian Gulf or the former Yugoslavia.

Casualty Evacuation (CASEVAC) is by ambulance either armoured or wheeled and driven by RLC personnel or by helicopter when such aircraft are available. A Chinook helicopter is capable of carrying 44 stretcher cases and a Puma can carry 6 stretcher cases and 6 sitting cases.

In late 1999 there were 12 x field ambulances/field hospitals in the regular army (3 in Germany and 9 in the UK) plus 10 field hospitals in the TA. The 1999 personnel total of the RAMC is approximately 2,500.

The Queen Alexandra's Royal Army Nursing Corps (QARANC)

On the 1st April 1992 the QARANC became an all-nursing and totally professionally qualified Corps. Its male and female officer and other rank personnel, provide the necessary qualified nursing support at all levels and covering a wide variety of nursing specialities. QARANC personnel can be found anywhere in the world where Army Medical services are required.

The 1999 QARANC personnel total is approximately 850.

Royal Army Dental Corps (RADC)

The RADC is a professional corps that in late 1999 consisted over just over 360 officers and soldiers. The Corps fulfils the essential role of maintaining the dental health of the Army in peace and war, both at home and overseas. Qualified dentists and oral surgeons, hygienists, technicians and support ancillaries work in a wide variety of military units - from static and mobile dental clinics to field medical units, military hospitals and dental laboratories.

The Adjutant General's Corps (AGC)

The Adjutant General's Corps was formed on 1 April 1992 and its sole task is the management of the Army's most precious resource, its soldiers. The Corps absorbed the functions of six existing smaller corps; the Royal Military Police, the Royal Army Pay Corps, the Royal Army Educational Corps, the Royal Army Chaplains Department, the Army Legal Corps and the Military Provost Staff Corps.

The Corps is organised into four branches, Staff and Personnel Support (SPS) Provost, Educational and Training Services and Army Legal Services. In late 1999, the AGC consisted of just over 7,000 officers and soldiers.

The Role of SPS Branch

The role of SPS Branch is to ensure the efficient and smooth delivery of Personnel Administration to the Army. This includes support to individual officers and soldiers in units by processing pay and Service documentation, first line provision of financial, welfare, education and resettlement guidance to individuals and the provision of clerical skills and information management to ensure the smooth day to day running of the unit or department.

AGC (SPS) officers are employed throughout the Army, in direct support of units as Regimental Administrative Officers or AGC Detachment Commanders. They hold Commander AGC (SPS) and SO2 AGC(SPS) posts in district/Divisional and Brigade HQs and fill posts at the Adjutant General's Information Centre (AGIC) and general staff appointment throughout the Army headquarters locations.

AGC (SPS) soldiers are employed as Military Clerks in direct support of units within the AGC Field Detachments, in fixed centre pay offices, in headquarters to provide staff support and in miscellaneous posts such as embassy clerks, as management accountants or in AGIC as programmer analysts.

The principal tasks of AGC(SPS) personnel on operations are:

a. The maintenance of Field Records, including the soldiers Record of Service, casualty reporting and disciplinary documentation.

b. Clerical and staff support to Battle Group HQs and independent Sub Units such as Engineer and Logistic Squadrons.

c. The issue of pay and allowances to personnel.

d. The maintenance of Imprest Accounts (the MoD Public Accounts) which involve paying local suppliers for services, receiving cash from non-Army agencies such as NAAFI and Forces Post Office receipts.

e. The deployment of a Field Records Cell which co-ordinates all personnel administration in the field.

f. AGC (SPS) personnel play a full part in operational duties by undertaking such tasks as local defence, guards and command post duties. In addition, Command Officers can employ any soldier in their unit as they see fit and may require AGC (SPS) personnel to undertake appropriate additional training to allow them to be used in some specialist roles specific to the unit, or as radio operators or drivers.

Currently, about 62% of AGC (SPS) soldiers are based in UK, 27% in Germany and 11% elsewhere. The majority, currently 70% are serving with field force units, with the remaining 30% in base and training units or HQs, such as MoD.

Members of AGC (SPS) are first trained as soldiers and then specialise as Military Clerks. AGC(SPS) officers complete the same military training as their counterparts in other Arms and Services, starting at the Royal Military Academy, Sandhurst. They are required to attend all promotion courses such as the Junior Command and Staff Course, and to pass the standard career exams prior to promotion to the rank of Major.

Organisation of a Regimental Administrative Office

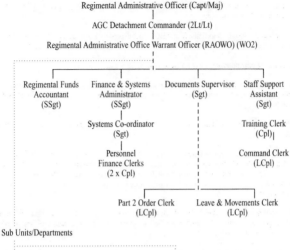

Regimental Administrative Officer (Capt/Maj)

AGC Detachment Commander (2Lt/Lt)

Regimental Administrative Office Warrant Officer (RAOWO) (WO2)

Regimental Funds Accountant (SSgt)

Finance & Systems Administrator (SSgt)

Documents Supervisor (Sgt)

Staff Support Assistant (Sgt)

Systems Co-ordinator (Sgt)

Training Clerk (Cpl)

Personnel Finance Clerks (2 x Cpl)

Command Clerk (LCpl)

Part 2 Order Clerk (LCpl)

Leave & Movements Clerk (LCpl)

Sub Units/Departments

Quartermaster's Department Clerk (Cpl)

Company/Light Aid Detachment Clerks (5 x Pte/Lcpl)

Quartermaster's Clerk (Pte)

The Role of the Provost Branch

The Provost Branch was formed from the formerly independent Corps of Royal Military Police (RMP) and the Military Provost Staff Corps (MPSC). Although they are no longer independent, they are still known as the AGC (PRO) and AGC (MPS) thus forming the two parts of the Provost Branch.

Royal Military Police

To provide the police support the Army requires the RMP has the following functions:

a. Providing operational support to units in the field.

b. Preventing crime.

c. Enforcement of the law within the community and assistance with the maintenance of discipline.

d. Providing a 24 hour response service of assistance, advice and information.

Operational support includes advising commanders and the staff who produce the operational movement plans. RMP traffic posts are deployed along the main operational movement routes and provide a constant flow of traffic information regarding the progress of front line troops and the logistical resupply. RMP with a vehicle to man ratio of 1:3 is also a valuable force for the security of rear areas. In addition there is a highly trained RMP close protection group that specialises in the protection of high risk VIPs.

The RMP provide the day to day police support for both the army in the UK and dependents and MoD civilians overseas. RMP units are trained and equipped to deal with the most serious crimes. The Special Investigation Branch (SIB) operates in a similar fashion to the civilian CID.

The Military Provost Staff

AGC (MPS) staff are recruited from within the Army are carefully selected for the leadership, management and training skills necessary to motivate the predominantly young offenders with whom they work. The majority of AGC (MPS) personnel are located in the Military Corrective Training Centre (MCTC) at Colchester where offenders sentenced by military courts are confined.

The Role of the ETS Branch

The AGC (ETS) Branch has the responsibility of improving the efficiency, effectiveness and morale of the Army by providing support to operations and the developmental education, training, support and resettlement services that the Army requires to carry out its task. ETS personnel provide assistance at almost all levels of command but their most visible task is the manning of Army Education Centres wherever the Army is stationed. At these centres officers and soldiers receive the educational support necessary for them to achieve both civilian and military qualifications.

The Role of the ALS Branch

The AGC(ALS) Branch advises on all aspects of service and civilian law that may affect every level of the Army from General to Private soldiers. Members of the branch are usually qualified as solicitors or barristers. In addition to the AGC personnel attached to major units throughout the Army the Corps is directly responsible for the following:

Smaller Corps

THE INTELLIGENCE CORPS (Int Corps) - The Int Corps deals with operational intelligence, counter intelligence and security.

THE ROYAL ARMY VETERINARY CORPS (RAVC) - The RAVC look after the many animals that the Army has on strength. Veterinary tasks in today's army are mainly directed towards guard or search dogs and horses for ceremonial duties.

THE ARMY PHYSICAL TRAINING CORPS (APTC) - Consists mainly of SNCOs who are responsible for unit fitness. The majority of major units have a representative from this corps on their strength.

THE GENERAL SERVICE CORPS (GSC) - A holding unit for specialists. Personnel from this corps are generally members of the reserve army.

SMALL ARMS SCHOOL CORPS (SASC) - A small corps with the responsibility of training instructors in all aspects of weapon handling.

CHAPTER 11 - UNITS OF THE REGULAR ARMY

The Cavalry
After the re-organisation following the Options for Change review, the cavalry consists of 11 armoured regiments and one mounted ceremonial regiment as follows:

The Household Cavalry
The Household Cavalry Regiment	HCR
The Household Cavalry Mounted Regiment	HCMR

The Royal Armoured Corps
1st The Queen's Dragoon Guards	QDG
The Royal Scots Dragoon Guards	SCOTS DG
The Royal Dragoon Guards	RDG
The Queen's Royal Hussars	QRH
9th/12th Royal Lancers	9/12L
The King's Royal Hussars	KRH
The Light Dragoons	LD
The Queen's Royal Lancers	QRL
1st Royal Tank Regiment	1 RTR
2nd Royal Tank Regiment	2 RTR

The Infantry
Divided into 40 general service battalions, plus six battalions of the Royal Irish Regiment which will be used only in Northern Ireland, and the Special Air Service Regiment.

The Guards Division
1st Bn Grenadier Guards	1 GREN GDS
1st Bn Coldstream Guards	1 COLM GDS
1st Bn Scots Guards	1 SG
1st Bn Irish Guards	1 IG
1st Bn Welsh Guards	1 WG

There are generally three battalions from the Guards Division on public duties in London at any one time. When a Regiment is stationed in London on public duties it is given an extra company to ensure the additional manpower required for ceremonial events is available.

The Scottish Division
1st Bn The Royal Scots	1 RS
1st Bn The Royal Highland Fusiliers	1 RHF
1st Bn The King's Own Scottish Borderers	1 KOSB
1st Bn The Black Watch	1 BW
1st Bn The Argyll & Sutherland Highlanders	1 A and SH
1st Bn The Highlanders	1 HLDRS

The Queen's Division
1st Bn The Princess of Wales's Royal Regiment (Queen's and Royal Hampshire)	1 PWRR
2nd Bn The Princess of Wales's Royal Regiment (Queen's and Royal Hampshire)	2 PWRR

1st Bn The Royal Regiment of Fusiliers	1 RRF
2nd Bn The Royal Regiment of Fusiliers	2 RRF
1st Bn The Royal Anglian Regiment	1 R ANGLIAN
2nd Bn The Royal Anglian Regiment	2 R ANGLIAN

The King's Division

1st Bn The King's Own Royal Border Regiment	1 KOBR
1st Bn The King's Regiment	1 KINGS
1st Bn The Prince of Wales's Own Regiment of Yorkshire	1 PWO
1st Bn The Green Howards	1 GH
1st Bn The Queen's Lancashire Regiment	1 QLR
1st Bn The Duke of Wellington's Regiment	1 DWR

The Prince of Wales's Division

1st Bn The Devonshire & Dorset Regiment	1 D and D
1st Bn The Cheshire Regiment	1 CHESHIRE
1st Bn The Royal Welch Fusiliers	1 RWF
1st Bn The Royal Regiment of Wales	1 RRW
1st Bn The Royal Gloucestershire, Berkshire and Wiltshire Regiment	1 RGBW
1st Bn The Worcestershire & Sherwood Foresters Regiment	1 WFR
1st Bn The Staffordshire Regiment	1 STAFFORDS

The Light Division

1st Bn The Light Infantry	1 LI
2nd Bn The Light Infantry	2 LI
1st Bn The Royal Green Jackets	1 RGJ
2nd Bn The Royal Green Jackets	2 RGJ

The Brigade of Gurkhas

| 1st Bn The Royal Gurkha Rifles | 1 RGR |
| 2nd Bn The Royal Gurkha Rifles | 2 RGR |

The Parachute Regiment

1st Bn The Parachute Regiment	1 PARA
2nd Bn The Parachute Regiment	2 PARA
3rd Bn The Parachute Regiment	3 PARA

The Royal Irish Regiment

| 1st Bn The Royal Irish Regiment | 1 R IRISH |
| 3rd/4th/5th/7th/8th/9th Royal Irish Regiment* | 3-9 R IRISH |

* The 3rd to 8th Bns The Royal Irish Regiment are employed exclusively in Northern Ireland and were formerly battalions of The Ulster Defence Regiment. The 4/5 Rangers is a TA Battalion stationed in Northern Ireland and wearing the Royal Irish capbadge.

There are three infantry training battalions at the Infantry Training Centre located at Catterick in North Yorkshire.

The Special Air Service Regiment
The 22nd Special Air Service Regiment   22 SAS

The SAS can be classed as an infantry unit but the members of the regiment are found from all arms and services in the Army after exhaustive selection tests.

The Royal Regiment of Artillery (RA)

1st Regiment Royal Horse Artillery	1 RHA	(Field)
3rd Regiment Royal Horse Artillery	3 RHA	(Field)
4th Regiment	4 REGT	(Field)
5th Regiment	5 REGT	(MLRS)
7th Regiment Royal Horse Artillery	7 RHA	(Parachute)
12th Regiment	12 REGT	(Air Def)
14th Regiment	14 REGT	(Training)
16th Regiment	16 REGT	(Air Def)
19th Regiment	19 REGT	(Field)
22nd Regiment	22 REGT	(Air Def)
26th Regiment	26 REGT	(Field)
29th Commando Regiment	29 REGT	(Field)
32nd Regiment	32 REGT	(MLRS)
39th Regiment	39 REGT	(MLRS)
40th Regiment	40 REGT	(Field)
47th Regiment	47 REGT	(Air Def)

The Corps of Royal Engineers (RE)

1st RSME Regiment	1 RSME REGT
3rd RSME Regiment	3 RSME REGT
21st Engineer Regiment	21 ENGR REGT
22nd Engineer Regiment	22 ENGR REGT
23rd Engineer Regiment (forming 2000)	23 ENGR REGT
25th Engineer Regiment	25 ENGR REGT
28th Engineer Regiment	28 ENGR REGT
32nd Engineer Regiment	32 ENGR REGT
33rd Engineer Regiment	33 ENGR REGT (EOD)
35th Engineer Regiment	35 ENGR REGT
36th Engineer Regiment	36 ENGR REGT
38th Engineer Regiment	38 ENGR REGT
39th Engineer Regiment	39 ENGR REGT

The total for the UK includes the 2 x RSME Training Regiments.

The Royal Corps of Signals (R SIGNALS)

1st (UK) Armd Div HQ and Signal Regiment	1 SIG REGT
2nd Signal Regiment	2 SIG REGT
3rd (UK) Div HQ & Signal Regiment	3 SIG REGT
7th (ARRC) Signal Regiment	7 SIG REGT
9th Signal Regiment (Radio)	9 SIG REGT
11th Signal Regiment (Trg Regt)	11 SIG REGT
14th Signal Regiment (Electronic Warfare)	14 SIG REGT
15th Signal Regiment	15 SIG REGT

16th Signal Regiment	16 SIG REGT
21st Signal Regiment (Air Support)	21 SIG REGT
30th Signal Regiment	30 SIG REGT

The Army Air Corps (AAC)

1st Regiment	1 REGT AAC
3rd Regiment	3 REGT AAC
4th Regiment	4 REGT AAC
7th Regiment	7 REGT AAC
9th Regiment	9 REGT AAC

THE SERVICES

The Royal Logistic Corps (RLC)

1 General Support Regiment	1 (GS) REGT
2 Close Support Regiment	2 (CS) REGT
3 Close Support Regiment	3 (CS) REGT
4 General Support Regiment	4 (GS) REGT
5 Territorial Army Training Regiment	5 (TRG) REGT
6 Support Regiment	6 (SP) REGT
7 Transport Regiment	7 (TPT) REGT
8 Artillery Support Regiment	8 (ARTY SP) REGT
9 Supply Regiment	9 (SUP) REGT
10 Transport Regiment	10 (TPT) REGT
11 Explosive Ordnance Disposal Regiment	11 (EOD) REGT
12 Supply Regiment	12 (SUP) REGT
13 Air Assault Support Regiment	13 (AIR ASSLT) REGT
14 Supply Regiment	14 (SUP) REGT
17 Port and Maritime Regiment	17 (PORT) REGT
21 Logistic Support Regiment	21 (LOG SP) REGT
23 Pioneer Regiment	23 (PNR) REGT
24 Regiment	24 REGT
27 Transport Regiment	27 (TPT) REGT
29 Regiment	29 REGT
89 Postal and Courier Regiment	89 (PC) REGT

Miscellaneous RLC Major Units

Training Regiment & Depot
Postal & Courier Depot
Army School of Ammunition
Cyprus Logistic Unit
3 Base Ordnance Depot

There are Combat Service Support Battalions with the Royal Marines 3 Commando Brigade, and the AMF(L) group.

Royal Army Medical Corps (RAMC)

1 Armoured Field Ambulance	1 ARMD FD AMB
2 Armoured Field Ambulance	2 ARMD FD AMB
3 Armoured Field Ambulance	3 ARMD FD AMB

16 Armoured Field Ambulance	16 ARMD FD AMB
24 Armoured Field Ambulance	24 ARMD FD AMB
4 Field Ambulance	4 FD AMB
5 Field Ambulance	5 FD AMB
14 Close Support Medical Regiment	14 CL SP MED REGT
21 Field Hospital	21 FD HOSP
33 Field Hospital	33 FD HOSP
34 Field Hospital	34 FD HOSP
84 Field Medical Equipment Depot	84 FMED

Military Bands

Following the 1993 re-organisation of military bands, on 1 April 1996 the Regular Army has 30 bands as follows:

Household Cavalry	-	70 musicians	- 2 bands
Grenadier Guards	-	49 musicians	- 1 band
Coldstream Guards	-	49 musicians	- 1 band
Scots Guards	-	49 musicians	- 1 band
Welsh Guards	-	49 musicians	- 1 band
Irish Guards	-	49 musicians	- 1 band
Royal Artillery	-	49 musicians	- 1 band
Royal Engineers	-	35 musicians	- 1 band
Royal Signals	-	35 musicians	- 1 band
Royal Logistic Corps	-	35 musicians	- 1 band
REME	-	35 musicians	- 1 band
Adjutant General's Corps	-	35 musicians	- 1 band
Army Air Corps	-	35 musicians	- 1 band
Royal Armoured Corps	-	140 musicians	- 4 bands
Scottish Division	-	70 musicians	- 2 bands
Queens Division	-	70 musicians	- 2 bands
Kings Division	-	70 musicians	- 2 bands
Prince of Wales's Division	-	70 musicians	- 2 bands
Light Division	-	49 musicians	- 1 band
Parachute Regiment	-	35 musicians	- 1 band
Royal Irish Regiment	-	35 musicians	- 1 band
Royal Gurkha Rifles	-	35 musicians	- 1 band

CHAPTER 12 - Recruiting, Selection and Training

"If any gentlemen, soldiers or others have a mind to serve Her Majesty, and pull down the French king; if any prentices have severe masters, any children have undutiful parents; if any servants have too little wages, or any husband too much wife, let him repair to the noble Sergeant Kite, at the sign of the Raven in the good old town of Shrewsbury...

Sergeant Kite 1704

Recruiting

Recruiting can best be described as the steps taken to attract sufficient men and women of the right quality to meet the Army's personnel requirements. Selection is the process that is carried out to ensure that those who are accepted into the Army have the potential to be good soldiers and are capable of being trained to carry out their chosen trade. Training is the process of preparing those men and women for their careers in the Army. Training is progressive and continues all the way through a soldier's career.

The Director General Army Manning and Recruiting (DGAMR), a Major General in The Ministry of Defence, is responsible for ensuring that the Army is properly manned and that sufficient men and women of the right quality are recruited to meet the needs of the service.

An MOD committee called the Standing Committee Army Manpower Forecasts (SCAMF) calculates the numbers that need to be enlisted to maintain the Army's personnel at the correct level. The Committee needs to take account of changing unit establishments, wastage caused by servicemen and women leaving the service at the end of their engagements, and those who might choose to leave before their engagements come to an end (PVR - Premature Voluntary Retirement). The number required in each trade in the Army is assessed and figures are published at six monthly intervals so that adjustments may be made during the year.

The Director of Army Recruiting (DAR), a Brigadier in The Ministry of Defence, and his staff located throughout the United Kingdom are then responsible for the recruiting and selection to meet the personnel targets.

Potential recruits are attracted into the Army in a number of ways including advertisements on the television, in cinemas and in the press. Permanently established recruiting teams from many Regiments and Corps tour the country and staff from the Army Career Information Offices (ACIOs) visit schools, youth clubs and job centres. Young, recently trained soldiers are also sent back to their home towns and schools to talk to their friends about life in the Army and are regularly interviewed by the local press.

During 1998-99 the total cost of recruiting for all three services was believed to have been over £100 million and, of this total, the Army figure was probably over £60 million. The approximate cost of recruits to each service was as follows:

Army	-	£5,000 per recruit
Royal Navy	-	£8,000 per recruit
Royal Air Force	-	£9,500 per recruit

Annual Army recruiting figures during the recent past are as follows:

	1993/94	1994/95	1995/96	1996/97	1997/98	1998/99
Officers	752	823	891	804	903	696
Soldiers	8,824	9,861	12,020	14,718	14,476	16,267

Outflow figures (personnel leaving the army) since 1995/96 are:

	1995/96	1996/97	1997/98	1998/99
Officers	1,289	1,095	1,030	1,353
Soldiers	14,154	14,259	13,348	15,662

Soldier Selection

Potential recruits are normally aged between 16 years and 6 months and 25 years, except when they are applying for a vacancy as an apprentice when the age limits are from 15 years 8 months to 17 years 6 months.

Under the latest selection system a potential recruit will have a preliminary assessment at the ACIO. Here, he or she will take the computer based Army Entrance Test (AET) which is designed to assess ability to assimilate the training required for the candidate's chosen trade. The staff at the ACIO will then conduct a number of interviews to decide on overall suitability for the Army. The ACIO staff will look at references from school or any employers and offer advice on which trade may be available and might suit the candidate. A preliminary medical examination will also be carried out that checks on weight, eyesight and hearing.

If these test and interviews are successfully passed, the candidate will be booked for further tests at the Recruit Selection Centre which is closest to his or her home. Recruit selection centres are at Glencorse in Scotland, Lichfield in Staffordshire, Pirbright in Surrey and Ballymena in Northern Ireland.

The candidates will remain at the RSC for an overnight stay and undergo another medical examination, a physical assessment test and an interview with a Personnel Selection Officer. The potential recruit will also see at first hand the type of training that they will undergo and the sort of life that they will lead in barracks if successful in getting into the Army. Physical fitness is assessed based on a timed run and some gymnasium exercises. After further interviews the candidate is informed if he or she is successful and, if so, is offered a vacancy in a particular trade and Regiment or Corps.

Phase 1 Training

Basic Recruit or Phase 1 training is the same for all soldiers whatever Regiment or Corps and whichever trade they are enlisted into. The course lasts for 10 weeks and is called The Common Military Syllabus (Recruit) (CMSR). It includes training in the basic military skills required of all soldiers and incorporates weapon handling and shooting, drill, physical fitness, field tactics, map reading, survival in nuclear, chemical and biological warfare and general military knowledge. It is an intensive course and requires the recruit to show considerable determination and courage to succeed.

The Army training organisation carries out centralised Phase 1 Training at 5 Army Training Regiments (ATRs). Each ATR is responsible for training all recruits enlisting into the following Regiments and Corps (with the exception of apprentices).

ATR Pirbright - The Household Cavalry, Infantry of the Guards Division, TheRoyal Logistic Corps, the Royal Electrical and Mechanical Engineers and the Royal Artillery.

ATR Bassingbourne - The Royal Engineers, The Royal Signals and Infantry of the Queen's Division.

ATR Winchester - The Royal Armoured Corps, Infantry of the Light Division, The Army Air Corps, The Adjutant General's Corps (including the Royal Military Police) and The Intelligence Corps.

ATR Glencorse - Infantry of the Scottish and King's Divisions.

ATR Lichfield - Infantry of the Prince of Wales's Division, The Parachute Regiment, Royal Army Medical Corps, Royal Army Veterinary Corps, Royal Army Dental Corps and Queen Alexandra's Royal Army Nursing Corps.

Phase 1 Training for the Royal Irish Regiment takes place at Ballymena in Northern Ireland.

Gurkha recruits now trained at Church Crookham following the closure of the Training Depot Brigade of Gurkhas in Hong Kong. The first intake of 153 men selected from 57,000 applicants started training in the UK during 1995.

Phase 2 Training
Phase 2 training is the 'Special to Arm' training that is required to prepare soldiers who have recently completed their basic Phase 1 training, to enable them to take their place in field force units of their Regiment or Corps. This phase of training has no fixed period and courses vary considerably in length.

Phase 2 training for the major Arms and Services is carried out as follows:

The Royal Armoured Corps - Takes place at Bovington Camp in Dorset. Recruits into the Household Cavalry Regiment also undergo equitation training.

Infantry - Infantry recruits do their 12 week Phase 2 Training at the Infantry Training Centre at Catterick.

The Royal Artillery - At the Royal School of Artillery at Larkhill in Wiltshire.

The Royal Engineers - At Cove in Hampshire and at the Royal School of Military Engineering at Chatham in Kent.

The Royal Logistic Corps - Drivers are trained at Leconfield, supply specialists at Blackdown, Cooks at Aldershot and Pioneers at Northampton.

The Adjutant General's Corps - Pay and Clerks are trained at the AGC Depot at Worthy Down near

Winchester and the Royal Military Police at Chichester.

Royal Electrical and Mechanical Engineers - Vehicle Mechanics are trained at Bordon and other trades at Arborfield.

Royal Signals - Training takes place at the Royal School of Signals at Blandford in Dorset.

Royal Army Medical Corps - At the RAMC Depot at Keogh Barracks, Aldershot.

Young Soldiers
Tradesman Apprentices Phase 1 and Phase 2 training which can last for up to two years is conducted at the Army Apprentice College. On entry, Apprentices are generally aged between 16 years and 17 years and 6 months.

The Army Foundation College (AFC) at Harrogate trains 16 and 17 year old recruits who wish to enter the Cavalry, Infantry and Royal Artillery. Those who successfully complete the 42 week course go straight to the Phase 2 training relevant to their arm. The first intake of 386 recruits started training in September 1998 and by the Army hopes that by 2002 about 1,300 recruits will be training at the AFC at any one time. Young soldiers attending the AFC are paid £138 per week.

Commissions
There are two main types of commission in the Army. These are:

a. THE REGULAR COMMISSION (Reg C) which is for those who wish to make the Army their permanent career. Regular Officers can normally expect their career to last until their 55th birthday.

b. THE SHORT SERVICE COMMISSION (SSC) which is for those who remain uncertain about their long-term career plans. The SSC lasts for a minimum of 3 years (6 for the Army Air Corps) but can be extended, if mutually agreed, to a maximum of 8 years.

The minimum educational requirements for a Regular Officer are currently 5 passes at GCSE which must include English Language, Mathematics and either a Science subject or Modern Language. Two of the passes must be at 'A' level grades A to E. Some Corps only accept candidates with appropriate degrees or professional qualifications.

The requirements for a Short Service Commission are less stringent requiring only 5 passes at GCSE grades A-C including English Language or Mathematics. Candidates for commissions should be over 17 years and 9 months and under 25 years old when they begin officer training.

c. SHORT SERVICE LIMITED COMMISSION - The SSLC is a commission that is aimed at those who have completed their 'A' Levels and have a gap year prior to entering University. The selection procedure at RCB has to be completed after which a three week course at Sandhurst is attended. Those who successfully complete the course join their chosen Regiment or Corps as 2nd Lieutenants for a minimum of 4 months and a maximum of 18 months with a front-line unit, but not on active service. The purpose of the SSLC is to create a pool of young men and women who will take a favourable impression of the Army into their careers.

d. LATE ENTRY COMMISSIONS - A number of vacancies exist for senior Non Commissioned Officers and Warrant Officers to be granted commissions known as Late Entry Commissions. Officers commissioned from the ranks are initially employed in exactly the same way as those granted direct entry commissions but, because of their age, generally do not rise above the rank of Major.

Officer Selection & Sandhurst

Candidates for commissions are normally advised of the options open to them by a Schools or University Liaison Officer who arranges for interviews and familiarisation visits to an appropriate Regiment or Corps. If the Regiment or Corps is prepared to sponsor a candidate they then guide him or her through the rest of the selection procedure. All candidates are required to attend the Regular Commissions Board (RCB) at Westbury, Wiltshire for a three day assessment prior to which they should have undergone a medical examination and attended a pre-RCB briefing so that they know what to expect.

RCB consists of a series of interviews and tests that assess the personality and the leadership potential in applicants. There is no secret in the selection procedures and details are available for all applicants.

RCB may, in some cases require further development in either leadership skills or academic standards prior to beginning officer training and this is conducted on a 12 week course at Rowallan Company at The Royal Military Academy Sandhurst (RMAS) which is at Camberley in Surrey.

All potential officers accepted for training attend the RMAS Common Commissioning Course which lasts for 44 weeks with 3 intakes a year in January, May and September. After successfully completing the Sandhurst course a young officer then completes a further specialist course with his or her chosen Regiment or Corps.

Females cannot be accepted in the Household Cavalry, The Royal Armoured Corps or the Infantry.

Welbeck College

Welbeck is the Army's sixth form college which offers two year 'A' Level courses for boys and girls who wish to gain commissions in the technical corps. The Welbeck course is science and engineering based and includes leadership training. Welbexians do not need to attend the Regular Commissions Board but simply require the recommendation of the Headmaster to gain entry to RMAS.

Army Training Overview

Responsible for Army Training is the Inspectorate General of Doctrine and Training (IGDT) based at Upavon in Wiltshire employing about 18,000 service and civilian personnel (the majority in the UK and Germany) with a budget of over £500 million annually. HQ IGDT has 103 military staff and 116 civilian personnel and is directly responsible to the Adjutant General.

Following basic Phase 1 and Phase 2 training, soldiers are posted to their units and progressive training is carried out on a continual basis. Training is geared to individual, sub-unit or formation level and units regularly train outside the UK and Germany. As would be expected there are specialist unit training packages for specific operational commitments such as Northern Ireland and Yugoslavia.

For example, the training package for personnel warned off for deployment to the former Yugoslavia consists of a 12 day special-to-mission package. The training is carried out by specialist training advisory teams at the Army's Combined Arms Training Centre at Warminster and for Germany based units at the Sennelager Training Centre.

The British Army's main training areas outside of the Europe are:

Canada - Suffield
British Army Training Unit Suffield (BATUS) has the responsibility to train battlegroups in the planning and execution of armoured operations through the medium of live firing and tactical test exercise. There are 6 x "Medicine Man" battlegroup exercises each year in a training season that lasts from March to November.

Canada - Wainright
The British Army Training Support Unit at Wainwright (BATSU(W)) provides the logistic and administrative support for Infantry units at the Canadian Forces training base in Western Canada. During the winter months the unit moves in its entirety to Fort Lewis in the USA where it carries out a similar function. There are usually 3 battalion group exercises at Wainright and 2 at Fort Lewis during the course of each training year.

Kenya
British Army Liaison Staff Kenya (BATLSK) is responsible for supporting Infantry battalion group exercises and approximately 3,000 British troops train in Kenya each year in a harsh unforgiving terrain ranging in altitude from 8,000 feet down to 2,300 feet. BATLSK has been based at its present site in Kahawa Barracks since Kenya's independence in 1963.

Belize
The British Army Training Support Unit Belize (BATSUB) was formed on 1 October 1994. Its role is to give training and logistic support to Land Command units training in a tropical jungle environment. In general terms BATSUB costs about £3 million per year.

Overseas Students
During any one year about 4,000 students from over 90 different countries take part in training in the United Kingdom. The charges for training depend on the length of the course, its syllabus and number taking part. Receipts from overseas governments for this training are believed to be in the region of £30-40 million.

Training Standards
Shooting - All ranks are required to take an annual personnel weapons test (APWT). Pass rates for 1992/93 (the only year for which unclassified figures are available) were:

Infantry	-	98%
Royal ArmouredCorps	-	85%
Royal Engineers	-	74%
Royal Artillery	-	78%
Royal Signals	-	88%
Royal Logistic Corps	-	89%
Army Average	-	86%

Basic Fitness Test - All soldiers of all ranks and ages are required to take a basic fitness test. This test involves a 1.5 mile run and walk (in a squad) on level ground and in training shoes, in 10 minutes for those under 30. There are gradually rising time limits for older personnel and recruits in training are given 10 mins and 30 seconds for the 1.5 mile run. The current standards for women are lower and female recruits are allowed to do the 1.5 mile run in 12 minutes and 50 seconds.

Recruit Training Assessments - During Recruit Training personnel are assessed at different stages of training as follows:

Test	Introduction	Interim	Final
Heaves	2	4	6
Sit Up Test	1 Min (20 reps)	2 min (42 reps)	3 min (65 reps)
1.5 Mile Run	11 min 30 sec	11 mins	10 min 30 sec

Career Profile - Soldier

As an illustration of the career that might be expected for a regular soldier, we have used a model based on the career of Thomas Atkins. A serving soldier about to retire after 22 years' service.

Age

17 - Left school at 16. Bored with life at home and not happy in his job with British Rail. Decides to join the Army, and takes selection tests at his local Army Careers Office. After a successful assessment at the Recruit Selection Centre he is sent to an Army Training Regiment to complete Phase 1 Common Military Syllabus (Recruit) Training lasting ten weeks. Following completion of the course he attends the Infantry Training Centre at Catterick for a further 12 week course where the specialist infantry skills are taught. After initial training Atkins is posted to a regular battalion of his regiment which is serving in Cyprus. Spends 18 months in Cyprus where he is employed as a rifleman in an infantry platoon.

19 - The battalion is posted to Tidworth in Hampshire. Rfn Atkins is transferred from an infantry platoon in "A" Company to the Anti-Tank Platoon in the Manoeuvre Support Company. Atkins sees this move as a career advancement, and from Tidworth completes a 6-month tour in Ulster. About two and a half years after arriving in Tidworth the battalion is posted to Belfast on an 18-month tour.

21 - Directly after the move to Belfast Rfn Atkins attends a battalion NCOs training course and is promoted to Lcpl. As a Lcpl he is the 2ic of an infantry section in a rifle platoon. After a year in Belfast, he is promoted to Cpl and attends a Weapons Instructors Course lasting 8 weeks at the Combined Arms Training Centre at Warminster.

23 - The battalion leaves Belfast on posting to Germany as an armoured infantry battalion mounted in Warrior armoured fighting vehicles. Cpl Atkins is posted to the Army Training Regiment where he is responsible for training recruits a section of recruits. After two years at the Army Training Regiment he re-joins his battalion that has two years of its four year tour left to serve.

25 - Spends one year in Germany commanding an infantry section mounted in a Warrior AIFV during which time the battalion spends six months on operations in support of NATO forces in the Former Yugoslavia. At the end of this year attends a Platoon Sergeants Course at the Combined Arms Training Centre, and on, rejoining the battalion after the course, is promoted Sergeant.

26 - Becomes 2ic of a rifle platoon, is responsible for the "on the job" training of a young officer and the welfare of the 30 soldiers in his care. On occasions, he commands the platoon in the absence of the officer platoon commander.

30 - Promoted to Colour Sergeant and becomes an instructor at the Royal Military Academy Sandhurst where he teaches officer cadets some of the fundamentals of soldiering. After Sandhurst, returns to the battalion now serving in Catterick where he runs the logistical support for an infantry company.

33 - Promoted WOII (Company Sergeant Major) and is almost entirely responsible for the discipline and administration of an infantry company of about 130 men.

36 - Appointed RQMS (Regimental Quartermaster Sergeant) and is now responsible for much of the logistic support for a complete infantry battalion.

38 - Promoted WOI (Regimental Sergeant Major). The most senior soldier in the battalion and very much the Commanding Officer's right hand man. Much feared by the scruffy and the idle, avoided by young officers with long hair, the reputation of the battalion is his personal responsibility.

40 - At the end of his service leaves the Army and returns to civilian life.

Note: Not all RSM's return to civilian life at the end of 22 years service. Many are offered commissions and fill important posts in both regiments and corps, often as Quartermasters responsible for equipment worth many millions of pounds. For example the Quartermaster of a cavalry regiment may be responsible for tanks, armoured vehicles and associated items on charge to the regiment worth some £300 million. As long ago as the First World War, Field Marshal Sir William Robertson (a commissioned warrant officer) became Chief of the Imperial General Staff.

Career Profile - Officer
To illustrate an officer's career, we have used a non graduate regular officer who has elected to serve in the infantry.

Age
19 - Having left school with 2 A Levels decides to join the Army and goes to the Regular Commissions Board (RCB) at Westbury in Wiltshire to undergo selection. On being passed by the RCB as a suitable candidate for a commission, is given a date to start at the Royal Military Academy, Sandhurst (RMA). At the RMA he completes a one year course, designed to give young officers a sound basic military education. Following graduation from Sandhurst he attends the 12 week Platoon Commanders Battle Course at the Combined Arms Training Centre.

20 - Posted to a battalion of his Regiment as a 2/Lt. The battalion is serving in Catterick and he commands a rifle platoon for two years. During his tour as a platoon commander the battalion serves in South Armagh on a six month tour and takes part in an exercise in Kenya. After two years is promoted to Lieutenant.

22 - Posted to the Infantry Training Centre where he commands a number of training platoons during a two year posting. Training platoons have experienced regular NCOs as instructors and their task is to take soldiers from the Army Training Regiments and turn them into infantrymen during a 12 week course.

24 - Returns to the battalion and commands the Mortar Platoon for a further 18 months, having undergone a conversion course at the Combined Arms Training Centre. During this time he is detached from the battalion for 4 months and works as a junior staff officer in Bosnia. At the end of this period is selected to become the Battalion Adjutant and is responsible for the day-to-day discipline and administration of the battalion.

27 - On appointment as Adjutant he is promoted Captain.

29 - After two years as Adjutant he is posted away from the battalion, and spends the next two years as an infantry exchange officer in the United States.

31 - Returns to the battalion now serving in Germany and becomes the 2i/c of an armoured infantry company. During this time he starts to prepare himself for an examination which if he passes will qualify him for promotion to Major, and if he does extremely well will qualify for a place at the Staff College.

32 - Becomes the Battalion Operations Officer, responsible to the Commanding Officer for preparing the battalion's war plans. Passes the Staff/Promotion exam and is given a place at the Staff College.

33 - Attends a course at the Staff College Camberley. After one year at the Staff College is promoted to major and posted to HQ 3 (UK) Division as a staff officer in the Operations Branch (SO2 G3)

36 - Returns to the battalion now serving in Tidworth where he commands a mechanised rifle company (mounted in Saxon APCs) for two years. During this period the battalion serves on six month tour in support of the UN in the Former Yugoslavia.

38 - Posted to HQ 1(UK) Armoured Division where he fills a staff officer's post in the Training Branch.

39 - Selected for promotion to Lieutenant Colonel and returns to the battalion once again serving in Germany. He now commands a Battlegroup composed of tanks, infantry, artillery and engineers.

42 - Promoted to Colonel and becomes a staff officer at PJHQ Northwood working for the Director of Joint Operations.

47 - Is promoted to Brigadier and commands an Armoured Brigade in Germany.

50 - Commands a Division as a Major General.

53 - Promoted to Lieutenant General and is appointed as Commander HQ Land.
55 - Retires as a Lieutenant General to become a television personality. Is constantly seen on BBC Newsnight commenting on newsworthy crisis situations.

CHAPTER 13 - RESERVE FORCES

Territorial Army (TA)

Strength of the Territorial Army (1 January 2000)

Armour	4 Regiments
Royal Artillery	7 Regiments (1)
Royal Engineers	5 Regiments
Infantry	15 Battalions
Special Air Service	2 Regiments
Signals	12 Regiments
Equipment Support	4 Battalions
Logistics	7 Regiments
Adjutant General's Corps	2 Regiments (2)
Intelligence Corps	1 Battalion
Aviation	1 Regiment
Medical	10 Field Hospitals

Notes: (1) Including HAC (2) Royal Military Police (3) Total is 70 major units.

TA ORDER OF BATTLE

Royal Armoured Corps

Royal Yeomanry
RHQ - London
Squadrons: Swindon; Leicester; Croydon; Nottingham; London.

Royal Wessex Yeomanry
RHQ – Bovington
Squadrons: Bovington; Salisbury; Cirencester; Barnstable.

Royal Mercian and Lancastrian Yeomanry
RHQ – Telford
Squadrons: Dudley; Telford; Chester; Wigan.

Queen's Own Yeomanry
RHQ – Newcastle
Squadrons: York; Ayr; Belfast; Cupar; Newcastle.

Royal Artillery

Honourable Artillery Company
RHQ – London
Squadrons: 5 all based in the City of London.

100 Regiment
RHQ – Luton
Batteries: Luton; Bristol; Nottingham.

101 Regiment
RHQ – Gateshead
Battalions: Blyth; Newcastle; South Shields.

103 Regiment
RHQ – St Helens
Batteries: Liverpool; Manchester; Bolton.

104 Regiment
RHQ – Newport
Batteries: Wolverhampton; Newport; Worcester.

105 Regiment
RHQ – Edinburgh
Batteries: Newtownards; Glasgow; Arbroath.

106 Regiment
RHQ – London
Batteries: Bury St Edmunds; London; Leeds: Southampton.

Central Volunteers HQ RA
London

<u>**Royal Engineers**</u>

Royal Monmouthshire RE (Militia)
RHQ – Monmouth
Squadrons: Cwmbran; Swansea; Warley.

71 Regiment
RHQ – Leuchars
Squadrons: Paisley; Newcastle.

73 Regiment
RHQ – Nottingham
Squadrons: Sheffield; Nottingham; Chesterfield; St Hellier (Jersey).

75 Regiment
RHQ - Failsworth
Squadrons: Birkenhead; Stoke on Trent; Walsall.

101 Regiment
RHQ – London
Squadrons: London; Rochester; Tunbridge Wells.

131 Independent Commando Squadron
London.

135 Topographical Squadron
Ewell.

412 Amphibious Engineer Troop
Hameln.

Central Volunteer HQ RE
Camberley.

Royal Signals

31 Signal Regiment
RHQ – London
Squadrons: Coulsdon; Eastbourne; London.

32 Signal Regiment
RHQ – Glasgow
Squadrons: Aberdeen; East Kilbride; Edinburgh.

33 Signal Regiment
RHQ – Huyton
Squadrons: Manchester; Liverpool; Runcorn.

34 Signal Regiment
RHQ – Middlesborough
Squadrons: Leeds; Darlington; Middlesborough.

35 Signal Regiment
RHQ – Coventry
Squadrons: Birmingham; Newcastle-Under-Lyme; Rugby; Shrewsbury.

36 Signal Regiment
RHQ – Ilford
Squadrons: Grays; Colchester; Cambridge.

37 Signal Regiment
RHQ – Redditch
Squadrons: Cardiff; Stratford-Upon-Avon; Manchester; Coventry.

38 Signal Regiment
RHQ – Sheffield
Squadrons: Derby; Sheffield; Nottingham.

39 Signal Regiment
RHQ – Bristol
Squadrons: Uxbridge; Banbury; Gloucester.

40 Signal Regiment
RHQ – Belfast
Squadrons: Belfast; Limavady; Bangor.

71 Signal Regiment
RHQ – London
Squadrons: Lincolns Inn; Bexleyheath; Chelmsford.

72 Signal Regiment
RHQ – Oxford
Squadrons: Bath; Windsor; Aylesbury.

1 Signal Squadron
Bletchley.

2 Signal Squadron
Dundee.

5 Communications Company
Chicksands.

63 Signal Squadron (SAS)

<u>Infantry</u>

The Tyne Tees Regiment
Bn HQ – Durham
Companies: Scarborough; Middlesborough; Bishop Auckland; Newcastle upon Tyne; Ashington.

The King's and Cheshire Regiment
Bn HQ – Warrington
Companies: Liverpool; Warrington; Manchester; Crewe.

51st Highland Regiment
Bn HQ – Perth
Companies: Dundee; Peterhead; Inverness; Dunbarton; Stirling.

52nd Lowland Regiment
Bn HQ – Glasgow
Companies: Edinburgh; Ayr; Glasgow; Galashiels.

The East and West Riding Regiment
Bn HQ – Pontefract
Companies: Huddersfield; Barnsley; Hull; York; Wakefield.

The East of England Regiment
Bn HQ – Bury St Edmunds
Companies: Norwich; Lincoln; Leicester; Mansfield; Chelmsford.

The London Regiment
Bn HQ – Battersea
Companies: Westminster; Edgeware; Balham; Camberwell; Mayfair; West Ham.

3rd (Volunteer) Battalion, The Princess of Wales's Royal Regiment (Queen's and Royal Hampshires)
Bn HQ – Canterbury
Companies: Farnham; Brighton; Canterbury.

The Royal Rifle Volunteers
Bn HQ – Reading
Companies: Oxford; Reading; Portsmouth; Milton Keynes.

The Rifle Volunteers
Bn HQ – Exeter
Companies: Gloucester; Taunton; Dorchester; Truro; Exeter.

The West Midlands Regiment
Bn HQ – Wolverhampton
Companies: Birmingham; Kidderminster; Burton upon Trent; Stoke-on-Trent; Shrewsbury.

The Royal Welsh Regiment
Bn HQ – Cardiff
Companies: Wrexham; Swansea; Cardiff; Colwyn Bay.

The Lancastrian and Cumbrian Volunteers
Bn HQ – Preston
Companies: Barrow in Furness; Blackburn; Workington; Preston.

The Royal Irish Rangers
Bn HQ – Portadown
Companies: Newtonards; Newtownabbey.

4th (Volunteer) Battalion, The Parachute Regiment
Bn HQ – Pudsey
Companies: London; Pudsey; Glasgow.

<u>**Army Medical Services**</u>

201 Field Hospital
RHQ – Newcastle upon Tyne
Squadrons: Newton Aycliffe; Stockton-on-Tees; Newcastle upon Tyne.

202 Field Hospital
RHQ - Birmingham
Squadrons: Birmingham; Stoke on Trent; Oxford; Shrewsbury.

203 Field Hospital
RHQ – Cardiff
Squadrons: Cardiff; Swansea; Abergavenny.

204 Field Hospital
RHQ – Belfast
Squadrons: Belfast; Ballymena; Newtownards; Armagh.

205 Field Hospital
RHQ – Glasgow
Squadrons: Glasgow; Aberdeen; Dundee; Edinburgh.

207 Field Hospital
RHQ – Manchester
Squadrons: Stockport; Blackburn; Bury.

208 Field Hospital
RHQ- Liverpool
Squadrons: Liverpool; Ellesmere; Lancaster.

212 Field Hospital
RHQ – Sheffield
Squadrons: Sheffield; Bradford; Nottingham; Leeds.

243 Field Hospital
RHQ – Keynsham
Squadrons: Keynsham; Exeter; Plymouth; Portsmouth.

256 Field Hospital
RHQ – Walworth, London
Squadrons: Walworth; Hammersmith; Kingston; Bow.

253 Field Ambulance
Belfast.

254 Field Ambulance
Cambridge.

152 Ambulance Regiment
RHQ – Belfast
Squadrons: Londonderry; Belfast; Bridgend.

C (144) Parachute Medical Squadron
London.

B (220) Medical Squadron
Maidstone.

B (250) Medical Squadron
Hull.

B (225) Medical Squadron
Dundee.

C (251) Medical Squadron
Sunderland.

C (222) Medical Squadron
Leicester.

HQ Army Medical Service TA
York.

Royal Logistic Corps

150 (Northumbria) Transport Regiment
RHQ – Hull
Squadrons: Hull; Tynemouth; Leeds; Doncaster.

151 (Greater London) Logistic Support Regiment
RHQ – Croydon
Squadrons: Romford; Sutton; Barnet; Southall.

156 (North West) Transport Regiment
RHQ – Liverpool
Squadrons: Liverpool; Birkenhead; Salford; Bootle.

157 (Wales and Midland) Logistic Support Regiment
RHQ – Cardiff
Squadrons: Cardiff; Telford; Swansea; Carmarthen; West Bromwich.

158 (Royal Anglian) Transport Regiment
RHQ – Peterborough
Squadrons: Peterborough; Kempston; Ipswich; Loughborough.

Scottish Transport Regiment
RHQ – Dunfermline
Squadrons: Dunfermline; Glasgow; Edinburgh; Glenrothes; Irvine.

168 Pioneer Regiment
RHQ – Grantham
Squadrons: Grantham; Cramlington; Coulby Newham.

CVHQ and HQ RLC TA
Grantham.

Royal Electrical And Mechanical Engineers

101 Battalion REME
Bn HQ – Queensferry
Companies: Prestatyn; Coventry; Clifton; Grangemouth.

102 Battalion REME
Bn HQ – Newton Aycliffe
Companies: Newton Aycliffe; Rotherham; Scunthorpe; Newcastle upon Tyne.

103 Battalion REME
Bn HQ – Crawley
Companies: Portsmouth; Redhill; Ashford.

104 Battalion REME
Bn HQ – Bordon
Company: Northampton.

HQ REME TA
Bordon

Adjutant General's Corps

4 Regiment, Royal Military Police
RHQ – Aldershot
Companies: West Bromwich; Brixton.

5 Regiment, Royal Military Police
RHQ – Livingston
Companies: Livingston; Stockton-on-Tees.

CVHQ AGC:
Worthy Down.

Intelligence Corps

3 (Volunteer) Military Intelligence Battalion:
BHQ – London
Companies: London; Edinburgh; York; Keynsham; Birmingham.

Special Air Service

21 and 23 Regiments SAS

Army Air Corps

7 Regiment AAC
Netheravon.

CVHQ ACC:
Netheravon

Officer Training Corps Units
Aberdeen University Officer Training Corps
Birmingham University Officer Training Corps
Bristol University Officer Training Corps

Cambridge University Officer Training Corps
East Midlands University Officer Training Corps
City of Edinburgh University Officer Training Corps
Exeter University Officer Training Corps
Glasgow and Strathclyde Universities Officer Training Corps
Leeds University Officer Training Corps
Liverpool University Officer Training Corps
London University Officer Training Corps
Manchester and Salford University Officer Training Corps
Northumbrian University Officer Training Corps
Oxford University Officer Training Corps
Queens University Officer Training Corps
Sheffield University Officer Training Corps
Southampton University Officer Training Corps
Tayforth University Officer Training Corps
University of Wales Officer Training Corps

TA Role

Currently the TA is approaching the end of a restructuring process that has seen personnel figures falling from around 59,000 in 1998 to a total of 41,200 on 1 November 1999.

In war, the 41,200 personnel of the Territorial Army could be reinforced by approximately 34,000 Individual Reservists (IRs) to a fully mobilised establishment of over 75,000. The TA acts as a General Reserve to the Army, with a secondary but vitally important function being the promotion of a nationwide link between the military and civilian community.

The MoD describes the mission of the TA as follows:

" The Territorial Army will have three roles. The role that first and foremost determines its structure is to be to provide individuals and formed units as an integral part of the deployable Army, with each unit having a clear mission to play an essential part alongside regular forces in operations in support of UK interests abroad. The distribution of units throughout the country, also enables the Territorial Army to provide a framework upon which larger reserve forces can be built should the country need them. Third, it contributes to promoting the link between the Army and the civilian community which it serves in practical and visible ways. This will mean that the future Territorial Army will have a new mission:

"to provide formed units and individuals as an essential part of the Army's order of battle for operations across all military tasks in order to ensure that the Army is capable of mounting and sustaining operations at nominated states of readiness. It is also to provide a basis for regeneration, while at the same time maintaining links with the local community and society at large".

During the 1980s and early 1990s plans appeared to place a large part of the defence of the mainland UK in the hands of the TA. TA soldiers were assigned national defence roles such as, guarding vital installations, undertaking reconnaissance and early warning, providing communications and damage control. However the emphasis is changing and in early 1995 a composite TA platoon served alongside the regular infantry component of the Falkland Islands garrison, and in Bosnia during late 1996 over 1,200 TA soldiers were serving with the Multi National Division (SW). TA soldiers continue to serve in Bosnia (mainly attached to regular units) and in mid 1999 a significant number were deployed to assist regular units operating in Kosovo. This is likely to continue into the longer term, and it is probable that with recruiting problems for the Regular Army being what they are, the use of TA personnel on operations outside of the UK will increase.

In the main TA Infantry Units have a General Purpose structure which will give them flexibility of employment across the spectrum of military operations. All Infantry Battalions, including Parachute Battalions, have a common establishment of three Rifle Companies and a Headquarters Company. Under the latest structural changes each rifle company will have a support platoon with mortar, anti-tank, reconnaissance, MMG and assault pioneer sections under command.

TA volunteers are paid at Regular Army rates (but with a reduced X Factor of 5%) for every full or part day of training. They receive:

a. One part day's pay for attending duties of two to four hours duration.
b. A whole day's pay for duties of eight hours or longer.

In addition, TA personnel can earn an annual tax-free bounty provided they have been available for call-out during the training year, attended a minimum amount of training, have passed certain tests and gained the Commanding Officer's Certificate of Efficiency.

The annual training commitment to qualify for bounty is:

Independent Units: 27 days including 15 days continuous at camp.
Specialist Units: 19 days including 15 days continuous at camp.

In each case individuals may attend one or more courses aggregated to at least eight days duration in lieu of camp, with the balance of seven days being carried out in extra out-of-camp training.

Some examples of bounty payments and commitments are:

	First Year	Second Year	Third Year	Fifth Year
Group A – Higher Commitment	£300	£650	£1,000	£1,050
Group A – Lower Commitment	-	£360	£555	£585
Group B – Officers, Officer Cadets and soldiers in the OTC	£100	£130	£155	£155

The Reserve Forces Act 1996
Under the Reserve Forces Act 1996 principal call out powers would be brought into effect in a crisis by the issue of a call out order. Members of the Reserve Forces are then liable for service anywhere in the world, unless the terms of service applicable in individual cases restrict liability to service within the UK.

Call out powers are vested in and authorised by Her Majesty the Queen who may make an order authorising call-out:

1 If it appears to her that national danger is imminent
1 Or that a great emergency has arisen
1 Or in the event of an actual or apprehended attack on the United kingdom.

The Secretary of State for Defence may make an order authorising call out:

1 If it appears to him that warlike preparations are in preparation or progress.
1 Or it appears to him that it is necessary or desirable to use armed forces on operations outside the UK for the protection of life or property.
1 And for operations anywhere in the world for the alleviation of distress or the preservation of life or property in time of disaster or apprehended disaster.

Under normal circumstances, the maximum continuous periods of permanent service which individuals can serve under the above powers are respectively 3 years, 12 months and 9 months. In exceptional circumstances the 3 years may be increased to 5 and the 12 months to 2 years but under the third power, no extensions can be ordered beyond the maximum of 9 months. Under each power, provisions also limit the maximum aggregated time a reservist can spend in permanent service over given lengths of time.

Reservists and employers may apply for deferral of or exemption from call out. It is recognised that those called out may not find the outcomes of their initial applications to their satisfaction. Therefore a system of arbitration has been set up.

The Reserve Forces Act 1996 introduces two new types of reserve categories: Higher Readiness Reserves and Sponsored Reserves.

1 **Higher Readiness Reserve (HRR):** these are individuals, serving either as members of the volunteer reserves or as individual reserves, who have taken additional liability for call out at any time. They have skills that are in short supply in both the regular and reserve forces. Typically these might be linguists, intelligence staff, media operations staff and specialist support staff.

1 To be a HRR, a reservist must sign an agreement to that affect and his civilian employer must agree in writing, to his doing so. An agreement, that may be followed by successive agreements, will be for one year. Whilst the agreement is in force the reservist may be called up to serve for up to nine months continuous service. As for other call-out powers, appeals against call-out by reservists or employers may be heard.

1 **Sponsored Reserves.** There are a number of support functions that are carried out by civilians but which in war are carried out by servivce personnel, because servicemen must carry out the function on operations. This new category of reserve will allow some of these tasks to be put out to contract, providing that the contractor employs in his workforce a sufficient number of employees willing to serve as a members of a reserve force in the Sponsored Reserve category. If the task was required to be carried out operationally, these employees could be called out to continue providing the required support as servicemen. Sponsored Reserves will have their own call out power and be subject to no other. This and their conditions of service will be tailored to the commercial aspects of the concept.

RFA 96 enables reimbursement to be made to Employers and Reservists for some of the additional costs of employees being called out. Some reservists will have financial commitments commensurate with their civilian salary and so provisions are in place to minimise financial hardship.

The MOD is also able to offset the indirect costs of employees being called out incurred by an employer, for example, the need to recruit and train temporary replacements. If employers or reservists are dissatisfied with the financial assistance awarded they may appeal to tribunals set up for this.

Full and Part Time Service: One provision of the RFA 96 is that reservists can now undertake periods of full or part time employment with the Armed Forces. This is not a call-out but a voluntary arrangement to make it possible for the Services to make more flexible use of their manpower assets. There are no fixed time limits. If a task needs doing, there is sufficient budget and a suitable volunteer is available for the job, then it can be done.

Pensions: Provision has been made in RFA 96 for the protection of Reservist pension rights in the event of call up. The MOD is permitted to pay the employers contributions to a civilian pension scheme.

TA soldiers are called-out using the same procedures as for Irs - ie. they are sent a Call-Out Notice specifying the time, date and place to which they are to report. If TA Units or Sub-Units are called-out, they form up with their vehicles and equipment at their TA Centres or other designated locations. They would then be deployed by land, sea and air to their operational locations in the UK or overseas. However, if TA personnel are called-out as individuals, they would report to a Temporary Mobilisation Centre where they would be processed before posting to reinforce a unit or HQ.

The Regular Reserve

Individual Reservists (IR) are former members of the Regular Army who after completion of their full-time service may be recalled to the Colours, or who volunteer after their legal Reserve obligation has expired. They have varying degrees of liability for recall and training depending upon factors such as period of Regular Army service, age and sex. Categories of IR are described below:

a. The Regular Army Reserve of Officers (RARO). Retired Regular, Army Emergency Reserve or TA Officers. Those granted Commissions from 1 April 1983 have a compulsory training liability for six years after leaving the Active List. Others may volunteer to train;

b. The Regular Reserve. Ex-Regular soldiers (male and female) who have a compulsory training liability (normally for six years after leaving the Colours) or who have volunteered to join it from other categories;

c. The Long-Term Reserve. Men (but not women) who have completed their Regular Reserve liability and who serve in this category until aged 45. They have no training liability;

d. Army Pensioners. Ex-Regular soldiers (male and female) who are in receipt of a Service pension. They have a legal liability for recall to age 60 (but only to age 55 would be invoked). They have no training liability.

Call-out Procedure

IR are required to keep at home an Instruction Booklet (AB 592A), their ID card and a personalised Booklet (AB 592B). The AB 592A provides IR with general instructions on what they have to do if mobilised. It contains a travel warrant and a special cash order. The AB 592A is computer produced and updated quarterly as required to take account of such changes as address, medical category and age. It explained where the reservist is to report on mobilisation and arrangements for pay and allotments, next-of-kin, clothing held etc.

Under present legislation IR may only be mobilised if called-out by Queen's Order. Mobilisation may involve only a few individuals/units or any number up to general mobilisation when all are called out. If mobilisation is authorised Notices of Call-Out are despatched to those IR concerned by Recorded Delivery as the legal notification. Announcements of call-out are also made by the press, radio and television.

Under the proposals for the new Reserve Forces Act, IR will be liable to call-out under the same new provisions as described above for the TA. In addition, the Act will bring the conditions relating to all three Services in line and will include officers and pensioners who are currently covered by separate legislation/Royal Warrants.

Training

Only Regular Reservists and some members of RARO have a liability to train. The legal liability is for up to 15 days plus four periods of 36 hours each year. This liability has not been enforced for many years.

The only training that is currently funded is for 1,500 man/weeks per year to enable the RARO and Regular Reservists who volunteer to take part in collective training with both Regular and TA Units. Payment is made at TA rates plus £215 (tax-free) bounty.

The Annual Reporting Exercises (ARCES), which required some RARO and all Regular Reservists to report for one day to have their clothing and documentation checked and undergo a brief 1+ hours training period also ceased in 1991. The reporting element has now been replaced by a postal system which provides a payment of £20 (taxed) to those who return an updated proforma.

Cadets

The Role of the CCF

The Combined Cadet Force (CCF) is a tri-Service military cadet organisation based in schools and colleges throughout the UK. Although it is administered and funded by the Services it is a part of the national youth movement.

The CCF receives assistance and support for it's training programme from the Regular and Reserve Forces, but the bulk of adult support is provided by members of school staffs who are responsible to head teachers for the conduct of cadet activities. CCF officers wear uniform but they are not part of the Armed Forces and carry no liability for service or compulsory training.

There are some 240 CCF contingents with 40,000 cadets, of whom some 25,000 are Army Cadets. The role of the CCF is to help boys and girls to develop powers of leadership through training which promotes qualities of responsibility, self-reliance, resourcefulness, endurance, perseverance and a sense of service to the community. Military training is also designed to demonstrate why defence forces are needed, how they function and to stimulate an interest in a career as an officer in the Services.

The Role of the ACF

The role of the Army Cadet Force (ACF) is to inspire young people to achieve success with a spirit of service to the Queen, country and their local community, and to develop the qualities of good citizenship, responsibility and leadership.

There are about 1,674 ACF detachments based in communities around the UK with a strength of around 40,000 cadets. The ACF is run by over 7,000 adults drawn from the local community who manage a broad programme of military and adventurous training activities designed to develop character and leadership.

CHAPTER 14 - MISCELLANEOUS

The Military Hierarchy

Rank	Badge	Appointment Example
General (Gen)	Crown, Star & Crossed Sword with Baton	Chief of the General Staff
Lieutenant General (Lt Gen)	Crown & Sword & Baton	Commander ARRC
Major General (Maj Gen)	Star & Sword & Baton	Divisional Commander
Brigadier (Brig)	Crown & 3 Stars	Brigade
Colonel (Col)	Crown & 2 Stars	Staff or School
Lieutenant Colonel (Lt Col)	Crown & 1 Star	Battle Group/Armoured Regiment/Infantry Bn
Major (Maj)	Crown	Sqn/Coy/Bty
Captain (Capt)	3 Stars	Squadron/Company 2ic
Lieutenant (Lt)	2 Stars	Troop/Pl Commander
2nd Lieutenant	1 Star (2/Lt)	Troop/Pl Commander
Warrant Officer First Class	Royal Coat of Arms on Forearm	Regimental Sergeant Major (WO 1) (RSM)
Warrant Officer Second Class	Crown on forearm	Company Sergeant Major (WO 2) (CSM)
Staff Sergeant (Ssgt)	Crown over 3 stripes	Coy/Sqn Stores (or Colour Sergeant)
Sergeant (Sgt)	3 stripes	Platoon Sergeant
Corporal (Cpl)	2 stripes	Section Commander
Lance Corporal	1 Stripe	Section 2ic (Lcpl)

Modes of Address

Where appropriate soldiers are addressed by their generic rank without any qualifications, therefore Generals, Lieutenant Generals and Major Generals are all addressed as "General". Colonels and Lieutenant Colonels as "Colonel", Corporals and Lance Corporals as "Corporal". Staff Sergeants and Colour Sergeants are usually addressed as "Staff" or "Colour" and CSMs as Sergeant Major. It would almost certainly be prudent to address the RSM as "Sir".

Private Soldiers should always be addressed by their title and then their surname. For example: Rifleman Harris, Private Jones, Bugler Bygrave, Gunner Smith, Guardsman Thelwell, Sapper Williams, Trooper White, Kingsman Boddington, Signalman Robinson, Ranger Murphy, Fusilier Ramsbotham , Driver Wheel, Craftsman Grease or Air Trooper Rotor. However, it should be remembered that regiments and corps have different customs and although the above is a reasonable guide it may not always be correct.

Regimental Head-Dress

The normal everyday head-dress of NCOs and Soldiers (and in some regiments of all ranks) is the beret or national equivalent. The norm is the dark blue beret. Exceptions are as follows:

a.	Grey Beret	The Royal Scots Dragoon Guards
		Queen Alexandra's Royal Army Nursing Corps
b.	Brown Beret	The King's Royal Hussars
		The Royal Wessex Yeomanry
c.	Khaki Beret	All Regiments of Foot Guards
		The Honourable Artillery Company
		The Kings Own Royal Border Regiment
		The Royal Anglian Regiment
		The Prince of Wales's Own Regiment of Yorkshire
		The Green Howards
		The Duke of Wellington's Regiment
d.	Black Beret	The Royal Tank Regiment
e.	Rifle Green Beret	The Light Infantry
		The Royal Green Jackets
		The Brigade of Gurkhas
		Adjutant General's Corps
f.	Maroon Beret	The Parachute Regiment
g.	Beige Beret	The Special Air Service Regiment
h.	Light Blue Beret	The Army Air Corps
i.	Scarlet Beret	Royal Military Police
j.	Cypress Green Beret	The Intelligence Corps

The majority of Scottish Regiments wear the Tam-O-Shanter (TOS) and the Royal Irish Regiment wear the Corbeen.

Regular Army Rates of Pay as at 1st April 1999

Officers	On Appointment	Rising To
University Cadet	8,989	12,472
Second Lieutenant	15,738	-
Lieutenant	20,805	22,995
Captain	26,539	30,831
Major	33,586	40,215
Lieutenant Colonel	47,366	52,359
Colonel	55,060	60,856
Brigadier	67,448	-

Notes:
Rates of pay apply to both male and female officers.
QARANC Officers are commissioned as Lieutenants.

Adult Soldiers	Band	Scale A (£ per week)	£ per Annum
Private Class 4	1	189.35	9,873
Private Class 3	1	213.08	11,110
Private Class 3	2	247.31	12,895
Private Class 3	3	285.32	14,877
Private Class 2	1	238.14	12,417
Private Class 2	2	272.65	14,216
Private Class 2	3	310.66	16,198
Private Class 1	1	259.00	13,505
Private Class 1	2	293.44	15,300
Private Class 1	3	331.38	17,279
Lance Corporal Class 1	1	296.52	15,461
Lance Corporal Class 1	2	330.96	17,257
Lance Corporal Class 1	3	371.91	19,392
Corporal Class 1	1	340.13	17,735
Corporal Class 1	2	374.29	19,516
Corporal Class 1	3	415.17	21,648
Sergeant	4	374.08	19,505
Staff Sergeant	5	432.60	22,557
Warrant Officer Class 2	6	510.16	26,601
Warrant Officer Class 1	7	588.84	30,703

Notes:

(1) Pay scales apply to both males and females.

(2) These rates only show the most common basic pay rates.

(3) From 1 January 1991 all recruits are enlisted on an Open Engagement. The Open Engagement is for a period of 22 years service from the age of 18 or the date of enlistment whichever is the later. Subject to giving 12 months notice, and any time bar that may be in force, all soldiers have the right to leave on the completion of 4 years reckonable service from the age of 18.

Length of Service Increments (LSI)

Daily Rates – After 9 years service personnel are eligible for extra daily long service increments of pay. These vary according to rank.

Rank	9 yrs £	12 yrs £	15 yrs £	18 yrs £	22 yrs £
Pte	0.97	1.28	1.28	1.28	1.28
LCpl	0.91	1.28	1.28	1.28	1.28
Cpl	0.91	1.28	1.56	1.56	1.56
Sgt	1.10	1.56	1.92	2.28	2.28
SSgt	1.10	1.56	1.92	2.64	2.64
WO2	1.10	1.56	1.92	2.64	3.01
WOI	1.10	1.56	1.92	2.64	3.46

Soldiers Pay Bands

All employments in the Army are grouped into Bands for calculating pay. Band 1 includes all recruits during training and the majority of employments. In general, the more skilled the employment, the higher the pay band.

Examples of Band 2 Employments are - Bandsman; Farrier; Driver Tank Transporter; Radar Operator(RA); Command Post Assistant(RA); Meteorologist; OP Assistant(RA); Surveyor(RA); Armoured Engineer; Amphibious Engineer; Bomb Disposal Engineer; Telecom Op (Linguist); Telecom Op (Systems); Student Nurse; Op Theatre Technician; Pharmacy Technician; Dental Technician; Operator Special Intelligence; Armourer, Blacksmith; Bricklayer; Carpenter; Construction Materials Technician; Draughtsman; Driver Specialist(RE); Electrician; Fitter; Gun Fitter; Metalsmith; Painter; Plant Operator; Plumber; Printer; Railwayman, Sheetmetal Worker; Shipwright, Vehicle Electrician; Vehicle Mechanic, Welder; Well Driller.

Examples of Band 3 employments are - Survey Technician; Telecom Op (Telegraph); Laboratory Technician; Physiological Measurement Technician; Registered General Nurse; Registered Mental Nurse; Telecom Op (Special); Telecom Technician; Physiotherapist; Aircraft Technician; Control Equipment Technician; Radar Technician; Marine Engineer; Radiographer; Avionics Technician; Instrument Technician; SAS Soldier.

Junior Entrants

Age	£ per week	£ per annum
16 but under 17 yrs	117.95	6,150
17 but under 17.5 yrs	143.15	7,464
17.5 years and over*	189.35	9,873

*While in apprentice training.

Charges

	£ per Week
Standard food charge	22.61

	£ per Week
Single Accommodation Charges (Grade 1)	
Major and Above	31.08

Captain & Below	25.20
Senior NCO	19.11
Cpl and Below	10.99
Junior Soldiers	8.68

The Royal Marines

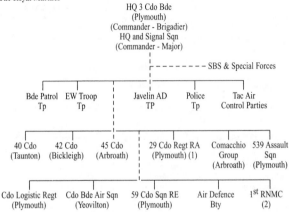

Note:
(1) 29 Cdo Regt RA has one battery stationed at Arbroath with 45 Cdo.
(2) 1st Bn The Royal Netherlands Marine Corps is part of 3 Cdo Bde for NATO assigned tasks.

Although the Royal Marines (RM) are an organisation that is part of the Royal Navy, they are trained and equipped for warfare on land, and it is very likely that they could be involved in operations and exercises with Army units. The Royal Marines number approximately 5,800 officers and men and their primary task is the reinforcement of Norway and NATO's Northern Flank, should a threat develop in that area.

The Royal Marines also have detachments on 12 ships at sea and a number of smaller units world-wide with widely differing tasks. However, the bulk of the manpower of the Royal Marines is grouped in battalion sized organisations known as Commando (Cdo). There are 3 Commando Groups and they are part of a larger formation known as 3 Commando Brigade (3 Cdo Bde).

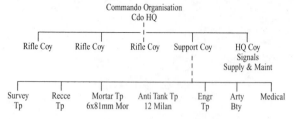

Commando Organisation
Cdo HQ

Rifle Coy | Rifle Coy | Rifle Coy | Support Coy | HQ Coy
Signals
Supply & Maint

Survey Tp | Recce Tp | Mortar Tp 6x81mm Mor | Anti Tank Tp 12 Milan | Engr Tp | Arty Bty | Medical

Note: A troop (Tp) equates to an army platoon. Each rifle company has three troops.

RAF Regiment

Currently the RAF Regiment exists to provide ground and short-range air defence for RAF installations, and to train all the RAF's combatant personnel to enable them to contribute to the defence of their units.

As of 1 April 1999 there were about 2,200 RAF Regiment personnel (including about 300 officers) in units are as follows:

No 1 Group (STC)

No 2 Squadron	Honnington	Field /Para Sqn
No 3 Squadron	Aldergrove	Field Squadron
No 1 Squadron	Honnington	Field Squadron
No 26 Squadron	Waddington	Rapier
No 37 Squadron	Bruggen	Rapier

No 11/18 Group (STC)

| No 15 Squadron | Leeming | Rapier |
| No 27/48 Squadron | Waddington | Rapier |

British Forces Cyprus (STC)

| No 34 Squadron | Akrotiri | Field Squadron |

Independent STC Units

| No 63 (QCS) | Uxbridge | Ceremonial/Field Squadron |

PTC Units

| RAF Regiment Depot | Honnington |
| Rapier Training Unit | Honnington |

Specialist RAF Regiment training for gunners is given at the RAF Regiment Depot at Honnington. On completion of training at the RAF College Cranwell officers also undergo further specialist training at RAF Honnington and, in some cases, the Combined Arms Training Centre at Warminster in Wiltshire or the Royal School of Artillery at Larkhill.

The RAF Regiment also mans the Queen's Colour Squadron which undertakes all major ceremonial duties for the Royal Air Force. These duties involve mounting the Guard at Buckingham Palace on an occasional basis, and providing Guards of Honour for visiting Heads of State. The Queen's Colour Squadron also has a war role as a field squadron. The 1998 SDR states that there will be a small reduction in the RAF Regiment's squadron structure from 14 (including RAF Regiment Reserve squadrons) to 13 but that the RAF will have an enhanced nuclear, chemical and biological role as part of a new Joint Service Capability.

There are now two basic RAF Regiment squadron organisations - the field squadron organised for ground defence against possible enemy ground action and the rapier squadron organised for defence against low-flying enemy aircraft. There are four dedicated field squadrons and 63 (QCS) Squadron with a dual ceremonial/field squadron role. Five Rapier squadrons defend RAF airbases and three Rapier squadrons have a role in defending USAF bases in the UK.

The Rapier system provides area, Low Level Air Defence (LLAD) over the area around the airbase to be defended. It consists of an Optical Tracker, a Fire Unit, a Radar and a Generator. The into-action time of the system is thought to be about 15 minutes and the radar is believed to scan out to 12 km. Each fire unit can therefore cover an Air Defence Area (ADA) of about 100 km?. Having discharged the 4 missiles on a Fire Unit, 2 men are thought to be able to carry out a reload in about 3 minutes. During the Falklands Campaign, Rapier was credited with 14 kills and 6 probables from a total of 24 missiles fired.

Rapier in service with the RAF Regiment has been upgraded from Field Standard B1(M) to Field Standard C (Rapier 2000). Rapier FSC offers significant enhancements to performance. The towed system launcher mounts eight missiles (able to fire two simultaneously at 2 separate targets) and is manufactured in two warhead versions. One of these warheads is armour piercing and able to deal with fixed-wing targets, while the other is a fragmentation warhead for the engagement of cruise missiles and RPVs. Rapier 2000 will have the Darkfire tracker and a tailor-made 3-dimensional radar system for target acquisition, developed by Plessey.

A Joint Service Rapier FSC OCU was formed at RAF Honnington to oversee both the RAF's and Army's conversion to the new system.

Rapier has now been sold to the armed forces of at least 14 nations. We believe that sales have amounted to over 26,000 missiles and over 600 launchers and 350 Blindfire radars.

Royal Auxiliary Air Force Regiment (RAuxAF Regt)

Airfield defence is further enhanced by squadrons of the RAuxAF Regt who are recruited locally and whose role is the ground defence of the airfield and its associated outlying installations. A RAuxAF Regiment Squadron has an all-up strength of about 120 personnel and costs approximately £500,000 a year to keep in service. As a general rule, a squadron has a headquarters flight, two mobile flights mounted in Land Rovers and two flights for static guard duties. RAuxAF Regt squadrons are as follows:

1310 Wing RAuxAF Regt	RAF Honnington	HQ Unit
2503 Sqn RAuxAF Regt	RAF Waddington	Ground Defence
2620 Sqn RAuxAF Regt	RAF Marham	Ground Defence
2622 Sqn RAuxAF Regt	RAF Lossiemouth	Ground Defence
2623 Sqn RAuxAF Regt	RAF Honnington	Training Squadron
2624 Sqn RAuxAF Regt	RAF Brize Norton	Ground Defence
2625 Sqn RAuxAF Regt	RAF St Mawgan	Ground Defence

Codewords and Nicknames

A Codeword is a single word used to provide security cover for reference to a particular classified matter, eg "Corporate" was the Codeword for the recovery of the Falklands in 1982. In 1990, "Granby" was used to refer to operations in the Gulf and Op Agricola is used for current operations in support of NATO forces in Kosovo. A Nickname consists of two words and may be used for reference to an unclassified matter, eg "Lean Look" referred to an investigation into various military organisations in order to identify savings in manpower.

Dates and Timings

When referring to timings the British Army uses the 24 hour clock. This means that 2015 hours, pronounced twenty fifteen hours, is in fact 8.15pm. Soldiers usually avoid midnight and refer to 2359 or 0001 hours. Time zones present plenty of scope for confusion! Exercise and Operational times are expressed in Greenwich Mean Time (GMT) which may differ from the local time. The suffix Z (Zulu) denotes GMT and A (Alpha) GMT + 1 hour. B (Bravo) means GMT + 2 hours and so on.

The Date Time Group or DTG can be seen on military documents and is a point of further confusion for many. Using the military DTG 1030 GMT on 20th April 1997 is written as 201030Z APR 97. When the Army relates days and hours to operations a simple system is used:

a. D Day is the day an operation begins.
b. H Hour is the hour a specific operation begins.
c. Days and hours can be represented by numbers plus or minus of D Day
Therefore if D Day is the 20th April 1997, D-2 is the 18th April and D + 2 is the 22nd April. If H Hour is 0600 hrs then H+2 is 0800 hours.

Phonetic Alphabet

To ensure minimum confusion during radio or telephone conversations difficult words or names are spelt out letter by letter using the following NATO standard phonetic alphabet.

ALPHA - BRAVO - CHARLIE - DELTA - ECHO - FOXTROT - GOLF - HOTEL-INDIA - JULIET - KILO - LIMA - MIKE - NOVEMBER - OSCAR - PAPA- QUEBEC - ROMEO - SIERRA - TANGO - UNIFORM - VICTOR - WHISKEY - X RAY - YANKEE - ZULU.

Military Quotations

Young officers and NCOs may find some of these quotations useful on briefings etc: There are two groups - Military and General.

Military

"The military value of a partisan's work is not measured by the amount of property destroyed, or the number of men killed or captured, but the number he keeps watching."
> *John Singleton Mosby 1833-1916*
> *Confederate Cavalry Leader*

"Peace - In international affairs, a period of cheating between two periods of fighting."
> *The Devils Dictionary 1911*

"A few honest men are better than numbers."
> *Oliver Cromwell*

" Mr Smith Sir! - As an obvious outsider what is your opinion of the human race?"
> *Drill Sergeant to a cadet at the Royal Military Academy 1998.*

"The beatings will continue until morale improves."
> *Attributed to the Commander of the Japanese Submarine Force.*

"When other Generals make mistakes their armies are beaten; when I get into a hole, my men pull me out of it".
> *The Duke of Wellington -after Waterloo*

"One might as well try to charge through a wall".
> *Napoleon - On St Helena - Regarding the British Infantry*

"Take short views, hope for the best and trust in God."
> *Sir Sydney Smith*

"There is no beating these troops in spite of their generals. I always thought them bad soldiers, now I am sure of it. I turned their right, pierced their centre, broke them everywhere; the day was mine, and yet they did not know it and would not run.
> *Marshal Soult - Albuhera 1811*

"Confusion in battle is what pain is in childbirth - the natural order of things".
> *General Maurice Tugwell*

"This is right way to waste money"
> *PJ O'Rourke - Rolling Stone Magazine*
> *(Watching missiles firing during an exercise)*

" This is just something to be got round - like a bit of flak on the way to the target".
> *Group Captain Leonard Cheshire VC - Speaking of his incurable illness in the week before he died.*

"Pale Ebenezer thought it wrong to fight, But roaring Bill, who killed him, thought it right".
> *Hillare Belloc*

"Everyone wants peace - and they will fight the most terrible war to get it".
> *Miles Kington - BBC Radio 4th February 1995*

"The easiest and quickest path into the esteem of traditional military authorities is by the appeal to the eye rather than to the mind. The `polish and pipeclay' school is not yet extinct, and it is easier for the medicore intelligence to become an authority on buttons than on tactics".

> *Captain Sir Basil Liddel Hart*
> *Thoughts on War 1944*

"Having lost sight of our objectives we need to redouble our efforts".
> *Anon.*

"The purpose of war is not to die for your country. The purpose of war is to ensure that the other guy dies for his country".
> *General Patton.*

"War is a competition of incompetence - the least incompetent usually win".
> *General Tiger -after losing Bangladesh.*

General

"Success is generally 90% persistence".
> *Anon.*

"Anyone sitting on a bus after the age of 30 should consider themself a failure".
> *Lady Westminster*

"It is only worthless men who seek to excuse the deterioration of their character by pleading neglect in their early years".
> *Plutarch - Life of Coriolanus - Approx AD 80*

" They say hard work never hurt anybody, but I figured why take the chance".
> *Ronald Regan*

"To applaud as loudly as that for so stupid a proposal means that you are just trying to fill that gap between your ears".
> *David Starkey - BBC (4 Feb 95)*

"Its always best on these occasions to do what the mob do".
"But suppose that there are two mobs?" suggested Mr Snodgrass.
"Shout with the largest" replied Mr Pickwick.
> *Pickwick Papers Chapter 13*

"Ah, these diplomats! What chatterboxes! There's only one way to shut them up - cut them down with machine guns. Bulganin, go and get me one!"
> *Joseph Stalin - As reported by De Gaulle during a long meeting.*

"The primary function of management is to create the chaos that only management can sort out. A secondary function is the expensive redecoration and refurnishing of offices, especially in times of the utmost financial stringency".
> *Theodore Dalrymple "The Spectator" 6 November 1993.*

"I consider myself to be the most important figure in the world."
> *His Royal Highness - Field Marshal Idi Amin Dada VC*

Abbreviations

The following is a selection from the list of standard military abbreviations and should assist users of this handbook.

AWOL	Absent without leave
accn	Accommodation
ACE	Allied Command Europe
Adjt	Adjutant
admin	Administration
admin O	Administrative Order
ac	Aircraft
AD	Air Defence/Air Dispatch/Army Department
ADA	Air Defended Area
ADP	Automatic Data Processing
AFCENT	Allied Forces Central European Theatre
AIFV	Armoured Infantry Fighting Vehicle
Airmob	Airmobile
ATAF	Allied Tactical Air Force
armr	Armour
armd	Armoured
ACV	Armoured Command Vehicle
AFV	Armoured Fighting Vehicle
AMF(L)	Allied Mobile Force (Land Element)
APC	Armoured Personnel Carrier
APDS	Armour Piercing Discarding Sabot
ARV	Armoured Recovery Vehicle
AVLB	Armoured Vehicle Launched Bridge
AP	Armour Piercing/Ammunition Point/Air Publication
APO	Army Post Office
ARRC	Allied Rapid Reaction Corps
ATGW	Anti Tank Guided Weapon
ATWM	Army Transition to War Measure
arty	Artillery
att	Attached
BE	Belgium (Belgian)
BGHQ	Battlegroup Headquarters
bn	Battalion
bty	Battery
BK	Battery Captain
BC	Battery Commander
BG	Battle Group
bde	Brigade
BAOR	British Army of the Rhine
BFG	British Forces Germany
BFPO	British Forces Post Office
BMH	British Military Hospital
BRSC	British Rear Support Command
C3I	Command, Control, Communications & Intelligence.
cam	Camouflaged
cas	Casualty

171

CCP	Casualty Collecting Post
CCS	Casualty Clearing Station
CASEVAC	Casualty Evacuation
cat	Catering
CAD	Central Ammunition Depot
CEP	Circular Error Probable/Central Engineer Park
CEPS	Central European Pipeline System
CET	Combat Engineer Tractor
CGS	Chief of the General Staff
CinC	Commander in Chief
CVD	Central Vehicle Depot
CW	Chemical Warfare
COS	Chief of Staff
civ	Civilian
CP	Close Protection/Command Post
CAP	Combat Air Patrol
c sups	Combat Supplies
CV	Combat Vehicles
CVR(T) or (W)	Combat Vehicle Reconnaissance Tracked or Wheeled
comd	Command/Commander
CinC	Commander in Chief
CPO	Command Pay Office/Chief Petty Officer
CO	Commanding Officer
coy	Company
CQMS	Company Quartermaster Sergeant
comp rat	Composite Ration (Compo)
COMSEN	Communications Centre
coord	Co-ordinate
CCM	Counter Counter Measure
DAA	Divisional Administrative Area
DTG	Date Time Group
def	Defence
DF	Defensive Fire
DK	Denmark
dml	Demolition
det	Detached
DISTAFF	Directing Staff (DS)
div	Division
DAA	Divisional Administrative Area
DMA	Divisional Maintenance Area
DS	Direct Support/Dressing Station
ech	Echelon
EME	Electrical and Mechanical Engineers
ECCM	Electronic Counter Measure
emb	Embarkation
EDP	Emergency Defence Plan
EMP	Electro Magnetic Pulse
en	Enemy
engr	Engineer
EOD	Explosive Ordnance Disposal

eqpt	Equipment
ETA	Estimated Time of Arrival
EW	Early Warning/Electronic Warfare
ex	Exercise
FRG	Federal Republic of Germany
FGA	Fighter Ground Attack
fol	Follow
fmm	Formation
FUP	Forming Up Point
FAC	Forward Air Controller
FEBA	Forward Edge of the Battle Area
FLET	Forward Location Enemy Troops
FLOT	Forward Location Own Troops
FOO	Forward Observation Officer
FR	France (French)
FRT	Forward Repair Team
FUP	Forming Up Place
GDP	General Defence Plan
GE	German (Germany)
GR	Greece (Greek)
GOC	General Officer Commanding
GPMG	General Purpose Machine Gun
HAC	Honourable Artillery Company
hel	Helicopter
HE	High Explosive
HEAT	High Explosive Anti Tank
HESH	High Explosive Squash Head
HVM	Hyper Velocity Missile
Hy	Heavy
IFF	Identification Friend or Foe
II	Image Intensifier
IGB	Inner German Border
illum	illuminating
IO	Intelligence Officer
INTSUM	Intelligence Summary
IRG	Immediate Replenishment Group
IR	Individual Reservist
IS	Internal Security
ISD	In Service Date
IT	Italy (Italian)
IW	Individual Weapon
JFHQ	Joint Force Headquarters
JHQ	Joint Headquarters
JSSU	Joint Services Signals Unit
LAD	Light Aid Detachment (REME)
L of C	Lines of Communication
LLAD	Low Level Air Defence
LO	Liaison Officer
Loc	Locating
log	Logistic

LRATGW	Long Range Anti Tank Guided Weapon
LSW	Light Support Weapon
MAOT	Mobile Air Operations Team
MBT	Main Battle Tank
maint	Maintain
mat	Material
med	Medical
mech	Mechanised
MFC	Mortar Fire Controller
MNAD	Multi National Airmobile Division
NE	Netherlands
MO	Medical Officer
MP	Military Police
MOD	Ministry of Defence
mob	Mobilisation
MovO	Movement Order
msl	missile
MV	Military Vigilance
NAAFI	Navy, Army and Air Force Institutes
NADGE	NATO Air Defence Ground Environment
NATO	North Atlantic Treaty Organisation
NCO	Non Commissioned Officer
nec	Necessary
NL	Netherlands
NO	Norway (Norwegian)
NOK	Next of Kin
ni	Night
NORTHAG	Northern Army Group
NTR	Nothing to Report
NBC	Nuclear and Chemical Warfare
NYK	Not Yet Known
OP	Observation Post
OC	Officer Commanding
OCU	Operational Conversion Unit (RAF)
OIC	Officer in Charge
OOTW	Operations Other Than War
opO	Operation Order
ORBAT	Order of Battle
pax	Passengers
POL	Petrol, Oil and Lubricants
P info	Public Information
PJHQ	Permanent Joint Head Quarters
Pl	Platoon
PO	Portugal (Portuguese)
PUS	Permanent Under Secretary
QM	Quartermaster
RAP	Rocket Assisted Projectile/Regimental Aid Post
RJDF	Rapid Joint Deployment Force
RTM	Ready to Move
RCZ	Rear Combat Zone

rec	Recovery
R & D	Research and Development
rebro	Rebroadcast
recce	Reconnaissance
Regt	Regiment
RHQ	Regimental Headquarters
RMA	Rear Maintenance Area/Royal Military Academy
rft	Reinforcement
RSA	Royal School of Artillery
RSME	Royal School of Mechanical Engineering
RTU	Return to Unit
SACUER	Supreme Allied Commander Europe
SATCOM	Satellite Communications
SDR	Strategic Defence Review
2IC	Second in Command
SH	Support Helicopters
SHAPE	Supreme Headquarters Allied Powers Europe
sit	Situation
SITREP	Situation Report
SIB	Special Investigation Branch
SLR	Self Loading Rifle
SMG	Sub Machine Gun
smk	Smoke
SNCO	Senior Non Commissioned Officer
SP	Spain (Spanish)
Sqn	Squadron
SP	Self Propelled/Start Point
SSM	Surface to Surface Missile
SSVC	Services Sound and Vision Corporation
STA	Surveillance and Target Acquisition
STOL	Short Take Off and Landing
tac	Tactical
tk	Tank
tgt	Target
TOT	Time on Target
TCP	Traffic Control Post
tpt	Transport
tp	Troop
TCV	Troop Carrying Vehicle
TLB	Top Level Budget
TU	Turkish (Turkey)
TUL	Truck Utility Light
TUM	Truck Utility Medium
UK	United Kingdom
UKMF	United Kingdom Mobile Force
UNCLASS	Unclassified
UXB	Unexploded Bomb
US	United States
U/S	Unserviceable
VCDS	Vice Chief of the Defence Staff

veh	Vehicle
VOR	Vehicle off the Road
WE	War Establishment
wh	Wheeled
WIMP	Whinging Incompetent Malingering Person
WMR	War Maintenance Reserve
WO	Warrant Officer
wksp	Workshop
X	Crossing (as in roads or rivers)

This publication was produced by R&F (Defence) Publications
Editorial Office Tel & Fax 01743-235079/241962
E Mail 113315.671@Compuserve.Com
Managing Editor: Charles Heyman; Deputy Editors Martin Osborne and John Ross
Other publications in this series are:

The Royal Air Force Pocket Guide 1994-95
The Armed Forces of the United Kingdom 1999-2000
The Territorial Army - Volume 1 1999

Further copies can be obtained from:
Pen & Sword Books Ltd
47 Church Street
Barnsley S70 2AS

Telephone: 01226-734222   Fax: 01226-734438

7th Edition January 2000

177

RECORDING HISTORY

Pen & Sword Books Ltd have unparalleled experience of publishing official regimental and Corps histories under their Leo Cooper imprint. Working in partnership with the regiments etc. concerned we advise on styles, edit, design and produce the highest quality books. We can also introduce professional authors where this is required. In addition to producing copies for the sponsor's use, Pen & Sword Books will market the books world-wide through our wholesale, retail and direct mail lists.

Recently published and future titles include: -

Wait for the Waggon	{Royal Corps of Transport}
Cold War Warriors	{The Duke of Edinburgh's Royal Regiment}
King's African Rifles	
Gentleman in Blue	{600 Squadron RAF}
Fly Navy	{Fleet Air Arm Officers' Association}
Long Range Desert Group	
Army Service Corps 1902-1918	
Second to None	{Coldstream Guards}
They Sustained - Arnhem 1944	{Royal Logistic Corps}

~~~

If your Ship, Regiment, Corps, Squadron or Association etc. has not got
a recent and readable history perhaps it should -
to find out more about this unique service
that we offer please contact:

Brigadier Henry Wilson,
Publishing Manager,
Pen & Sword Books Ltd
47 Church Street,
Barnsley,
South Yorkshire, S70 2AS,

Tel: 01226 734241, Fax: 01226 734438.

The History of Landmines

MIKE CROLL

The History of Landmines takes the reader from ancient Rome to the colonial wars and from the American Civil War to the Gulf War explaining why increasing numbers of these devices have been used and how they have become more sophisticated. The genesis of the present humanitarian crisis is fully described along with the problems of clearing landmines today.

Mike Croll, a former Royal Engineer Officer and an experienced deminer is particularly well fitted to write about landmines. He has a balanced, dispassionate perspective and this book will greatly contribute to the understanding of the subject.

ISBN: 0 85052 628 0
176 pages
Illustrated throughout
£18.95 hardback

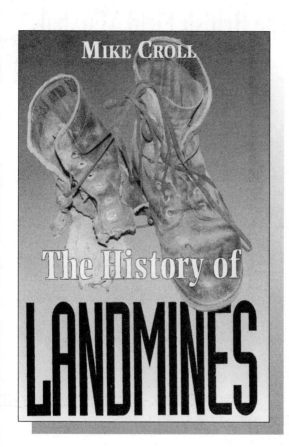

MIKE CROLL

The History of

LANDMINES

The British Field Marshals
1736-1997
A Biographical Dictionary

T A HEATHCOTE

FOREWORD BY
GENERAL SIR CHARLES GUTHERIE, GCB, LVO, OBE, ADC GEN

Following the UK Government's decision not to appoint any further Field Marshals, the time is right for a definitive book covering all holders of this illustrious rank. The author describes in the most readable fashion the lives, achievements, successes and failures of all the 138 Field Marshals appointed since the creation of the rank in 1736. He unearths rich seams of fact and controversy and his accounts will educate and amuse.

- The complete Who's Who of all holders of the most senior rank attainable, in British History
- Authoritative and definitive yet readable and entertaining
- Covers the history of British feats of arms over the last 250 years plus
- Valuable as a work of reference, educational tool or simply as 'a good read'

ISBN: 0 85052 696 5
384 pages
£25.00 hardback

THE BRITISH FIELD MARSHALS

1736-1997

A Biographical Dictionary

T A HEATHCOTE

Foreword by
GENERAL SIR CHARLES GUTHRIE, GCB, LVO, OBE, ADC GEN

THE ARMED FORCES
of the
UNITED KINGDOM
1999-2000
CHARLES HEYMAN

The Armed Forces of the United Kingdom 1999-2000
covers all the vital aspects of the organisations and
equipment of the UK Army, Royal Navy and the
Royal Air Force.

Silhouette outlines for major equipment and wiring
diagrams showing the details of all national military
organisations including an RN frigate, and RAF
squadron and an Army infantry battalion.

1999-2000 edition contains all the details of the UK
Government's 1998 Strategic Defence Review.

ISBN: 0 85052 621 3
200 pages
Illustrated throughout
£5.95 paperback

Charles Heyman

THE ARMED FORCES of the UNITED KINGDOM
1999-2000